D1221898

Best Practices for Supporting Adjunct Faculty

BEST PRACTICES FOR SUPPORTING ADJUNCT FACULTY

Edited by

Richard E. Lyons
Faculty Development Associates

ANKER PUBLISHING COMPANY, INC.
Bolton, Massachusetts

Best Practices for Supporting Adjunct Faculty

Copyright © 2007 by Anker Publishing Company, Inc. All rights reserved. Printed in the United States of America. No part of this publication may be reproduced or distributed in any form or by any means, electronic or mechanical, including photocopying, recording, or by any information storage or retrieval system, without the prior written consent of the publisher.

ISBN 978-1-933371-27-9

Composition by Jessica Holland
Cover design by Borges Design

Anker Publishing Company, Inc.
563 Main Street
P.O. Box 249
Bolton, MA 01740-0249 USA

www.ankerpub.com

Library of Congress Cataloging-in-Publication Data

Best practices for supporting adjunct faculty / edited by Richard E. Lyons.
    p. cm.
  Includes bibliographical references and index.
  ISBN 978-1-933371-27-6
  1. College teaching—Vocational guidance—United States. 2. College teachers, Part-time—Training of—United States. 3. Education, Higher—United States. I. Lyons, Richard E., 1946-

  LB1778.2.B475 2007
  378.1'2—dc22
                                        2007002587

*To Janet, for her dedication to my work and her gentle coaching
that helps it connect with part-time instructors, and those
who champion their teaching.*

TABLE OF CONTENTS

ABOUT THE AUTHORS

THE EDITOR

Richard E. Lyons is the Senior Consultant with Faculty Development Associates, through which he has provided workshops on college and university campuses throughout North America, and feature presentations at an array of academic conferences. He is also a principal in AdjunctSuccess.net that provides support services online for the part-time faculty members of client institutions. Since 1972 he has served as an adjunct instructor, professor of management, department chair, instructional dean, and coordinator of faculty development. Focusing his mid-1990s dissertation research on the development of adjunct faculty, he has since authored three books—*Success Strategies for Adjunct Faculty* (Allyn & Bacon, 2004), *Teaching College in an Age of Accountability* (Allyn & Bacon, 2003), and *The Adjunct Professor's Guide to Success* (Allyn & Bacon, 1999), as well as a number of articles and book chapters on developing the potential of adjunct faculty.

Dr. Lyons earned his bachelor's degree in business administration and master's degree in business education at Western Kentucky University, and his Ed.D. in curriculum and instruction at the University of Central Florida. He can be reached at lyons@adjunctsuccess.net.

THE CONTRIBUTORS

Joni Allison has served since 2001 as the assistant director of the Delphi Center for Teaching and Learning at the University of Louisville. Prior to her current position, she served as the director of adult learning and program development and distance learning with the community college system in Tennessee. She earned her master's degree in educational psychology, with an emphasis in adult education at the University of Tennessee. Joni can be contacted at joni.allison@louisville.edu.

Keith Barker has been involved in curriculum design and education technology for more than 40 years. With a background in electronic and computer engineering, he has taught at the Universities of Sheffield (UK) and Connecticut. As associate vice provost for undergraduate education and the director of UConn's Institute for Teaching and Learning, he is currently responsible for all faculty development, including teaching assistants, technology in the classrooms, and widespread support for undergraduate education across all of its campuses. His Institute can be visited at www.itl.uconn.edu, and he can be reached at keith.barker@uconn.edu.

Helen Burnstad is director emeritus of staff and organization development at Johnson County Community College, in Overland Park, Kansas. Highly active in the National Council for Staff, Professional and Organizational Development (NCSPOD) as president, membership vice president, and treasurer, and the Professional and Organizational Development (POD) Network, Helen has presented on adjunct faculty issues at academic conferences for more than 20 years. She has also researched, written, and consulted with an array of institutions, and served as a facilitator for the Chair Academy. A principal in AdjunctSuccess.net, Helen can be reached at burnstad@adjunctsuccess.net.

Marie Carter is vice president for enrollment management at Shepherd University. She holds an M.Ed. in student personnel services from the University of South Carolina and an Ed.D. in higher education administration from West Virginia University. Marie can be reached at mcarter@shepherd.edu.

Milton D. Cox is director of the Center for the Enhancement of Learning and Teaching at Miami University, where he founded and directs the Lilly Conference on College Teaching, and is founder and editor-in-chief of the *Journal on Excellence in College Teaching*. Director of a FIPSE dissemination grant establishing faculty learning community programs, he is coeditor of *Building Faculty Learning Communities* (Jossey-Bass, 2004). Milt received the certificate of special achievement from the Professional and Organizational Development Network in Higher Education in recognition of notable contributions to the profession. He can be reached at coxmd@muohio.edu.

Frank Harber is the chair of the business management department at Indian River Community College. After 20 years in the business world, he began his teaching career as an adjunct instructor at IRCC. Three years later, he accepted a full-time position and has since served regularly on the adjunct faculty committee. In 2004–2005, his dissertation research at the University of South Florida culminated in "A Study of the Effects of Completing an Instructor Effectiveness Course on the Accountability Measures of Adjunct Community College Faculty." Frank can be reached at iharber@ircc.edu.

Ben Hayes has taught sociology and criminal justice at the college and university level since 1970. He began serving on the Kansas City Kansas Community College Faculty Development Committee in the early 1980s, eventually becoming its chair. That role evolved into full-time director of faculty and staff development, a position that Ben has held since 1999. Ben has served as president of the National Council for Staff, Program, and Organizational Development (NCSPOD) and is a charter member of the Kansas City Professional Development Council. He received his B.A. from Fort Hays State University, and his M.A. and Ph.D. from the University of Kansas. He can be reached at bhayes@kckcc.edu.

Shannon Holliday serves as project coordinator in the Center for Teaching and Learning at Shepherd University, working to enhance faculty development and success. She holds a B.A. in English and can be reached at shollida@shepherd.edu.

Cindy Hoss, a college educator for more than 30 years, currently serves as assistant dean of instruction and curriculum in the School of Professional and Graduate Studies at Baker University. She served two terms as president of the National Council for Staff, Program, and Organizational Development (NCSPOD), is a peer reviewer for the Higher Learning Commission of the North Central Association of Colleges and Schools, and serves on the editorial board of the Chair Academy *Leadership Journal.* She earned B.A. and M.A. degrees from Fort Hays State University, and her Ed.D. in administration, curriculum and instruction from the University of Nebraska–Lincoln. She can be reached at choss@bakeru.edu.

Marianne Hutti began teaching in 1977 at Spalding University. At the University of Louisville School of Nursing since 1979, she is a professor of nursing and a women's health nurse practitioner, practicing one-half day/week in a local gynecologic private practice. Her bachelor's and master's degrees in nursing are from the University of Kentucky, and her doctoral degree in nursing is from Indiana University. Dr. Hutti is a nationally known NIH-funded nurse-researcher in the area of pregnancy/perinatal loss, and a university and national award-winning teacher. In Fall 2005 she became associate director of the Delphi Center for Teaching and Learning in charge of faculty development.

H. Edward Lambert has been a Faculty Teaching Associate in Miami University's Center for the Enhancement of Teaching and Learning (CELT) and is a member of the departments of educational leadership and business technology. He has been facilitator of CELT's Part-Time and Adjunct Teaching Enhancement Program (PATEP). Having retired from a career as a business executive and lawyer, Ed now teaches career development courses on the Oxford and Middletown campuses. His interests include teaching techniques based upon recent developments in brain research, as well as scholarly teaching techniques in general, and scholarly teaching of part-time faculty.

Evelyn Lauterbach is a graduate student at the University of Louisville, expecting to earn her master of education in college student personnel in 2007. Evelyn has a B.A. in secondary education and history and was the salutatorian of Bellarmine University's class of 2004. She has internship, volunteer, and/or graduate assistantship experience at three institutions (Bellarmine University, University of Louisville, and Indiana University Southeast) and is passionate about pursuing a lifetime career in higher education. She can be reached at thefullenkampbird@hotmail.com.

Tom Lux, after 26 years in the corporate world, left his position as a corporate vice president to form a successful commercial consulting company where he traveled the country doing sales training seminars. In addition, he accepted positions at Moraine Valley Community College and at Governors State University as an adjunct professor. Over the past few years at GSU, he has developed and taught a course to prepare graduate students in the communication program for teaching positions in nearby community colleges.

Dan Mercier is the assistant director of the Institute for Teaching and Learning and the director of instructional design and development at the University of Connecticut. Dan has worked in higher education since 1996, and has extensive experience in faculty development, instructional design, and distance education. He received his M.A. in education from the University of Connecticut and can be reached at dan.mercier@uconn.edu.

Gayle K. Nolan is the coordinator of faculty and staff development and associate professor of academic affairs at Delgado Community College. She has written widely on academic topics and Delgado's experiences surviving Hurricane Katrina, and has been published in *Change* magazine, the *Community College Journal of Research and Practice*, and *Leadership Abstracts*. Gayle's bachelor's and master's degrees, and teaching experience were in special education. She can be reached at gnolan1@dcc.edu.

Daryl Peterson is the director of ScenariosOnline at Valencia Community College in Orlando, Florida. Since 2002 he has managed the development and delivery of online scenarios-based faculty development courses for Valencia and many other colleges. Previously Daryl spent 15 years managing student success initiatives and faculty support, including development and delivery of online workshops for faculty, for a major textbook publishing company. He can be reached at dpeterson8@valenciacc.edu.

Laura Renninger is the coordinator for music history and music appreciation at Shepherd University. Dr. Renninger also teaches courses in music psychology, world music, and women in music. She received her bachelor's of music degree in performance from Miami University and both her master's of music and Ph.D. degrees in musicology from the University of Illinois at Urbana–Champaign. She is currently serving as the interim dean of teaching and learning at Shepherd University. She can be reached at lrenning@shepherd.edu.

Gale S. Rhodes is assistant university provost and director of the Delphi Center for Teaching and Learning at the University of Louisville. She earned a B.S. degree (1973) in sociology, her M.S. (1975) in college student personnel from the University of Tennessee, and an Ed.D. in counseling and higher education (1994) from the University of Louisville. Gale has more than 20 years of experience working with adult learning and development programs. She has presented seminars and workshops and published research in the area of diversity and sexual harassment. Her primary area of research is in prejudice reduction.

Nancy Richard, a published fiction writer, has taught English at Delgado Community College since 1990. Currently she also serves as adjunct mentoring coordinator for English and developmental faculty, and as editor for the College's Southern Association of Colleges and Schools (SACS) Compliance Certificate and Quality Enhancement Plan. Formerly she taught as a graduate assistant at the University of Louisiana–Lafayette and at the University of North Carolina–Greensboro, where she also served as fiction editor for the *Greensboro Review.* She received her B.A. and M.A. from the University of Louisiana–Lafayette and her M.F.A. in creative writing from the University of North Carolina–Greensboro.

Russell Richardson, a college teacher for more than 30 years, began teaching at College of the Canyons in 1987, and currently serves as a professor of political science. Involved in professional development programs throughout his career, he has served as the coordinator of the Associate Program since 1989. A founding member of the College of the Canyons Institute of Teaching and Learning, he is now its director. He received his B.S. and M.A. from Western Kentucky University and an Ed.D. in higher education from Texas Tech University.

Jason Schwartz has taught anatomy and physiology at Indian River Community College (Florida) and other colleges since 2002, after retiring from his 24-year career as a practicing physician. He earned his B.A. from Fordham University and a doctorate from the University of the State of New York, New York Chiropractic College. He can be reached at Drjasonpschwartz@yahoo.com.

Cynthia Siegrist has worked at Delgado Community College in New Orleans, Louisiana, as an ESL instructor, department head, and faculty developer since 1991. At Delgado, she has served as the chair of the Faculty Evaluation and Improvement of Instruction Committee and as a member of the Professional Development Committee. She received a B.A. in French from the University of Michigan and a MATESOL from the School for International Training in Brattleboro, Vermont.

Jeanne C. Silliman has been teaching at Ivy Tech Community College for 20 years. Currently a professor of skills advancement reading, she has been involved in faculty development with the college for many years and has served as chair of the faculty development team. She now coordinates adjunct faculty development initiatives being implemented in the Ivy Tech Evansville region under a grant from the Lilly Foundation. She serves on a statewide Ivy Tech Community College committee for Lilly adjunct faculty support initiatives and chairs the subcommittee planning faculty development programs. She received a B.A. in English from St. Benedict College and her M.A. in education from the University of Evansville. She can be reached at jsillima@ivytech.edu.

Ann-Marie West serves as the Preparedness and Planning Manager for Disaster Services at the Northeast Florida Chapter of the American Red Cross, but remains active in higher education circles. She served on the Kansas City Professional Development Council and the National Council for Staff, Program and Organizational Development (NCSPOD) for two years, and has been certified by the latter as a NCSPOD practitioner. She earned her A.A. in liberal arts at Gulf Coast Community College, and an A.S., B.S. in management/logistics, and an M.B.A. in international business at Park University.

Kevin Yee has been teaching in the postsecondary environment since 1992, as a graduate student, instructor, visiting assistant professor, and adjunct faculty member at a variety of institutions, including Pomona College, Duke University, the University of Iowa, the University of California–Irvine, and the University of Central Florida. He received his B.A. and Ph.D. in German literature from UC–Irvine. He became a full-time faculty developer in 2004 at the University of Central Florida, and can be reached at kevinyee@ucf.mail.edu.

Cynthia Zutter is an anthropologist and the chair of the Department of Anthropology, Economics, and Political Science at MacEwan College in Edmonton, Alberta. She has taught at the college since 1996, has been involved with the faculty development committee since 2000, and served as the coordinator of the Faculty Mentoring Program since it was initiated in 2001. She welcomes any comments and suggestions at zutterc@macewan.ca.

Preface

In recent years, the percentage of course sections taught by part-time faculty members in North American institutions of higher education has increased dramatically. As it has, some have sought to influence a reversal in that trend by claiming that part-time faculty's teaching quality was inherently inferior to that of full-timers. The available data do not substantiate that point. Our colleges and universities are under increasing pressure from state legislatures, the business community, and individual citizens to serve increasing numbers of place- and time-challenged students, align educational programs with economic development goals, and achieve additional accountability measures. Where they are properly trained and supported, adjunct instructors provide a flexible, affordable way to achieve those objectives.

It is incumbent on each institution to ensure that each faculty member who enters its classrooms is systematically prepared and supported, so that the highest quality educational outcomes can be achieved. *Best Practices for Supporting Adjunct Faculty* has been developed to show the reader a number of ways in which this preparation and support are being provided, in strategic, affordable ways. The initiatives highlighted herein have proven effective in a wide array of environments: at research universities, liberal arts colleges, and community colleges; at single-campus settings, multiple-campus arrangements, and even through a consortium of highly diverse institutions; at publicly funded and private institutions; in highly urbanized areas and small towns; in the United States and Canada. The practices can be categorized loosely into orientation protocols, short-term courses providing a foundation of teaching and classroom management skills, mentoring initiatives, workshops delivered in various packages, recognition programs, and comprehensive initiatives that meld multiple components.

In the literature of higher education, our part-time colleagues are usually called "adjunct faculty." Coupled often with such adjectives as "invisible" and "marginalized," the term likely conjures up an image to many—both inside and outside academe—of a monolithic, facelss and nameless cohort of distressed "less than somethings." The opening chapter of this book seeks to refute that paradigm. Since adjunct faculty members teach largely evening and weekend course sections, and in locations that are often removed from the primary campus, the effective professional development initiatives highlighted in this book seek strategically to foster a sense of belonging among their part-time instructors. The best practices included here display other commonalities as well.

Each best practice was developed and launched with a modest investment of financial, physical, and human resources, but has provided disproportionately valuable rewards. Each of those included is grounded in sound research—both primary and secondary, and driven by clearly identified objectives. Each has achieved success in no small part because its insightful leaders recognized the need to secure support from both top-level administration, instructional leaders who interface with part-timers on a regular basis, and the full-time faculty. Each initiative incorporated regular data-gathering into its management system, so that potential improvements were identified early and integrated continuously into improving its effectiveness. Last, but arguably most critical, each best practice had one or several "champions"—someone at the institution who made it a top priority, who looked proactively for opportunities to communicate its mission, and who advocated on the behalf of the institution's adjunct instructors to align processes and services with their needs.

The first of the book's 15 chapters frames the discussion, reviews insightful literature on the issue of developing adjunct faculty members, and highlights the four adjunct faculty member profiles introduced by Judith Gappa and David Leslie, in *The Invisible Faculty* (Jossey-Bass, 1993). A major premise is that institutions developing initiatives should design a process that addresses the needs of its particular cohort of part-time faculty members.

Chapter 2 showcases a multiple approach program for orienting busy, new adjunct faculty members into the culture of the University of Central Florida, based in Orlando, where there is a highly competitive market for part-time instructors.

Chapter 3 highlights a six-session program instituted in September 2005 at the University of Louisville, located in an urban area that has a competitive market for academic labor. This program provides new adjunct faculty members training in using active learning strategies, integrating technology into teaching, and other topics identified as critical through its extensive needs assessment process.

Chapter 4 features an online resource developed at Valencia Community College, in Orlando, which builds upon participants' existing knowledge to enhance their classroom effectiveness to build an effective faculty that has deep roots in the community.

The following two chapters highlight programs that utilize different approaches to provide novice part-timers with mentoring opportunities. Chapter 5 highlights a traditional one-to-one initiative employed at MacEwan College, in Alberta, Canada. Chapter 6 showcases the team approach taken by Delgado Community College, in New Orleans, in which a senior full-time faculty member mentors all of the new part-timers within his or her instructional division for an academic year.

Chapter 7 showcases a consortium of diverse institutions located in metropolitan Kansas City that joined forces in 1994 to provide faculty development opportunities. It has since expanded its programming to embrace the needs of adjunct faculty members.

Chapter 8 highlights the entrepreneurial approach taken by Governors State University (Illinois) to prepare part-time faculty members of the community colleges in its geographical area.

The next two chapters feature initiatives that provide proven part-time instructors with the opportunity to expand their value to the institution and, in the process, earn added status. Chapter 9 focuses on the Associate Program implemented at California's College of the Canyons, in 1989. Chapter 10 highlights the Adjunct Faculty Associates Program instituted at the University of Connecticut.

Chapter 11 showcases a program at the Evansville, Indiana, campus of Ivy Tech Community College that combines a thorough orientation protocol with an online course titled Teaching in the Learning College, and a mentoring element to deliver an integrated, comprehensive support system.

The comprehensive program installed at Florida's Indian River Community College, in 1996, is highlighted in Chapter 12. It includes an orientation structured by a standardized checklist, a short course titled Instructor Effectiveness Training, a system of mentoring opportunities, a professional development library designed with part-timers in mind, brown bag professional development luncheons, and a spring reception that incorporates a recognition program for outstanding adjunct faculty members.

Chapter 13 provides information on how Shepherd University in West Virginia designed and launched a new professional development program for its part-time faculty members, and the results it was able to attain in only one year.

Chapter 14 highlights the process that Miami University–Ohio employed to develop its adjunct faculty development initiative and the achievements it attained in its first two years.

The closing chapter provides the perspective of an adjunct professor who has taught at two different institutions—one with a proven program that prepared and supported him well, the other that was just beginning to provide support. His perceptions of the role that the programming available at each institution had on his job satisfaction are enlightening.

Best Practices for Supporting Adjunct Faculty is not designed to provide a template for what should be implemented at your institution. Instead, it seeks to demonstrate what can be accomplished by committed leaders, with limited resources, when they are driven by the desire to integrate proven community resources more fully into the instructional culture of the institution. Hopefully copies of the book will circulate your campus and spark a discussion that will lead to the implementation of a modest initiative that addresses your institution's specific needs—an initiative that, once proven, will expand and take its place as a fixture of your institutional culture. When the full potential of your adjunct faculty is approached, benefits will accrue to instructional leaders, full-time faculty members, the community, but most important, to students, that far outweigh the resources required to plan your initiative thoroughly and get it implemented fully.

ACKNOWLEDGMENTS

No project that requires such advance planning and ongoing cooperation and commitment as the writing of a book of contributed chapters can be successful without the participation of many selfless individuals. First and foremost, we acknowledge those who crafted the chapters that appear in *Best Practices for Supporting Adjunct Faculty.* They worked through already busy duty times, and in many cases off-duty times, to produce and revise their chapter drafts, and often responded on short notice to issues required to get the project to the "finish line." Their commitment to their respective individual initiatives and their desire to lift up the value of their work to a wider audience were no doubt the driving factors in making this tenuous balancing act work to the extent that it has. Personally I am indebted to my colleagues Frank Harber and Ray Carpenter, who provided me flexibility in other duties to accommodate the need to get the manuscript to final status, Desna Wallin, in whom I have found a colleague to discuss these ideas, and my mentor, Marcy Kysilka, who first encouraged me to find my voice. Lastly I want to acknowledge Jim Anker, Carolyn Dumore, and Wendy Swanson of Anker Publishing Company, who provided the ideal combination of "loose" and "tight" oversight to bring the manuscript to final status.

Richard E. Lyons
February 2007

Deepening Our Understanding of Adjunct Faculty

Richard E. Lyons

In steadily increasing numbers, they meander through college and university corridors, seemingly searching for a room number or a resource for information. Their faces—except for those of Oprah Winfrey, James Carville, or a locally prominent public servant—are recognized by precious few, perhaps only the department chairperson or dean who hired them. Like the new student who in midyear took a seat next to us in our high school history class, we usually fail to welcome them in the way we would hope others would welcome us. Instead we simply take note of their presence, ask ourselves what course they might be teaching, and scurry along attending to our duties and full-time colleagues.

They are our part-time faculty members. Most colleges and universities could not function efficiently or effectively without their playing an active role in our instructional delivery system. Adjunct faculty provide expertise in critical courses that perhaps no full-time member on staff possesses; their evening and weekend availability enable us to expand class schedules to serve our evermore time- and place-challenged students; their passion for sharing their expertise enables our students to achieve more effective real-world perspectives; and they do it all for often embarrassingly modest remuneration and with a shameful lack of support.

By most accounts, approximately 600,000 part-time instructors are employed regularly in North American colleges and universities (Almanac Issue, 2006; Mullens, 2001). At many urban institutions, they staff an increasing share of course sections—especially the introductory courses that tenured full-timers often decry, but that are so critical to ultimate student success and the institution's accountability outcomes. Although adequate statistics do not yet exist, it would surprise few of us if it were discovered that adjunct instructors—many geographically removed from the student population—are teaching a majority of online classes across North America. As publicly supported colleges and universities respond to reduced support, and as baby boomers move toward retirement age, the number of part-time faculty members is likely to expand even further.

These instructors are called by various titles, each with nuanced differences of meaning, depending upon the institution for which they teach and other factors. But none of these commonly used titles seems completely appropriate. Although they are sometimes called "part-time faculty," a good many cobble together teaching assignments from several institutions to carve out a full-time living. In Canada, they are commonly referred to as *sessional faculty*—a term that to some also includes temporary full-time instructors (Mullens, 2001). Recently some have begun referring to them as *contingent faculty*. Most seem to use the terms *adjunct faculty, adjunct instructor, adjunct professor*—perhaps even integrating a ranking system that includes *assistant* or *associate* within the title—or the more pejorative *adjunct*. While these each have a connotation of being an extension to something more important, this group of terms seems to have the widest recognition and acceptance.

In hopes of elevating the title to reflect the significant contribution that adjunct faculty make to their institutions' teaching mission, some colleges and universities, including two represented in this book, have adopted the term *associate faculty*. At Metropolitan State University in Minnesota, they are called *community faculty*, to differentiate them from their full-time *campus faculty* colleagues. Additional terms will no doubt come into use as additional institutions begin to recognize the valuable role our part-time instructors provide our system of higher education.

Although some people may know very few adjunct professors as individuals, readers of this book are likely to appreciate—more than many—how crucial they are to the education of our students. It is increasingly common for adjunct faculty to deliver more than half of the course sections offered by an institution. Evening and weekend students at some colleges and universities may graduate having had every one of their courses taught by a part-timer. Why then, are part-timers so much less likely than full-time faculty members to receive the professional development and other forms of support that we all realize is required for success? Is it an "out of sight, out of mind" paradigm among those who could effect change in the status quo? Or is it the lack of power that part-timers wield, as evidenced by their low pay rates, their contingent work status, or our repeatedly hiring them at the last minute? Or is it perhaps a lack of leadership, unwilling to stand tall and build a case for their valuable role? And how can we not challenge our full-time faculty for blaming adjunct faculty for a perceived decline in the overall quality of instruction when the data demonstrate that the quality of their teaching shows no significant difference from that of full-timers in spite of little support at most institutions (Leslie & Gappa, 2002)? The wise people among us realize that it is time for each institution to address this issue locally and become part of the solution rather than part of the problem. But where do we start? The logical place would seem to be by seeking to understand our adjunct instructors more deeply (Covey, 1989).

CRITICAL RESEARCH FINDINGS

Not so long ago, there was little research available on issues related to part-time faculty. That changed substantially in 1993 with the publication of the extensive research generated by Judith Gappa and David Leslie at varied institutions throughout North America. Published as *The Invisible Faculty*, their findings included a long-standing typology of part-time instructors based upon their lifestyles and motivation to teach.

Specialists, experts, or *professionals* denote part-time instructors who are employed full-time outside of their teaching and who are driven to teach by the desire to share their expertise, network with community members, and/or repay a psychological debt to an educator from their background. This profile includes businesspeople and those from medical professions and the public sector who teach in career-oriented programs, as well as people who perhaps majored in one discipline that has remained an avocation throughout their lives. This is the largest cohort of adjunct faculty nationwide, approaching half of all those who teach part-time in a postsecondary institution.

Freelancers are those who, by choice, are employed in multiple part-time jobs, including a regular college or university teaching assignment. They thrive on the variety and the unique psychological rewards that they derive from their classroom experiences, and they also depend somewhat on the income that it generates. This category includes artists of many types, for example, the musician who plays in the local symphony, gives private lessons, plays special functions, and teaches regularly at a local college or university.

Numerically freelancers are commonly thought to be the smallest group of part-timers.

While *career enders* are approaching the end of their work lives, they want to maintain a connection to the energy of a serious endeavor. Although their teaching assignments are typically linked to their careers, many are removed geographically from their place of employment. Staying connected requires continuous updating and maintaining relationships from their previous career environments. While career enders have been a rather small and quiet group of part-time instructors, their ranks are being increasingly boosted by retiring baby boomers who were grounded in the civil rights, antiwar, and women's movements.

The remaining profile of adjunct professors is the *aspiring academics.* Having recently completed, or about to fulfill, the requirements of their graduate programs, aspiring academics teach largely for the income it generates and to build their potential for pursuing a full-time teaching position. Although they represent an estimated 20%–25% of part-time instructors across all disciplines and institutions, their ratios are perceived to be higher within urban areas that are home to large universities and within certain disciplines—especially the humanities. Aspiring academics receive the most press attention, which fosters a perception among the public of being the largest or even the exclusive profile of adjunct professors. Their ratio is also likely to be overestimated by academics themselves, who often began their careers as adjunct instructors and perceive that they were the rule rather than the exception. In need of cash to repay student loans and defray living expenses, aspiring academics often seek and obtain positions with multiple institutions concurrently and are thus sometimes referred to as "roads scholars," "freeway flyers," or "gypsy scholars." Given their lifestyles, aspiring academics are the most likely of the four profiles to need higher salaries and fringe benefits provided by their employing institution and to be the most politically active in their pursuit of improved working conditions.

Given their teaching at nontraditional times and places, adjunct instructors are likely to feel an estrangement from the institution and a sense of isolation from other faculty members. According to Pam Schuetz (2002), "Part-timers are more weakly linked to their students, colleagues, and institutions than full-timers" (p. 44). She points out that adjunct faculty members are almost twice as likely as full-timers to have no contact with colleagues and that they generally have less awareness of students' needs or campus support services. Schuetz suggests that good teachers are more likely to have strong connections to colleagues and the institution and that increasing those connections will ultimately improve teaching.

Admittedly, many part-time instructors have other occupations that prevent them from participating in the full life of the faculty; in addition, many are transient and will not remain with the college. Even though these characterizations do not apply to a large proportion of adjunct faculty, colleges unfortunately paint the entire group with the same brush and assume these conditions mitigate any investment in the future of part-time faculty members. Some colleges appear to view them as expendable, interchangeable components of a Tinker Toy system of staffing with little regard for the quality of teaching that this approach produces. However, Leslie and Gappa (2002) report that part-timers are a much more stable portion of the workforce than many assume, with 30% reporting more than 10 years of teaching experience at their *current* institution.

Because part-time faculty play such an influential role in instruction, the quality of their teaching and the opportunities they have for professional development should be key concerns for academic leaders. However, given the variety of logistical and economic roadblocks associated with adjunct faculty development programs, most institutions never mount an offensive (Roueche, Roueche, & Milliron, 1995). Because most adjunct faculty have weak ties to the institution, some educators argue that the benefits of such programs are inconsequential.

In *Strangers in Their Own Land,* Roueche, Roueche, and Milliron (1995) made a convincing counterargument: Part-timers need equal opportunities to grow and develop as professionals. The authors wrote that adjunct instructors

> should be integrated into the college community and recognized as increasingly important players in the teaching and learning process in the interest of providing quality instruction to the growing number of full- and part-time students who will sit in their classrooms, in the interest of appreciating the investment value of the part-time faculty, and ultimately in the interest of establishing and maintaining the college's reputation for teaching excellence. (Roueche, Roueche, & Milliron, p. 120)

The sheer number of classes assigned to adjunct professors makes a powerful argument that responsible colleges and universities should invest in their teaching lives. Even as the financial survival of the institution relies increasingly on adjunct faculty, so too does the academic quality of the teaching and learning enterprise. If good teaching that produces evidence of student learning is to be anything other than random, institutional policies must deliberately support the development of all instructors. Many institutions adhere to this path by providing resources and training for their full-time faculty, but if these programs ignore the adjunct instructors, a large gap in educational quality is likely to appear (Grubb & Associates, 1999). A key to the future success of higher education institutions lies in their ability to change part-time teaching into a rewarding, collegial experience.

One of the earliest attempts to make that change, which is chronicled in chapter 9, was initiated by California's College of the Canyons in 1989. News of its and others' successes at academic conferences, the publication of *The Invisible Faculty* (Gappa & Leslie, 1993), and the perceived cost of doing nothing contributed to additional initiatives being launched. Best practices for supporting adjunct faculty, including those featured in the remaining chapters of this book, tend to display some common characteristics.

Effective initiatives are grounded in sound research, both that of nationally focused researchers like Judith Gappa and David Leslie, as well as institution-specific research. For example, a study of the adjunct faculty at a Florida college (Lyons, 1996) found that part-time instructors require:

- A thorough orientation to the institution, its culture, and its practices

- Adequate training in fundamental teaching and classroom management skills

- A sense of belonging to the institution

- Both initial and ongoing professional development

- Recognition for quality work that is perceived as appropriate and adequate

To help readers develop an effective orientation instrument and to systemize a process for integrating their part-time instructors more efficiently and effectively into the institutional culture, templates are included in the appendix of this chapter. These templates will enable your institution to develop a process to capture data that will prove useful in making improved course section assignments and assimilate new part-timers so they become effective members of your instructional staff. With so many adjunct instructors hired on short notice, it is critical to put a system into place that enables them to become acclimated as quickly as possible.

The remaining chapters of this book focus on initiatives that help achieve one or more of the identified needs of adjunct instructors. These initiatives share some common characteristics. Early in its planning, each initiative identified a mission and measurable outcomes. Each made a concerted effort to generate support from the top administration, from its department chairs, and from the faculty as a whole. All were launched with modest budgets. Each generated feedback from its participants, and fed their suggestions back into improving their programs on a continuous basis.

Finally, and arguably most important, each initiative had one or more champions—someone willing to advocate for their part-time colleagues, often in the face of people who viewed supporting adjunct faculty as inappropriate. These champions view adjunct faculty as providing valuable perspectives to students, knowledge of current trends within critical career fields, and a connection to employers within the community. These champions tend to be realists—knowing that the trends that encourage the use of part-time faculty are not going to subside in the foreseeable future—and have committed to working within the existing system until a perceived ideal world arrives in which all professors are well paid and full-time.

Maximizing the Potential of Your Adjunct Faculty

With the quality of higher education under increased criticism from key circles (Jaschik, 2006) and rising pressure from regional accrediting associations, it is essential that instructional leaders include part-time faculty in their strategies for improving institutional effectiveness. Throughout this chapter, we have noted the potential increased contribution that adjunct faculty members can provide to instructional programs—expertise in critical fields, passion for sharing their real world perspectives, scheduling flexibility, and others. Strategic-minded leaders have begun to see the wisdom in leveraging these potential benefits to deepen student learning, improve student retention and other accountability outcomes, and achieve the rising expectations of accrediting associations, employers, and other stakeholders. These benefits can accrue only when adjunct faculty members are equipped with basic teaching and classroom management skills, supported with resources that foster continuous self-improvement, and acknowledged as colleagues.

But part-timers' potential for contributing to your effectiveness extends far beyond their teaching alone by driving support toward the institution. Because the largest ratio of adjunct faculty members are specialists, experts, or professionals, many of them provide connections to community employers who might provide internships and jobs for students, support specialized programs, and serve on various boards and committees. Adjunct instructors who are career enders tend to be opinion leaders with long-term ties to citizens who have the resources needed to support fundraising activities.

Besides facilitating the flow of resources toward your institution, a well-developed cohort of adjunct faculty has potential for communicating your message to opinion leaders within your community. When a new instructional program or fundraising initiative has been implemented, what better group of "mavens" and "connectors" could be engaged to reach a tipping point of support than your adjunct faculty members (Gladwell, 2002)? They often have established relationships with civic, spiritual, and business organizations that have potential to move such initiatives toward successful outcomes much more quickly than would have otherwise been possible.

One of the beauties—and sometimes challenges—of the North American system of higher education is that institutions are so diverse in mission, culture, student population, and other critical factors. There is no "one size fits all" solution to increasing the effectiveness of your institution's adjunct faculty. Hopefully this chapter and the ones that follow will provide you with valuable ideas for expanding professional development opportunities for part-time instructors at your institution, which will in turn enhance student learning, improve your accountability outcomes, and increase community support.

References

Almanac Issue 2006–2007. (2006, August 25). *The Chronicle of Higher Education, 53*(1).

Covey, S. R. (1989). *The 7 habits of highly effective people: Powerful lessons in personal change.* New York, NY: Fireside.

Gappa, J. M., & Leslie, D. W. (1993). *The invisible faculty: Improving the status of part-timers in higher education.* San Francisco, CA: Jossey-Bass.

Gladwell, M. (2002). *The tipping point: How little things can make a big difference.* New York, NY: Back Bay Books.

Grubb, W. N. & Associates (1999). *Honored but invisible: An inside look at teaching in community colleges.* New York, NY: Routledge.

Jaschik, S. (2006, September 7). Mediocre grades for colleges. Retrieved December 11, 2006, from the *Inside Higher Ed* web site: http://insidehighered.com/news /2006/09/07/reportcard

Leslie, D. W., & Gappa, J. M. (2002). Part-time faculty: Competent and committed. In C. L. Outcalt (Ed.), *New directions for community colleges: No. 118. Community college faculty: Characteristics, practices, and challenges* (pp. 59–67). San Francisco, CA: Jossey-Bass.

Lyons, R. (1996). *A study of the effects of a mentoring initiative on the performance of new, adjunct community college faculty.* Unpublished doctoral dissertation, University of Central Florida.

Mullens, A. (2001). The sessional dilemma. *University Affairs, 42*(5), 10–13, 25.

Roueche, J. E., Roueche, S. D., & Milliron, M. D. (1995). *Strangers in their own land: Part-time faculty in American community colleges.* Washington, DC: Community College Press.

Schuetz, P. (2002). Instructional practices of part-time and full-time faculty. In C. L. Outcalt (Ed.), *New directions for community colleges: No. 118. Community college faculty: Characteristics, practices, and challenges* (pp. 39–46). San Francisco, CA: Jossey-Bass.

Appendix 1.1

Template: Adjunct Instructor Information

Use this template to develop an instrument for aiding instructional leaders within a given department/division/program in making course section assignments to adjunct instructors.

Adjunct Instructor Name _____ Date _____
E-mail Address _____ Telephone Number ( ) _____--_____
Area of residence _____ Location of employment _____

1. Available times (check all that apply, add details if appropriate, e.g., after 6 p.m.):

Monday:	Morning ___	Afternoon ___	Evening ___
Tuesday:	Morning ___	Afternoon ___	Evening ___
Wednesday:	Morning ___	Afternoon ___	Evening ___
Thursday:	Morning ___	Afternoon ___	Evening ___
Friday:	Morning ___	Afternoon ___	Evening ___
Saturday:	Morning ___	Afternoon ___	Evening ___

2. Assume that a section of a course is scheduled to begin 48 hours from now. On a scale of 0 (neither background nor interest in teaching course) to 10 (proven expertise and high interest), evaluate your ability to teach the following courses successfully:

XXX 1001	Introduction to XXX	___
XXX 2001	XXX for Non-Majors	___
XXX 2002	Intermediate XXX	___
XXX 3001	Special Topics in XXX	___
XXX 3003	Seminar in XXX	___
XXX 4001	Advanced Applications of XXX	___
Etc.		

3. Place a check mark in the blank beside the profile that best explains your lifestyle and reasons for teaching:

    ___ *Specialist, expert, professional:* Employed full-time or nearly full-time outside of teaching at the college; teach part-time primarily as a strategy for sharing expertise with others, making contacts, and generating additional income.

___ *Career ender:* Retired or nearing retirement; teaching for personal fulfillment, sharing expertise with students, and generating additional income.

___ *Freelancer:* By choice, work several part-time jobs, including teaching, because of the variety and rewards it provides.

___ *Aspiring academic:* Teach part-time as a strategy for gaining a full-time teaching position at the college or university level.

Template: Adjunct Instructor Orientation Checklist

Resources Provided and Explained:
___ College/university catalog
___ Adjunct Faculty Handbook
___ Academic calendar/Course schedule/Department brochure
___ Teaching and Learning Center brochure
___ Other?

Administrative Issues:
___ Personnel file? Note missing items:
___ Teaching eligibility process completed? Note missing items:
___ Faculty ID card, parking sticker, library card issued?
___ Other?

Instructional Issues:
___ Institutional/program mission? Relationships with other institutions?
___ Profile of students? Typical class size? Receipt of official class rolls?
___ Course enrollment procedures? Drop/add procedures? Course "make" policy?
___ Schedule of required meetings, professional development opportunities?
___ Student support resources: library, computer labs, academic coaching?
___ Classroom issues: keys/security codes, housekeeping, equipment, etc.
___ Parking, security issues, and personnel access? Protocols for reporting incidents?
___ Student recruitment and retention guidelines, student counseling protocols?
___ Evaluation of instructor performance protocols?
___ Grading protocols, final grade rolls, submission procedures?
___ FERPA and ADA protocols?
___ Auxiliary resources: printing, audiovisual equipment? Computer labs?
___ Other?

Academic Unit Issues:
___ Organizational chart? Communications system? Mentoring protocol?
___ Role of assigned course in curriculum? Prerequisites? Required/elective?
___ Course syllabus/outline, standard learning objectives?

__   Textbook, ancillary materials? Adoption process? Prices?
        Bookstore logistics?
__   Office, storage space? Work areas? Meeting space with students?
__   Clerical/administrative assistance? Roles/protocols?
__   Mailbox, materials distribution system?
__   Specialized facilities, equipment, resources?
__   Introduction to key people?
__   Critical issues facing academic unit?
__   Other?

2 | Ensuring an Effective Start for Adjunct Faculty: Orientation With Multiple Options

Kevin Yee

The University of Central Florida (UCF) faces the kinds of challenges in adjunct faculty development that are commonly seen at other institutions of higher learning around the nation. There are three main issues that pose obstacles to adjunct faculty development: steady turnover, a population of adjunct faculty members with great diversity in experience and disciplinary backgrounds, and a decentralized hiring system that adds complexity to the challenge of identifying new adjunct faculty and offering timely development. As the seventh largest university in the nation, the University of Central Florida (UCF) currently hosts 45,000 students on several campuses. The Orlando campus is supplemented by growing campuses in Daytona Beach, Cocoa, and several other regional campuses and centers, many in cooperation with onsite community colleges. The hiring of faculty members, both full-time and part-time, has grown with the university in recent years, and UCF employed 305 adjunct faculty in a recent semester. Many of these part-time instructors are new each semester.

The adjunct faculty members hired each year come from different disciplines and have different goals. An effective first step to understanding the population of adjunct faculty and their needs can be asking them to identify themselves by the categories first created in Judith Gappa and David Leslie's (1993) seminal work *The Invisible Faculty*:

- *Aspiring academics*—Teach part-time while developing their credentials and teaching and research skills in preparation for an anticipated full-time teaching career.

- *Freelancers*—Maintain more than one part-time employment position by choice (examples: professional musicians, soccer moms, consultants).

- *Specialists, experts, or professionals*—Teach primarily for the ability to network themselves into their communities and grow their careers.

- *Career enders*—About to retire from full-time work; motivated to teach as a way to give something of themselves back to their careers.

When asked which category best reflected their own situation, the adjunct instructors attending UCF responded as shown in Table 2.1.

Table 2.1. *Self-Reported Adjunct Type (Gappa/Leslie Categories)*

Aspiring Academics	32%
Freelancers	18%
Specialists, Experts, or Professionals	33%
Career Enders	17%

The various types of adjunct instructors have differing levels of experience in academic settings. Aspiring academics, for example, are more likely to be familiar with classroom management techniques, often assembled over time by a process of trial and error. Although these instructors may have more experience, they are also the group most likely to seek more ideas for teaching strategies because many of them are hoping to become full-time professors and plan to teach for years to come. Specialists, experts, or professionals sometimes have no classroom experience prior to this teaching engagement. While some institutions may find it useful to customize development opportunities after identifying adjunct instructors by category, UCF has adopted a more inclusive approach. Even though adjunct faculty may think they have diverse goals when they first participate in faculty development offerings, in practice most groups of adjunct faculty end up having similar needs to full-time faculty, and their training and development may not need to be customized.

Yet challenges remain for faculty developers. The turnover in any given term constitutes dozens of adjunct faculty members, implying a renewed need each session for orientation and development opportunities. As is common around the country, each department or program at UCF separately hires faculty, including adjunct faculty, as their needs and budgets permit. As a consequence, there are no convenient methods for knowing when adjunct faculty have been hired or how to contact them, because many adjunct faculty use their own private email accounts rather than a university account. One of the primary challenges is identifying the adjunct faculty to advertise training and development opportunities. The combined effect of these challenges—different types of adjunct faculty, steady turnover, and hiring practices—argues against a single unified orientation program. Instead, at UCF there are multilayered opportunities for adjunct faculty to receive assistance and attend training sessions of varying lengths and commitments.

ADJUNCT INSTRUCTORS AT UCF

The University of Central Florida employs more than 1,600 faculty annually, broken down as shown in Table 2.2. Within the academic year 2005–2006, 72% of the adjunct instructors who worked in the first semester also worked in the second semester. This continuity of adjunct faculty within the academic year was accompanied by a burst of additional hiring during spring semester 2006, with the result that 41% of the second semester's total had not worked in that position the previous term.

Table 2.2 *UCF Faculty by Category*

Academic Year 2005–2006	
Full-Time Faculty—Tenured and Tenure-Earning	848
Full-Time Faculty—Visitors	160
Full-Time Faculty—Instructors	202
Adjunct Faculty	305
Graduate Teaching Assistants (FTEs)	169
Total	*1,684*

Source: Integrated Postsecondary Education Data System (www.nces.ed.gov/ipeds/)

From year to year, the number of returning adjunct faculty fluctuates. At the start of the 2005–2006 academic year, 48% of the adjunct faculty had not been in that position the previous semester. In fact, only 37% of the adjunct faculty teaching in spring 2006 had been teaching at UCF in spring 2005.

The adjunct faculty members were distributed around the university as shown in Table 2.3 at the start of the academic year 2005–2006.

Table 2.3. *Distribution of Adjunct Faculty*

Portion of the Total Pool of Adjunct Faculty	College
34%	Arts and Humanities
27%	Health and Public Affairs
18%	Education
7%	Engineering and Computer Science
6%	Hospitality Management
4%	Business Administration
2%	Sciences
1%	Biomedical Sciences
1%	Other

With such a wide array of disciplines and teaching experience in the adjunct faculty population, training is best accomplished by employing multiple solutions and providing various resources for information. At the institutional level, the Office of the Provost and the vice president for academic affairs maintain an online faculty handbook consisting of an overview of the institution, an introduction to the university's organizational structure, and guidelines for academic and employment information such as regulations, policies, procedures, and benefits. There are also links to pedagogical, research, and campus resources maintained elsewhere on campus. At the local level, some departments create and annually maintain their own handbooks for adjunct faculty. Though often unbound, these packets are detailed and highly tailored, often covering the entire adjunct faculty experience from entering the department to leaving it. The Department of Public Administration at UCF has created an adjunct faculty handbook covering common questions by new part-time instructors, divided by topics such as hiring, department policies on keys and photocopies, and teaching specifics such as ordering books and finding rosters (see Appendix 2.1 for the table of contents). Because some of this information overlaps with other offices and units on campus, portions of the handbook must be revised each year. The benefits to the adjunct faculty receiving the handbook are significant, leaving few questions unanswered.

The Faculty Center for Teaching and Learning at UCF also invites adjunct faculty members to an orientation for new faculty. In addition, the faculty center created several professional development opportunities specifically for adjunct faculty. In an effort to address the needs of the many part-time constituencies, each with varying degrees of availability and different desires for the breadth and depth of orientation and development, the faculty center has adopted a three-pronged approach. Adjunct faculty may come to the program that best suits their schedule and desire to learn more about the university. Some elect to come to all three. However, all are voluntary.

OPPORTUNITY #1: ONE-HOUR WORKSHOPS AND THE FACULTY CENTER WORKBOOK

The faculty center at UCF hosts numerous one-hour workshops just before and just after the start of each semester. These sessions are designed to address the important nuts and bolts at the institution. They also provide plentiful handouts that point to additional resources on campus and other handouts that offer teaching tips. In short, faculty developers provide resources so that adjunct faculty will know where to turn when they need more assistance and ideas. These workshops are provided at no cost to the participant.

The faculty center sponsors a single-day development retreat for adjunct faculty. Several handouts were used so often that over the years they evolved into a workbook that encourages adjunct faculty to continue their development on their own. Adapted from a series of worksheets into more of a self-guided discovery of teaching and pedagogical techniques, the 150-page workbook is broad enough to be used for varied faculty and instructional audiences at UCF, not just adjunct faculty. It is provided free of charge to teachers (see Appendix 2.2 for the table of contents). This document, like the adjunct faculty handbook from the Department of Public Administration, requires occasional updating and is best not preprinted in massive quantities in case information changes throughout the year.

Some of these materials are available on the Faculty Success web site, which provides easily accessible links to many of the resources adjunct faculty would need. The web site is divided into five sections: Getting Started, Helpful Resources, Important Information, Policies and Procedures, and Student Resources (it can be accessed by the general public at www.fctl.ucf.edu/success).

During the one-hour workshops, adjunct faculty are provided with the workbooks and the Faculty Success URL, though participants are free to direct the discussion as their needs dictate. Often, the non-UCF pedagogical resources of the workbook are deferred for later study, and adjunct faculty choose to use the workshop time to explore UCF-specific details, such as campus and electronic resources available to them.

OPPORTUNITY #2: SINGLE DAY-LONG RETREAT

The primary orientation and training of adjunct faculty at UCF occurs during a full-day retreat near the start of every term. This eight-hour retreat dedicates one-third of the time to campus resources and institution-specific information and the remaining two-thirds of the time to pedagogical topics such as course design, syllabus writing, crafting assessments, interactive teaching methods, and classroom management. Adjunct faculty from all disciplines around the university are invited, but attendance tends to be approximately 40 participants per retreat. The retreat is organized into a series of 30- and 75-minute workshops on various topics, with some overlap of the themes in the faculty center workbook, making the workbook a good choice for the primary text used in this retreat (see Appendix 2.3 for the itinerary of the retreat).

Participants are paid a stipend for attending, because adjunct faculty sometimes hold other jobs, and a day spent on professional development might mean a day when another source of income is forfeited, and because additional expenses (such as child care) might be incurred by choosing to attend. Furthermore, the stipend reaffirms the university's belief in the importance of professional development for all teaching faculty at UCF.

UCF offers the full-day workshop on Saturday to provide for adjunct faculty who work full-time during the normal workweek. Participants are given a copy of *The Adjunct Professor's Guide to Success* (Lyons, Kysilka, & Pawlas, 1999), a prominent how-to book, to read and adopt on their own. As an alternative, participants may request a copy of *Teaching Tips* (McKeachie & Svinicki, 2006) or *A Handbook for Adjunct/Part-Time Faculty and Teachers of Adults* (Greive, 2002).

A study of the effectiveness of this single-day retreat began in spring 2006. The purpose of the study is to gauge adjunct faculty's self-reported knowledge in five areas (identifying campus resources, locating campus resources, teaching effectively, required syllabus components, and FERPA compliance) on identical pre- and postsurveys. The surveys are administered to adjunct faculty who attend the single-day retreat and agree to participate in the study. The presurvey is administered at the start of the day, just after the study is announced and explained, and before participants have seen the agenda for the retreat. The postsurveys are administered at the end of the same day upon completion of the agenda. Participants self-select a four-digit code to enable comparisons between pre- and postsurveys.

The pre- and postsurveys contain the same five questions, asking participants to gauge how well they know campus and pedagogical resources. These questions are answered on a 5-point Likert scale: 5 = *agree strongly*, 4 = *agree*, 3 = *neutral*, 2 = *disagree*, and 1 = *disagree strongly*. Preliminary data reveal an average pretest score of 3.40 and an average posttest score of 4.59, indicating a significant increase in participants' self-reported knowledge as a result of the retreat.

Part of the same study that began in 2006 is a direct assessment of participants' knowledge of general pedagogical principles and specific UCF policies. Once again, the identical test is used before and after the same-day retreat (see Appendix 2.4). The results of the nine questions of the knowledge test are shown in Table 2.4.

The retreat, therefore, generated improvement not only in the participants' perception of their knowledge, but also their direct knowledge. The results do have some limitations. The data do not account for long-term recall of the concepts and information provided at the retreat, because the posttest was administered on the same day. The questions posed in the survey and test do not directly address the retreat's perceived utility, though written comments

Table 2.4. *Percentage of the participants who answered correctly*

	Pretest	Posttest
Question 1	88%	100%
Question 2	56%	100%
Question 3	38%	100%
Question 4	31%	94%
Question 5	94%	94%
Question 6	31%	69%
Question 7	81%	81%
Question 8	100%	94%
Question 9	81%	94%
Average	67%	92%

on informal event evaluations indicate that the majority of adjunct faculty find the retreat to be highly useful.

Participants who attend the retreat are provided with a letter of partici-pation and encouragement to continue their professional development through additional association with Faculty Center activities. This letter can be helpful in the adjunct faculty member's teaching and professional portfo-lio. The face-to-face interaction at the retreat creates a sense of community among the adjunct faculty members, who as a group might otherwise strug-gle to identify with other faculty members on campus. As Roueche, Rouche, and Milliron (1995) note, adjunct faculty integration into every campus community is desired and necessary for the institution's overall health. Howard and Hintz (2002) call for a more formalized mentoring program to ease the transition from orientation to self-sufficiency for adjunct faculty.

OPPORTUNITY #3: ONLINE COURSE

An online course was also developed in summer 2006 and was made available to all adjunct faculty and other teaching faculty on campus. Administered through a free, open-source course-management platform named Moodle (www.moodle.org), this online course provides a modular approach to campus resources and pedagogical topics that are explored at greater length (sometimes with several layers of additional information available via optional hyperlinks). As with any online course, this one benefits users by being accessible anywhere and at any time. Also, the modular approach allows for self-directed learning. The modules can be reinforced with online course tools such as electronic quizzes, discussion forums, and assignments that may easily be submitted online for grading. Using templates, the participants may design an entire course from the beginning. They can also build their own teaching portfolios to showcase their experiences and abilities. An additional goal is to sharpen their beliefs and practices in teaching (or, in some cases, to begin to craft those beliefs and practices). Although it was designed for the UCF audience, the course is open to the public and visitors are free to explore without creating an account: http://courses.fctl.ucf.edu.

One challenge to the developers of the course was to provide information at a self-guided pace for faculty who may be seeking different depths of information. For example, not every faculty member will open this web site intending to read all the course modules or to complete the course at all; such adjunct faculty may merely be seeking an abbreviated explanation of essential information, such as the syllabus components required by the university. Others may want to pursue additional links and access not only practical applications common in teaching, but also the relevant theoretical underpinnings. For such adjunct faculty, the online course offers much more than a point of reference; it becomes an active source of investigating pedagogical issues. Helen Burnstad (2003) recommends the use of refresher orientations for adjunct faculty every few years, and this online course provides such an opportunity.

The course was developed as a group of stand-alone modules. The use of additional links to learn more details provides the needed balance between too much and too little information. Although this web site can be used as an equivalent of a course, there is no transcript credit for completion, and the course operates without a schedule. Participants may begin or end at any time or take as long to complete the material as they desire. This online offering may be the only orientation for some adjunct faculty, particularly if their scheduling precludes attending the one-hour workshops or the full-day retreat. As a result, the online course covers some familiar content addressed in the workbook and the one-day retreat, though it is organized into a modular approach (see Appendix 2.5).

SUMMARY

The faculty center attempts to advertise its development offerings for adjunct faculty to as many of them as possible. In addition to print and online advertisements through the university-wide email list and a faculty center newsletter (the same outlets used to advertise regular workshops), the faculty center also requests a list of adjunct faculty a few weeks prior to the start of classes from the Office of Institutional Research at UCF. Because hiring is ongoing and sometimes occurs just before the start of the term, the complete adjunct faculty list is difficult to obtain before the start of the semester. This list includes departmental information and email addresses. Adjunct faculty can then be emailed directly and informed of the various development opportunities available to them. Another successful method is to contact department chairs to inform them directly of the orientation options. Chairs know whom they have hired and who is likely to want or need orientation, and they are happy to forward the email to interested adjunct faculty.

The population of adjunct faculty at UCF is varied by discipline, employment situation, and experience in the classroom. Because adjunct faculty have wide differences in availability for training and scheduling, the faculty center at UCF has responded with a three-tiered system designed to offer development in a variety of depths and schedules: short-duration workshops, a medium-duration retreat, and a long-duration online course (which can also be used as a quick online reference tool). The hope is that a diverse set of offerings will address the needs of all adjunct faculty, regardless of experience, availability, and schedule.

References

Burnstad, H. M. (2003). Part-time faculty development at Johnson County Community College. In G. E. Watts (Ed.), *New directions for community colleges: No. 120. Enhancing community colleges through professional development* (pp. 17–25). San Francisco, CA: Jossey-Bass.

Gappa, J. M., & Leslie, D. W. (1993). *The invisible faculty: Improving the status of part-timers in higher education.* San Francisco, CA: Jossey-Bass.

Greive, D. (2002). *A handbook for adjunct/part-time faculty and teachers of adults* (4th ed.). Cleveland, OH: INFO-TEC.

Howard, B., & Hintz, S. (2002, May 24). *Adjunct faculty orientation and mentoring: Developing and retaining the best!* Paper presented at the annual meeting of the National Institute for Staff and Organizational Development, Austin, TX.

Lyons, R. E, Kysilka, M. L., & Pawlas, G. W. (1999). *The adjunct professor's guide to success: Surviving and thriving in the college classroom.* Boston, MA: Allyn & Bacon.

McKeachie, W. J., & Svinicki, M. (2006). *Teaching tips: Strategies, research, and theory for college and university teachers* (12th ed.). Boston, MA: Houghton Mifflin.

Roueche, J. E., Roueche, S. D., & Milliron, M. D. (1995). *Strangers in their own land: Part-time faculty in American community colleges.* Washington, DC: Community College Press.

APPENDIX 2.1

Adjunct Faculty Handbook
UCF's Department of Public Administration

Table of Contents

    o.   Grievances
    p.   Department Evaluation

IV. The Department Office
    a.   Copy Machines
    b.   Print Shop Processes

V. Campus Resources
    a.   University Testing Center
    b.   Library
    c.   Computer Labs
    d.   Faculty Center for Teaching & Learning
    e.   Student Disability Services
    f.   University Writing Center

VI. Appendices
    a.   Program Curriculum and Requirements
    b.   Departmental Certificates
    c.   Important Web Resources
    d.   Speakers/Topic Presenters
    e.   Computer Lab Locations
    f.   Example of Semester Timeline
    g.   Sample Adjunct Performance Evaluation Form
    h.   Sample UCF Bookstore Order Form
    i.   Instructions for Reserving Items at the Library

APPENDIX 2.2

Faculty Center Workbook

Table of Contents

I.   Learners and Learning
    Learning Theories
    Learner Differences
    Bloom's Taxonomy of Educational Objectives

II. Teaching
    Course Design
    Syllabus Design
    Effective Lectures

Leading a Discussion/Lab
Collaborative Learning
Problem-Based Learning (PBL)
101 Interactive Techniques
Final Course Evaluations (Sample)
Midterm Evaluation

III. Managing Roles and Relationships
Academic Freedom and Integrity
Academic Dishonesty
Legal Matters
Interacting with Students with Disabilities
Atmosphere
Classroom Management Scenarios
Diversity
Case Studies
Testing and Grading
Managing Grades
Grading with Rubrics
Online Gradebook: myUCF Grades

IV. The Teaching Portfolio
Teaching Portfolio Overview
Teaching Philosophy Sample
Sample Narrative

V. Campus and Online Resources
Timeline of the Semester: Deadlines and Preparing for the First Day of Class
Questions to Ask Your Chair or Department Representative
Printing Photos of Your Students
Offices on Campus
Online Resources

Appendix 2.3

Itinerary at Full-Day Adjunct Retreat

I. Online and Campus Resources
Faculty Center workbook
Overview of the Faculty Center services
UCF Portal: rosters, eCommunity, other programs

WebCT: grade reporting, using it for online office hours, etc.
Faculty Center Web site and resources
Wireless network at UCF
Parking and parking stickers
Identification card and library card
Interactive campus map

II.　Teaching Portfolios / Teaching Philosophy
　　Importance and composition of a teaching portfolio
　　Peer observations
　　Teaching philosophy statement

III.　Classroom Technology: Demonstration of the Classroom Console Computer

IV.　Course Design, Goals & Objectives
　　Inventory of teaching goals
　　Aligning course goals
　　Goals vs. objectives

V.　Syllabi & Lesson Plans
　　Lesson plans and course objectives
　　What elements should be on every UCF syllabus?
　　Reverse-engineering an inherited syllabus

VI.　Lunch: Discussion of Case Study

VII.　The Diverse Classroom Environment
　　Learner differences: Learning Styles inventories

VIII.　Instructional Methodologies, Assessment Techniques
　　Teaching large classes
　　Classroom Assessment Techniques (CATs)
　　PowerPoint practices
　　Group work, PBL, collaboration

IX.　Cheating, Plagiarism, and Disruptive Conduct
　　Academic freedom, academic integrity
　　"Problem students" and classroom management
　　End of semester evaluations / "midterm evaluations"

APPENDIX 2.4

UCF General Knowledge Test for Adjunct Instructors

1. At UCF, all classes are required to use the plus/minus grading system.
    a.   True
    b.   False
    Pre-test: 88% of the participants answered correctly
    Post-test: 100% of the participants answered correctly

2. Objectives are different from goals in that:
    a.   Goals should be met before objectives are attempted.
    b.   Objectives should be met before goals are attempted.
    c.   Objectives are measurable; goals may not be.
    d.   There is no difference between goals and objectives.
    Pre-test: 56% of the participants answered correctly
    Post-test: 100% of the participants answered correctly

3. Twenty-four hours after a class where only lecture was employed, how much material does the average student remember?
    a.   5%
    b.   10%
    c.   20%
    d.   25%
    Pre-test: 38% of the participants answered correctly
    Post-test: 100% of the participants answered correctly

4. Which of these is not a major section of a teaching portfolio?
    a.   Statement of Teaching Philosophy
    b.   Statement of Teaching Practices
    c.   Narrative
    d.   Appendices
    Pre-test: 31% of the participants answered correctly
    Post-test: 94% of the participants answered correctly

5. It is legal to post student grades outside a lecture hall only if grades are listed by:
    a.   The last four digits of the Social Security number
    b.   UCF ID number
    c.   Random code
    d.   Any of the above is legal.

Pre-test: 94% of the participants answered correctly
Post-test: 94% of the participants answered correctly

6. Which of the following is most true?
    a. The syllabus should be seen as the instructor's contract with the students.
    b. The syllabus should not be seen as the instructor's contract with the students.
    c. The syllabus will often be seen as the instructor's contract with the students and should be given an overt tone of legalese.
    d. The syllabus will often be seen as the instructor's contract with the students but should not be given an overt tone of legalese.
    Pre-test: 31% of the participants answered correctly
    Post-test: 69% of the participants answered correctly

7. Which of the following is NOT one of Bloom's Taxonomy of Educational Objectives?
    a. Interpretation
    b. Comprehension
    c. Analysis
    d. Synthesis
    Pre-test: 81% of the participants answered correctly
    Post-test: 81% of the participants answered correctly

8. The online resource at UCF where you can see the faces of your students before the semester begins is called:
    a. WebCT
    b. myUCF
    c. SocialNet
    d. eCommunity
    Pre-test: 100% of the participants answered correctly
    Post-test: 94% of the participants answered correctly

9. On the first day of class, a student tells you she has dyslexia and would like additional time to take all the tests. Your correct response is to:
    a. Administer a diagnostic test to discover if the student really has dyslexia.
    b. Point out that it would be unfair to other students to grant additional time.
    c. Agree to the student's request and find a solution you can both live with.
    d. Defer answering the question for now and refer the student to the Office of Student Disability Services.
    Pre-test: 81% of the participants answered correctly
    Post-test: 94% of the participants answered correctly

Appendix 2.5

Outline of Online Course for Adjunct Instructors

Module 1—Introduction to Campus Resources
Module 2—The First Day of Class, Nuts and Bolts of the Semester, Deadlines, Due Dates
Module 3—Legal Policies and Classroom Management; Interactions with Students
Module 4—Building a Course From Scratch; Writing Goals and Objectives
Module 5—Creating a Syllabus (Plus: How to "Translate" an Inherited One)
Module 6—Creating a Lesson Plan
Module 7—Effective Lectures
Module 8—Instructional Technologies: WebCT and PowerPoint
Module 9—Tests, Rubrics, Midterm Evaluations
Module 10—Interactive "Classroom Assessment Techniques"
Module 11—Addressing Multiple Learning Styles
Module 12—Collaborative Learning
Module 13—Active Learning Strategies
Module 14—Learning Theories
Module 15—Teaching Portfolios: Definitions, Templates, Samples

3 | THE PART-TIME FACULTY INSTITUTE: STRATEGICALLY DESIGNED AND CONTINUALLY ASSESSED

Marianne H. Hutti, Gale S. Rhodes, Joni Allison, Evelyn Lauterbach

The growing body of literature related to part-time faculty suggests that one of the ways to make part-time faculty members feel more valued and respected is to provide them with faculty development programming created specifically for their needs. This chapter describes the assessment process used to evaluate the needs of the part-time faculty at the University of Louisville (Kentucky), and the year-long faculty development program that was developed to meet those needs. The program and its evaluation will be described, evaluation tools will be provided, and plans for future programming based on a second needs assessment will also be identified.

The mission of the University of Louisville (U of L) is to be Kentucky's premier, nationally recognized, metropolitan research university. Established in 1798, U of L has 21,760 students, 5,764 faculty and staff, and more than 100,000 alumni around the world. U of L has approximately 539 part-time and 1,445 full-time faculty members. The literature reports many problems that part-time faculty identify related to their work. These problems include lack of office space (27%), lack of office telephone (26%), lack of computer access (42%), lack of access to photocopying or library services (8%), and no support for professional development (72%; Townsend & Hauss, 2002). Additionally, part-time faculty members are seldom assigned to faculty mentors, and administrators do not evaluate their work. Therefore, excellent part-time faculty members receive no recognition, and substandard teachers get no direction (Nutting, 2003). Further, part-time faculty often teach larger, and often lower level classes than full-time faculty (Nutting, 2003). As a group, part-time faculty are underpaid, overworked, and frequently feel unappreciated and disrespected (Woodson, 2005).

The literature is also full of ideas for assisting part-time faculty to feel more valued. Universities should focus on creating a sense of community for part-time faculty by improving communication with them; routinely including them in department and school events and meetings; providing adequate office space for advising and paperwork; offering part-time faculty adequate telephone, copying, and computer access; providing an updated faculty handbook designed specifically for part-time faculty; recognizing them for teaching excellence and years of service; considering to offer privileges such as tuition benefits, travel subsidies, and other incentives (Bach, 1999; Woodson, 2005); and investing in faculty development programming specifically tailored to part-time faculty (Hickey, 2005).

UNIVERSITY OF LOUISVILLE
PART-TIME FACULTY NEEDS ASSESSMENT

Part-time faculty members are critical to the teaching mission of the University of Louisville. The university recognized the need to retain and continue to develop its part-time faculty, and it wanted to help them feel more valued and appreciated. As a result, the Delphi Center for Teaching and Learning worked with the Part-Time Faculty Subcommittee of the University of Louisville Faculty Senate to develop a needs assessment for their part-time faculty during the spring 2004 semester, which was then administered to the part-time faculty. Professional development programming specific to the needs of the part-time faculty was developed based on this assessment using the top six needs that were identified.

No doubt, like many large institutions, the University of Louisville does not have an email list of all of its currently employed part-time faculty members. Therefore recruiting participants for the needs assessment depended upon a list of part-time faculty kept by the Part-Time Subcommittee of the Faculty Senate, which was generated through self-identification by part-time faculty members. Items for the needs assessment were developed then administered to the 278 part-time faculty on the senate's part-time faculty Listserv via an email-based software survey program called Zoomerang. A 15.8% response rate (n = 44) was obtained. Participants were asked about their perceived learning needs, preferred timing of programming, and incentives, if offered.

Results of the Initial Part-Time Faculty Needs Assessment

The majority of the part-time faculty respondents (58%) had taught at U of L for one to six years. During this time, 66% reported they had received training on teaching methodologies. The most common training received was related to the Blackboard Learning Management System (77%), instructional design (33%), planning course strategies (33%), syllabus development (33%), and departmental policies and procedures (30%). A large majority (90%) reported they would be interested in attending a faculty development program specifically tailored to part-time faculty.

The top learning needs identified in the needs assessment included:

1. Facilitating student engagement in the classroom
2. Instructional design
3. Diversity in the classroom
4. Teaching with technology
5. Testing and evaluation
6. Designing online learning

These top identified needs became the topics delivered to the faculty during the Part-Time Faculty Institute, based on the decision of the associate director of the Delphi Center. The majority (63%) of participants requested weekday programming, but more than one-third (35%) preferred evening programming. Therefore, as the sessions were planned, they were offered twice monthly, once in the late afternoon from 3:00–5:00 p.m. and again on a different day from 5:30–7:30 p.m. to maximize attendance. Hors d'oeuvres were offered in the late afternoon, and a buffet supper was offered in the evening session. The institute, including stipends, was funded through the Delphi Center for Teaching and Learning.

When asked about stipend preference, respondents preferred a monetary stipend (60%) over an iPod (21%) or a personal digital assistant (PDA; 19%). Therefore, the program was developed with a $300 stipend as the incentive after faculty members completed five of the six sessions in the series to encourage part-time faculty participation. A certificate of completion was also awarded.

The purpose of the Part-Time Faculty Institute is to provide high-quality faculty development to U of L part-time faculty at a time and in a manner that they desire. Therefore, each year when the faculty learning needs are reanalyzed to plan for the subsequent year, participants are also asked how often they wish to meet, what time of day is most convenient for them, and the meeting format and type of incentive they prefer. This assists the planners to continue to bring faculty-centered programming to the part-time faculty annually and helps to ensure the success of the program.

During the initial planning of the program, the literature on part-time faculty was reviewed to discover what benchmark institutions were doing for their part-time faculty. This information helped the planners discover what to ask the faculty in terms of the choices they could be given. However, the plan always was to develop the program around the desires of the faculty, rather than what others were doing, with the assumption that they would be more likely to take advantage of a program that they helped to design.

The instructors for the institute were recruited from U of L faculty members who had won at least one university-level teaching award in the past five years. These award-winning faculty members were then sent a list of the topics that were planned for the institute, and if they had the background and interest in teaching any of the specific topics for their part-time colleagues. Instructors were easily found among this group, even though they were offered a minimal stipend of $200 for sessions they taught. The associate director of the program met with the faculty presenters and discussed the expectation that each session would be interactive and the faculty presenters would role-model active teaching strategies as they taught—regardless of topic. Each session also left at least 30 minutes for participants to apply the information presented.

The participants in the Part-Time Faculty Institute are all volunteers and are accepted on a first-come, first-served basis. Participation was not limited in 2005. A total of 93 part-time faculty participated in the institute in its first year. Of these, 42 were male (45%) and 51 were female (55%). A total of six sessions were offered during the two semesters of the institute, and faculty could join the institute in the fall or the spring semester. Table 3.1 indicates the number of participants who attended one or more of the sessions offered (attendance at five of six sessions was required for completion and the stipend) and the university schools that these part-time faculty represented.

Table 3.1.

Number of Participants Attending	
6 sessions = 24	3 sessions = 9
5 sessions = 17	2 sessions = 17
4 sessions = 11	1 session = 15

Representing the Following Schools:	
32	School of Arts and Sciences
14	Kent School of Social Work
9	School of Education
9	Nonacademic Departments/Unknown
8	School of Dentistry
7	School of Business
4	School of Medicine
4	School of Music
3	Speed School of Engineering
2	School of Nursing
1	Libraries
0	School of Law
0	School of Public Health
93	*Total Part-Time Faculty Members*

Second Part-Time Faculty Needs Assessment

A second needs assessment was completed during sessions four, five, and six of the initial (2005–2006) Part-Time Faculty Institute to determine learning needs for 2006–2007. Part-time participants were asked if any changes should be made in the format of the institute, particularly related to how often the institute met, the number of sessions, the timing of the sessions, and incentives offered. Only faculty who had participated in the institute

were included in this needs assessment. Sixty-one faculty members responded to the second needs assessment (79.2% response rate; n = 77). The second needs assessment was developed based on a review of the
teaching/learning literature and included 85 choices. An example of the
needs assessment used to evaluate the part-time faculty can be found in
Appendix 3.1. The top learning needs identified for the second year of the
institute included:

1. Teaching to different learning styles
2. Strategies for enhancing active learning
3. Motivating students
4. Teaching for deeper learning
5. The art of leading an effective discussion
6. Engaging the quiet student

The majority of participants (40 of 61) continued to prefer monthly "meet
and eat" sessions. Twenty-five respondents suggested changing the format to
faculty learning communities that would meet periodically to learn about
teaching issues of their choosing, and nine preferred one or two day-long
conferences annually for faculty development.

PART-TIME FACULTY INSTITUTE

The Part-Time Faculty Institute held its first session in September 2005. The
institute was comprised of three sessions in the fall and three sessions in the
spring semesters. Once again, each session was taught twice, from either
3:00–5:00 p.m. or from 5:30–7:30 p.m. Again, hors d'oeuvres were offered
in the late afternoon session and supper was offered in the early evening session. All sessions were designed to be very interactive and to role-model the
types of teaching it was hoped that the part-time faculty would utilize in
their classrooms. Institute teachers were award-winning University of
Louisville full- and part-time faculty who were carefully selected based on
their topic knowledge and their ability to teach.

Topics taught were identified by the 2005 needs assessment administered to the institute participants. Fall topics included Facilitating Student
Engagement in the Classroom (September; n = 43), Designing Experiential

Learning (October; n = 47), and Diversity in the Classroom (November; n = 47). Spring topics included Teaching With Technology (February; n = 77), Testing and Evaluation (March; n = 56), and Designing Online Learning (April; n = 50). All faculty members who taught in the Part-Time Faculty Institute were required to submit two to three learning objectives by which their programs were evaluated. As indicated by the sample evaluation form in Appendix 3.2, participants evaluated the degree to which they perceived the session objectives to have been met, as well as the degree to which the content contributed to their knowledge of teaching. Participants were also asked to rate the relevance of the content to their teaching and whether they anticipated the content would help them teach more effectively. Participants' overall satisfaction with the instructors' presentations, opportunities for participation, and course materials were routinely evaluated. In addition, participants were asked to rate their use of the strategies presented *before* they attended the institute at the beginning session of each semester. The evaluators continued to rate the participants' use of these strategies at each evaluation point as the semester progressed. The evaluation form found in Appendix 3.1 was slightly modified each time it was used so that strategies that were utilized over the course of the semester could be evaluated.

Findings From Fall 2005

Table 3.2 identifies the objectives and participant responses from the fall 2005 sessions. The table indicates that participants generally rated the November session highest (Diversity in the Classroom), followed by September (Facilitating Student Engagement) and October (Designing Experiential Learning). Participants rated Objective 5 the highest overall, indicating that the knowledge they gained from the fall sessions would help them teach more effectively. Objective 1 was the second highest rated, indicating that participants believed the objectives of the fall sessions were fully met.

Table 3.2. *Objectives 1–6 (1 = Strongly Disagree to 5 = Strongly Agree)*

Objectives	Sept.	Oct.	Nov.	*(Mean)*
Objectives of the program were fully met.	4.0	3.6	4.1	*(3.9)*
Content of program contributed to my knowledge of teaching.	4.0	3.72	4.0	*(3.9)*
I plan to use the information I gained from this session in my teaching.	3.8	3.36	3.87	*(3.67)*
Information from this session was highly relevant to the teaching that I do.	3.76	3.6	4.1	*(3.82)*
I believe that the knowledge I gained will help me teach more effectively.	4.15	3.72	4.1	*(3.99)*
I anticipate changing the way I teach (even small ways count!) as a result of this program.	3.76	3.27	4.25	*(3.67)*
(Mean)	*(3.91)*	*(3.54)*	*(4.07)*	

Table 3.3. *Teaching Strategies (1 = Never to 5 = Always)*

Baseline/September	Oct.	Nov.	Strategy
2.4	2.2	2.0	Lecture without discussion
2.8	3.6	3.8	Active learning strategies
2.9	3.6	3.9	Reinforce key points
3.0	3.5	3.97	Use phases of student engagement
2.5	—	3.57	Encourage serious conversations among diverse groups
2.6	—	3.39	Include diverse perspectives

Table 3.3 contains the teaching strategies that were addressed in the fall 2005 semester. The September 2005 ratings were used as the baseline for the rest of the semester. As indicated by Table 3.3, the use of lecture without discussion decreased, as hoped, over the course of the fall semester. However, the use of active teaching strategies and other strategies taught as part of the program content increased over time during fall 2005.

Participants also had an opportunity to rate the presenter's overall presentation, the opportunity for participation, and course materials. The objectives were rated on a scale of 1 (*poor*) to 5 (*excellent*) as shown in Table 3.4. Once again, the November presentation on Diversity in the Classroom received the highest overall ratings for presentation, opportunity for participation, and course materials (mean score = 4.4) with the presentation on Facilitating Student Engagement in the Classroom coming in a close second (mean score = 4.38).

Table 3.4. *Overall Evaluation of Presentation (1 = Poor to 5 = Excellent)*

Objective	Sept.	Oct.	Nov.	(Mean)
Instructor's presentation was:	4.3	3.3	4.4	(4.0)
Opportunity for participation was:	4.38	4.2	4.5	(4.36)
Course materials were:	4.46	4.1	4.3	(4.28)
(Mean)	(4.38)	(3.86)	(4.4)	

Findings From Spring 2006

Sessions for spring 2006 included Teaching With Technology (February), Testing and Evaluation (March), and Designing Online Learning (April). Table 3.5 identifies the objectives and participant responses from these sessions. The most highly rated session occurred in March, followed by February and April. All objectives were rated as greater than 4 on a scale of 1–5 (*strongly disagree* to *strongly agree*) except for Objective 6, which asked participants if they anticipated changing the way they teach as a result of this program. The mean score for this objective was 3.52/5.0.

Table 3.5. *Objectives (1 = Strongly Disagree to 5 = Strongly Agree)*

Objectives	Feb.	Mar.	Apr.	(Mean)
Objectives of the program were fully met.	4.6	4.46	4.56	*(4.54)*
Content of the program contributed to my knowledge of teaching.	4.6	4.5	4.54	*(4.54)*
I plan to use the information I gained from this session in my teaching.	4.47	4.59	3.95	*(4.12)*
Information from this session was highly relevant to the teaching that I do.	4.10	4.31	3.95	*(4.12)*
I believe the knowledge I gained will help me teach more effectively.	4.3	4.53	4.35	*(4.39)*
I anticipate changing the way I teach (even small ways count!) as a result of this program.	3.50	3.8	3.26	*(3.52)*
(Mean)	*(4.26)*	*(4.36)*	*(4.17)*	

Table 3.6 contains the teaching strategies that were addressed in the spring 2006 semester. The February 2006 ratings were used as the baseline for the remainder of the semester. These ratings were computed by taking the overall results for each session on each objective and then multiplying the total number of participants in each associated subcategory with the number assigned to that category (e.g., 4 = *very frequently,* 3 = *frequently,* 2 = *seldom,* 1 = *never*) on our Likert scale. Each of the subtotals was then summed and divided by the total number of respondents to get a mean score for that objective.

As in the fall, the results showed that the use of the teaching strategies taught during the spring semester increased over time from the baseline measurement point in February to the final measurement point in August 2006. The April session related to Designing Online Learning and used a variety of teaching methods in the online environment. This was the last class session. Therefore, how faculty members were using the knowledge at that time could not be evaluated. A follow-up email-based survey was sent to institute participants in August 2006 to evaluate their use of the strategies they learned about in April 2006. A response rate of 61% was obtained.

Table 3.6. *Use of Teaching Strategies Over Time (1 = Never to 5 = Always)*

Baseline/February	Mar.	Apr.	Aug.	Strategy
2.5	3.10	3.05	—	Utilize various forms of technology in the classroom.
2.11	2.3	2.6	2.6	Develop and use grading rubrics.
1.5	—	2.4	2.7	Develop effective multiple-choice exams.
1.72	—	—	2.3	Design online instruction.
1.77	—	—	2.4	Use a variety of mediums in online instruction to effectively meet needs of learners.

As indicated in Table 3.6, part-time faculty continued to grow in their knowledge from the baseline measurement in February 2006 and the final measurement in August 2006. While they did not increase their use of rubrics over the summer term (between May and August 2006), some of them did not teach during that time, so they did not report a decrease in their use of rubrics. From the baseline in February to the final measurement in August 2006, their self-report of design of online instruction increased from a mean of 1.72 to 2.3. Their use of a variety of mediums and methods in online teaching to better meet the needs of their learners increased from 1.77 to 2.4 in this same time period. Their self-reported ability to develop effective multiple-choice exams increased from 1.5 to 2.7.

Table 3.7. *Overall Evaluation of Presentation (1 = Poor to 5 = Excellent)*

Objectives	February	March	April	(Mean)
Instructor's presentation was:	4.8	4.61	4.66	(4.69)
Opportunity for participation was:	4.73	4.26	4.39	(4.46)
Course materials were:	4.57	4.48	4.39	(4.41)
(Mean)	(4.7)	4.45)	(4.45)	

Instructors' presentations in spring 2006 were well received by participants. On a scale of 1 (*poor*) to 5 (*excellent*), participants rated both their opportunities for participation and their course materials as "good" or better (greater than 4.0). The February presentation on Teaching With Technology was rated the highest of the three spring presentations in terms of overall instructor presentation, opportunity for participation, and course materials.

Appendix 3.2 is an example of the evaluation form used for the Part-Time Faculty Institute. Faculty were evaluated using the learning objectives that they submitted in Section I, as well as general program outcome objectives in Section II. Specific evaluation of the presentation, the opportunity for participation, and handouts are requested in Section III. Section IV is an evaluation of the use of the teaching strategies in the upcoming sessions. Section IVa requests an assessment of the participants' knowledge of the teaching strategies prior to any of the sessions and captures baseline data for the learner group. Section IVb requests a personal assessment of how much participants learned about each teaching strategy in the sessions provided and serves as perceived program outcome data for faculty who participate in the institute.

Limitations

This evaluation is limited in that all of the assessment is based on measures of self-assessment. No objective measures of change in teaching were used. These findings cannot be generalized beyond this sample.

CONCLUSIONS

The Part-Time Faculty Institute was well received by participants. Teaching strategies that were presented in fall 2005 and spring 2006 demonstrated increasing use by participants over the course of the fall and spring semesters. The Part-Time Faculty Institute will be continued in 2007 utilizing the top learning needs identified in the spring 2006 needs assessment. Additional unexpected benefits of the institute include creating a sense of community among the part-time faculty and encouraging a relationship of assistance and mentorship between the full-time faculty and the part-time faculty participants.

References

Bach, P. (1999). Part-time faculty are here to stay. *Planning for Higher Education, 27*(3), 32–40.

Hickey, R. (2005). Giving part-time online instructors what they need. *Distance Education Report, 9*(24), 6–8.

Nutting, M. M. (2003). Part-time faculty: Why should we care? In E. Benjamin (Ed.), *New directions for higher education: No. 123. Exploring the role of contingent instructional staff in undergraduate learning* (pp. 33–41). San Francisco, CA: Jossey-Bass.

Townsend, R. B., & Hauss, M. E. (2002, October). The 2002 AHA-OAH survey of part-time and adjunct faculty. *Perspectives.* Retrieved December 15, 2006, from: www.historians.org/perspectives/issues/2002/0210/0210aha3.cfm

Woodson, N. (2005). What do adjunct faculty want? *Community College Week, 18*(5), 4–5.

Appendix 3.1

Part-Time Faculty Needs Assessment

Campus: _____

Delphi Center for Teaching and Learning
Faculty Needs Assessment: Spring 2006

Directions: Please indicate the top 3 areas you would like to learn more about by placing a 1, 2, or 3 by your top three interests. Place a checkmark by any other topics of interest to you. Please indicate the campus on which you teach in the right upper corner of this form. On the back, please indicate the way in which you would prefer to have this information brought to you in the coming months. Thank you!

_____ Learning theories: How students learn
_____ Adult vs. traditional learners: How they differ
_____ Developing learning objectives
_____ Course design
_____ Syllabus development
_____ Engaging the Online Learner
_____ Group Dynamics in the Classroom
_____ Engaging the quiet student
_____ Developing assessment/grading rubrics
_____ Grading practices
_____ Responding to student incivility in class
_____ Structure and spontaneity: The art of leading an effective discussion
_____ Teaching for deeper learning
_____ Responding to student writing
_____ Reading strategies for students
_____ Creating effective assignments and exams in the sciences
_____ Planning for the First Day of Class
_____ Addressing the issue of students' prior knowledge
_____ Professional conduct
_____ Teaching academically diverse students
_____ Fielding students' questions
_____ Maintaining instructional quality with limited resources
_____ Teaching to different learning styles
_____ Copyright guidelines for college teachers

_____ Preserving academic honesty in the classroom and online
_____ Making the most of office hours
_____ University resources outside the classroom for students
_____ Motivating your students
_____ Web resources for faculty
_____ Peer networking
_____ Effective time management for faculty
_____ Strategies for enhancing active/engaged learning
_____ Teaching problem solving
_____ Writing to learn activities and assignments
_____ Collaborative learning: Group work and study teams
_____ Helping students learn
_____ Evaluating students' written work
_____ Allaying students' anxiety about tests
_____ Getting your students to do the readings
_____ Making the most of instructional aids and technology
_____ Assessing students' learning
_____ Test construction/writing test questions/understanding the item analysis
_____ Preparing students for tests/test anxiety
_____ Evaluation: tests, assignments, and course performance—best practices and alternatives
_____ Evaluating and documenting teaching effectiveness
_____ Establishing and maintaining a positive classroom environment
_____ Designing your course for higher level learning
_____ Balancing the teaching, service, and research role of faculty
_____ Clarifying the expectations for promotion and tenure
_____ University resources for faculty teaching
_____ Making the lecture a learning experience
_____ Questioning techniques for learning and assessment
_____ Writing letters of recommendation
_____ Academic advising and student mentoring

Other topic ideas:_____

_____

_____

_____

Directions: HOW would you prefer that this information be brought to you? Please indicate your interests in methods by order of preference using 1, 2, and 3. Thank you! (NOTE: All meals provided by Delphi Center)

_____ Faculty Learning Communities where small groups of faculty get together periodically to learn about cutting edge teaching methods and issues of their choosing. (Frequency of meeting set by Learning Community)

_____ **Monthly** "Lunch and Learn" or "Eat and Meet" sessions where faculty meet in groups for a meal and a speaker or facilitator presents a topic of interest.

_____ **Free Day-long Conferences** held yearly _____ or at the beginning _____ or end _____ of each semester before or after students are in classes to discuss cutting edge teaching strategies and issues.

_____ **One-on-one consulting** with Center staff regarding teaching issues or problems

_____ **Quarterly** "Lunch and Learn" or "Eat and Meet" sessions as described above

_____ **At what times** are you most available for monthly or quarterly meetings? (check all that apply)

_____	Breakfast	_____	Mid-morning
_____	Lunch	_____	Mid-afternoon
_____	Supper	_____	Evening (after supper)

APPENDIX 3.2

Example of Evaluation Form Used in the Part-Time Faculty Institute

University of Louisville
Delphi Center for Teaching and Learning Evaluation Form
Part-Time Faculty Institute Program

Name of Program:
Date of Program:
Name of Presenter(s):

Section I—Objectives:
1.
2.
3.

1	2	3	4	5
strongly disagree	somewhat disagree	somewhat agree	agree	strongly agree

Section II—*Related to the response scale above, from strongly disagree (1) to strongly agree (5), please rate your level of agreement with the following statements:*

1. The objectives of this program were fully met.   1   2   3   4   5

2. The content of this program contributed to my knowledge about teaching.   1   2   3   4   5

3. I anticipate using the information I gained from this program in my teaching.   1   2   3   4   5

4. The information from this program was highly relevant to the teaching that I do.   1   2   3   4   5

5. I believed that the knowledge I gained will help me teach more effectively.   1   2   3   4   5

6. I anticipate changing the way I teach (even small ways count!) as a result of this program.   1   2   3   4   5

Section III

Overall, the course was:	Poor	Below Average	Average	Good	Excellent
The instructor's presentation was:	1	2	3	4	5
Opportunity for participation was:	1	2	3	4	5
The course materials were:	1	2	3	4	5

Section IVa
Please rate your knowledge/use of the following teaching strategies/information BEFORE you attended the Part-Time Faculty Institute (list strategies that have not yet been taught).

	None	Little	Average	Above Average
7. List strategies here	1	2	3	4
8. List strategies here	1	2	3	4
9. List strategies here	1	2	3	4

Section IVb
Please rate your knowledge/use of the following teaching strategies/information SINCE you attended the Part-Time Faculty Institute (list strategies taught in previous sessions).

	None	Little	Average	Above Average
10. List strategies here	1	2	3	4
11. List strategies here	1	2	3	4
12. List strategies here	1	2	3	4

4

A PROVEN PROGRAM FOR SUPPORTING ADJUNCT FACULTY ONLINE

Daryl Peterson

If good teaching that produces evidence of student learning is to be anything other than random, institutional policies must deliberately support the development of teachers. Many colleges follow this path by providing resources and training for their full-time faculty, but if these programs ignore the adjunct faculty, a large gap in educational quality is likely to appear (Grubb & Associates, 1999). When academic leaders realize that a professional development initiative in their part-time faculty members is a wise investment, they must then factor in the adjunct faculty's availability to participate in the design and implementation strategy of the institution's program. Two categories of part-timers—specialist, expert, or professionals and freelancers—are by definition employed extensively outside their teaching assignments. Aspiring academics sometimes teach at more than one institution concurrently, and even career enders lead busy lives (Gappa & Leslie, 1993). An effective program that serves a significant portion of its intended audience would do well to consider the potential of providing its professional development offerings in a way that maximizes convenience.

The statistics regarding the steady increase in the amount of adjunct faculty-led instruction nationally are well known. Estimates indicate that up to 60% of college instruction is now adjunct faculty led (Wallin, 2005). Valencia Community College is not exempt from these statistics. The percentage of sections taught by full-time teachers is near 60%. However, like most colleges, the college struggles to get ratios anywhere close to 60% in first-year courses, especially in developmental math, reading, and writing. While college wide, 43% of Valencia course sections are taught by adjunct faculty (Office of Institutional Research, 2004a), the ratios in developmental sections shift considerably. For example, on one of the largest campuses 87% of college prep mathematics and 56% of college prep reading and writing were taught by adjunct faculty (Office of Institutional Research, 2004b). With approximately three-quarters of its incoming class (first-time college students) testing into developmental education (college prep) courses, creating stability and consistency in this level of instruction becomes extremely important.

Meanwhile, Valencia has made a strategic move to make faculty compensation considerably more competitive—and learning related. With this added investment, it is likely its overall ratios of full-time faculty will have to be reduced over the coming years. As the utilization of adjunct faculty increases, partnering more effectively with them to maintain and increase the quality of instruction becomes exceptionally important.

While some areas of the country have a fairly stable and consistent pool of adjunct faculty available, Central Florida is very competitive when it comes to recruiting part-time faculty. In addition to 385 full-time faculty, Valencia employs approximately 1,000 adjunct instructors. In recruiting those part-times, they compete with three other community colleges, the University of Central Florida, and numerous for-profit institutions. As a result, Valencia often scrambles to find faculty to teach courses at the last minute. And they estimate an approximate 10% turnover rate for their adjunct instructors each term.

ADJUNCT PROFESSIONAL DEVELOPMENT HISTORY

Valencia's history of development for adjunct faculty was basically ad hoc, featuring in-service, face-to-face events that adjunct faculty found difficult, if not impossible, to attend. Many times, seminars were offered on the day a presenter was available and topics were often selected for other than strategic reasons. Attendance was very limited, sometimes peaking at 20–30 adjunct faculty, approximately 2%–3% of the adjunct staff, which generally represented the "choir." It became obvious that if Valencia was not only going to maintain, but in some areas increase, adjunct faculty ratios, they must make a meaningful investment in their development and create ways to engage a much larger percentage of them in the college learning community.

The current strategic adjunct outreach and partnership program has its history in the private sector as well as the Valencia community. In 1999, Houghton Mifflin Company's Faculty Development Programs partnered with WisdomTools, Inc. to begin development of a series of online workshops for faculty utilizing the Scenarios software from Indiana University.

With its unique story, case study, and problem-based learning approach, the software provided an excellent vehicle for the development of content for this project. The partnership included faculty developers from Valencia, the University of Minnesota, Indiana University, and Buena Vista University in Iowa. The result was a Teaching in College Scenarios course with separate editions for community college faculty, university faculty, and university teaching assistants. At the same time, consultants from the TLT Group formed a development team to create a Scenarios course for faculty who were moving to teaching online. Houghton Mifflin's attempts to market these courses to colleges in 2000 achieved only moderate success.

In 2000 Valencia President Sandy Shugart initiated discussions with Houghton Mifflin regarding utilization of the Teaching in the Community College course at Valencia as part of the adjunct faculty outreach program. In addition he envisioned an entrepreneurial role for the college in disseminating the course to other community colleges. With those ends in mind, a series of pilots was launched in the 2001–2002 academic year to gauge the effectiveness of the courses. The analysis of the pilots showed clearly that faculty had gained both in knowledge and experience during the course and that Scenarios was a very useful tool in promoting deep learning and meaningful conversations on teaching and learning. It was recommended that the program be updated, expanded, and renamed Teaching in the Learning College.

Negotiations during spring 2002 resulted in Valencia Community College acquiring the sublicense for the use of Scenarios software in the educational marketplace from WisdomTools, Inc. and the rights to the Teaching in College courses, most important, Teaching in the Learning College from Houghton Mifflin. And during summer 2002, Houghton Mifflin's vice president of faculty development and technology moved to Orlando to establish ScenariosOnline, a business unit within the college charged with developing new Scenarios courses and marketing them to community colleges in North America.

During the succeeding four years, new courses for adjunct faculty and full-time faculty were added including Creating an Individual Learning Plan and Creating a Competence-Based Portfolio for new full-time faculty, Succeeding With Online Group Projects, Making It All Add Up, and Doing the Write Thing for adjunct and interested full-time faculty. Partnerships with other colleges to use existing ScenariosOnline courses and develop new programs were launched. Partners currently include Miami Dade College, North Harris Montgomery Community College District, Richland

Community College, the Community Colleges of the University of Hawaii System, Kentucky Community and Technical College System, Guilford Technical Community College, Bucks County Community College, Lake-Sumter Community College, Daytona Beach Community College, and others. New ScenariosOnline courses currently in the development process with partner schools include Supervisory Skills, Serving Students, Assessment, Teaching Online, and a series of human resource scenarios courses.

ASSOCIATE FACULTY PROGRAM

Background

In developing its partnership with adjunct instructors, Valencia embarked in 2003 on an ambitious plan to create an inclusive, comprehensive adjunct faculty development program. The "blended learning" program, with Scenarios courses as the key component, was developed via an "innovation management process." As is the case with most community colleges, Valencia had some pockets of innovative practices that had developed spontaneously. During the effort to become more of a learning college, they tried to follow Terry O'Banion's (1997) advice to "round up the innovations." This is now recognized as a three-phase process that helps the college discover which innovations will truly support the goal of improving student learning.

In Phase 1 an innovative practice must be pilot tested and assessed for effectiveness; in the case of adjunct faculty development this meant a number of pilots and betas of both the online Teaching in the Learning College and the face-to-face seminars. These initiatives were grant funded. In the innovation management process, successful Phase 1 initiatives that show the potential to bring systemic change are then funded by a combination of external grants and internal minigrants. Phase 2 initiatives must show increasing levels of effectiveness to be moved forward to the next phase. Such was the case with the adjunct outreach and development initiatives and finally, in Phase 3, the adjunct program was brought to scale, funded by "hard money" from the operational budget and institutionalized at the beginning of the 2005–2006 academic year.

In the summer of 2005, planning for ways to create incentives for part-time teachers to connect with the college around the central goal of improving student learning became reality. The result was the Associate Faculty

Program that provides a step in pay and a new title for adjunct faculty in exchange for a significant commitment to professional development that is focused on improving student learning. The program rests on three years of pilot testing and the collaboration of many areas of the college, including finance, human resources, and academic affairs.

This new program does not make the causal argument that if you participate in faculty development, you will be a better adjunct instructor. No faculty development program will be a panacea. But there is evidence locally at Valencia and nationally that enhanced faculty teaching skills have a positive effect on reducing college student departure (Braxton, Bray, & Berger, 2000). The goal then was to create professional development that would significantly enhance adjunct faculty's level of engagement, quality of instruction, and ultimately their students' persistence and success.

A significant hurdle in launching a comprehensive faculty development program for adjunct faculty was committing to investing resources in a previously unsupported but huge contingent of instructional faculty. Although Valencia has developed an extremely successful, comprehensive three-year tenure track, Teaching and Learning Academy, for new full-time faculty, cultivating a mind-set that valued the same commitment of support for adjunct instruction was no easy matter. But the ultimate consensus was that all faculty need time, resources, and support to:

- Help make good on the promises of the "open door"

- Learn about diversity and how to build inclusive learning communities

- Understand learning styles to support the development of diverse teaching strategies

- Design learning activities that motivate and engage students

- Develop assessments that reflect more than information recall

The Valencia Associate Faculty Program is a blended learning certification program that focuses on creating community and on connecting adjunct faculty to the college and to full-time faculty by combining an online (ScenariosOnline) faculty development curriculum with the face-to-face (Faculty to Faculty) seminars.

The addition of the online curriculum was driven by the necessity of making quality professional development an available, accessible, and convenient learning experience, in which the adjunct faculty would be eager to engage. In addition to quality and accessibility, the online learning opportunities have proven to be very cost effective. Valencia is able to offer adjunct faculty the 60 hours of coursework necessary for certification for one-fourth of the cost of funding their attendance at a conference. And they are able to engage 15 faculty members in 30 hours of collaboration with their peers for approximately the same cost as bringing in a consultant to work with faculty in a four-hour seminar.

All of the components of the Associate Faculty Program are designed to move faculty development beyond a "seat-time" approach to a "product-based" approach. Some examples include syllabus development, teaching philosophies, and group projects in ScenariosOnline courses and Digital Dossiers in Faculty to Faculty seminars.

Adjunct Faculty Certification

The Adjunct Faculty Program moves Valencia away from a stipend model for workshops and seminars toward a compensation model that is aligned with a proposed full-time faculty compensation enhancement for professional development.

The current adjunct pay scale has become step one, with no faculty development necessary.

Step two provides an increase in adjunct faculty pay of $33 per credit hour taught (a three-credit course would provide a $99 increase) after 60 hours of faculty development have been accumulated. The new title of associate faculty is earned at that point. The 60 hours are earned by completing combinations of the following:

- Faculty to Faculty (three seminars)—20 hours

- ScenariosOnline courses:
    - Teaching in the Learning College (required)—30 hours
    - Succeeding With Online Group Work—20 hours
    - Doing the Write Thing (developmental writing)—20 hours
    - Making It All Add Up (developmental math)—20 hours
    - Teaching Online and Assessment courses will be added in 2007

- Other approved faculty development and technology workshops—hours variable

- Facilitation of approved faculty development—hours variable

The total of 60 hours for the associate faculty status includes the requirement of Teaching in the Learning College, the foundational course in community college teaching. It is possible to earn the 60 hours within one academic year. Adjunct faculty who have already accomplished 60 hours of this work will be granted credit and brought into the system as associate faculty. A three-year time limit applies to hours earned as well as the associate faculty status. Renewal of the status depends on accomplishing 60 additional hours during the three years following achievement of the status (for example, taking 20 hours per year would keep the status current for an additional three years).

A modification of Valencia's Atlas student information system allows them to offer faculty a professional development transcript of approved completed courses, workshops, and other activities. Upon receipt of the transcript showing 60 hours, the faculty member notifies human resources to award the new title and approve the increment in pay beginning with the following term.

Figure 4.1 represents the process involved in initially achieving associate faculty status and maintaining it over the three-year cycle.

Figure 4.1. *Flow Diagram for Achieving and Maintaining Associate Faculty Status*

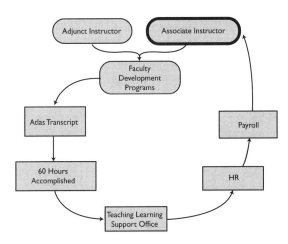

Faculty to Faculty

Faculty to Faculty is a successful series of topical seminars offered to Valencia's adjunct faculty during the January semester. Two hundred thirty-two participants attended the 2005 seminars. The series is facilitated by full-time faculty members who lead the discussions and provide oversight for the faculty presentations while they gain experience in faculty development and provide leadership and informal mentoring to adjunct faculty. Seminar topics are determined by surveys of Valencia adjunct faculty. The 2005 series included the use of technology in the classroom and course assessment. The 2006 series focused on technology for learning and developing student critical thinking. The seminars include a showcase of faculty work in the topics presented.

One of many positive outcomes of the Faculty to Faculty seminars has been the development of a Digital Dossier, an electronic teaching portfolio that allows adjunct faculty members to put their best professional work forward where the entire academic community can view it. The Digital Dossier is an electronic collection of materials that provide a perspective of a faculty member at Valencia. It includes a list of the individual's goals in professional development (Goals), a record of what has been accomplished in faculty development (Professional Development Record), a compilation of teaching artifacts created to use in the faculty member's courses (Teaching Artifacts), the individual's personal views on teaching (Teaching Philosophy), and a section in which individuals post their thinking about professional development activities and the effect they have had on faculty work in and out of the classroom (Reflections). Examples of Valencia faculty Digital Dossiers are located at http://net2.valenciacc.edu/cp/adjunct_faculty_public/list.cfm.

The Digital Dossier also offers Valencia's faculty development office a key opportunity for assessment of the Associate Faculty Program. It was first employed in the spring term of 2006. In the fall term of 2006 and each term thereafter, the Digital Dossiers online will be scored with a holistic rubric. The scores will not be made public, but exemplary dossiers will be recognized and rewarded. Faculty members with portfolios that are found to be inadequate or incomplete will be contacted by the faculty development office and offered a variety of opportunities to improve their work. Any development or training program that awards a certificate and monetary benefits needs to prove its worth. The Digital Dossier is one of the program assessment methods that grant some insight into what the participants learned and how they are using their new skills. It is necessary to evaluate the quality of these portfolios and apply a strategy to bring additional support to those faculty members whose work on display indicates a need for further improvement.

ScenariosOnline

To establish a partnership with adjunct faculty, it is imperative that the professional development offered to them not only respects them as professionals but also:

- Is available and accessible

- Models good pedagogy

- Is grounded in proven learning theory

- Provides strategies for immediate classroom application

To achieve those goals, Valencia selected WisdomTools Scenarios, an e-learning tool combining technology and story, as the vehicle for creating online faculty learning communities. The unique courses created with this tool are case-based narratives that provide authentic contexts for asynchronous, collaborative conversations and group insights among faculty. While all of the current courses utilize Scenarios, Valencia continues to explore and evaluate additional delivery vehicles that may prove to be valuable supplements to current courses and/or provide a more effective venue for certain types of development.

ScenariosOnline course features provide participants in Valencia's faculty development programs with a number of significant benefits:

- *Accessibility.* ScenariosOnline courses are asynchronous and convenient and rich with useful tools for faculty. They make connections among faculty who are generally very isolated. They provide the flexibility and accessibility needed in the delivery of professional development to adjunct faculty (and full-time faculty). A comprehensive, effective online program is an essential feature of outreach to adjunct faculty who find it difficult, if not impossible, to attend face-to-face events. New courses on teaching online, topics such as assessment, and a course for midcareer faculty will be added in the coming year.

- *Modeling.* In addition to convenience, ScenariosOnline courses allow Valencia to offer their faculty learning programs that model the collaboration the college wants for students and the deep learning that story and problem-based learning foster. The courses also introduce faculty to the concept of an online learning community that facilitates the transition to an online environment in their own classrooms.

- *Theory-based.* The courses are designed for situations such as classroom instruction where procedures are "shades of gray" and context based with a set of options, not a single solution. The course objectives, then, are a function of the faculty member's goals. For example, Valencia is committed to assisting faculty in understanding learning centeredness and using that understanding as the context for their instruction to enhance student learning. The scenario/story and associated resources and activities will lead the group to new insights on strategies they might employ in their own classrooms. While faculty are generally experts in their content and technical areas, many do not have a working understanding of how learning really happens. They have had limited professional development experiences that focused on student learning. ScenariosOnline courses include a rich variety of resources that provide the foundation for the development of strategies for creating a positive classroom learning environment.

- *Applicability.* Course topics focus on a variety of teaching methodologies and include course planning and syllabus development, classroom management, learning styles and dealing with a diverse student population, active learning, and assessment issues. Many course activities and assignments foster immediate application. They facilitate "action learning" (Marquardt, 1999), which engages small groups in using what they are learning to solve real problems while simultaneously reflecting on the learning process itself. For example, participants review the course resources, revise their syllabi, making them more learning centered, and then share their syllabi with their colleagues. They also select Classroom Assessment Techniques (CATS), try them in their classes, and discuss their effectiveness with their group.

ScenariosOnline Course Structure

The unique structure of courses embedded in the Scenarios software is shown in Appendix 4.1, Figures 4.2, 4.3, and 4.4. The course takes the form of a story that is best described as a play with three or four acts or episodes. Within each act or episode there are numerous scenes that feature a variety of characters. Each scene has a narrative and associated resource links that are utilized in the interactive conversation space.

Collaborative activities within the Scenarios conversation space take the form of discussion forums (Appendix 4.1, Figure 4.4, lower right and Figure 4.5) or point of view (point-counterpoint). These may also be supported by surveys or quizzes. The activities effectively promote deep learning and also provide a model of scenario-based learning that faculty may employ in their own classrooms. However, promoting deep learning and scenario-based learning is difficult because students often resist taking responsibility for their own learning. Students generally have not been prepared for learning that is contextual, relevant, and research oriented rather than lecture and test driven.

The course structure provides faculty participants with the opportunity to be a student in a collaborative work team as they engage in a story of instructional experiences and what that means in terms of student learning. This experience is invaluable, if not essential, for faculty who hope to establish a classroom environment that reflects the nature of learning centeredness. Strategies emerging from the faculty collaboration hopefully will be directly applicable in promoting student collaboration.

To effectively utilize story as a vehicle for generating insight and deep learning in an asynchronous learning environment, three characteristics (Siegel, 2005; Siegel, Ellis, & Lewis, 2004) are essential:

- *Authenticity.* A story must be realistic; it must ring true and connect directly to the listener's work and/or personal life. The story may be about student issues, classroom management, or any number of topics, but whatever the theme, it must be situated in the listener's setting. A community college math instructor will be more interested in stories related to his or her instructional setting than stories about student financial aid. A university faculty member will be more engaged in a story about balancing research and teaching than other less relevant topics. Authenticity increases listener attention and identification. Even with a fictitious story, the listener will identify with the characters and scenes if they are authentic. An authentic story offers the opportunity for learning to happen informally as well as formally.

- *Collaboration.* The power of story emerges from the shared wisdom of the faculty participants, so it is important for more than one person to interact with the story. The story provides the perspectives of multiple characters, and members of the faculty work team provide their own perspectives. It is from this collaborative effort that insights emerge. The wisdom is in the collective.

- *Conversation.* An authentic story presented to a collaborative faculty work team prompts a conversation. The hypothesis is that the conversation initially serves to bond the team and create norms for interaction. The first conversations are about the story, but as the story unfolds, the conversations deepen. Deep conversation leads to insight, emerging from a new story being created by the team. The real story is not the original one, but the one that evolves from the team. Each insight transforms the story and leads to the next insight.

ScenariosOnline courses are the critical online component of all of Valencia's development programs. Adjunct faculty who aspire to be associate faculty are required to complete Teaching in the Learning College and may participate in other elective courses, including Making It All Add Up (for developmental math faculty), Doing the Write Thing (for developmental writing faculty), and Succeeding With Online Group Projects (for faculty who are moving to online or blended instructional settings). Valencia's Teaching and Learning Academy for new tenure-track faculty includes two custom ScenariosOnline courses, Creating an Individual Learning Plan and Creating Competency-Based Portfolios.

PARTICIPANT EVALUATIONS AND REACTIONS

Valencia's work with adjunct faculty has been built upon their well researched and assessed approach to full-time faculty development (Nellis, Clarke, DiMartino, & Hosman, 2001), which was modified for the context of part-time instructors. As with full-time faculty programs, recording of participant reactions is essential for the evolution of faculty development initiatives and the documentation of return on investment.

From dissertation survey research of spring 2004 (Bosley, 2004), Valencia learned:

- 93% of the 241 respondents are satisfied or very satisfied with adjunct teaching at Valencia

- 91% stated that they are likely to encourage a good friend to seek an adjunct faculty position at Valencia

- 82% report that Valencia's professional development activities met their needs

- 90% (36% of the sample) who participated in ScenariosOnline courses rated them as good or excellent

Faculty to Faculty feedback survey approval ratings have been consistently higher than 90% since the program was initiated. Participants clearly felt that the meetings met their expectations, contained ideas they could apply, and were effectively presented in engaging formats (Office of College and Community Relations, 2005). Some insight into participant learning was also gained through the assignments. In each spring series of seminars, participants demonstrate learning by creating and displaying a classroom-based assessment technique, a use of technology to enhance learning, or a strategy for enhancing student critical thinking.

Although gauging how much participants in faculty development learn is not always easy, ScenariosOnline course effectiveness has been evaluated extensively since 2001. Participants who finish the courses will have completed at least 80% of the activity assignments. Those who complete Teaching in the Learning College will have produced a new and improved syllabus for at least one course that contains three items that make it more learning centered. They will also have used at least one Classroom Assessment Technique (CAT) in a course and evaluated its effectiveness, plus incorporated at least one developmental advising (LifeMap) activity in a course and evaluated its effectiveness.

One evaluation method employed is to download the online participant dialogue and analyze it for the quality of exchange and to see if any new learning is evident. This learning measure is conducted during the spring term offering of Teaching in the Learning College. Each year the findings indicate that adjunct faculty have a true "aha" experience with CATs and a greater understanding of the need for and methods of creating more active learning in their classrooms. Another pattern from past evaluation is that the adjunct faculty engagement with Valencia's developmental advising system (LifeMap) is tentative at best. There seems to be some gain in terms of comprehension-level acquaintance with LifeMap concepts, but to bring faculty into developmental advising practices may call for a more intensive and, likely, a face-to-face professional development context. However, results from the latest Teaching in the Learning College alumni survey (see below) indicate that some progress is being made in this area.

In the course evaluations of the Valencia pilots and betas of Teaching in the Learning College in 2001 and 2002 (Nellis, Hosman, King, & Armstead, 2002), participants liked the course, found the resources useful, felt more connected to the college and to colleagues, and applied their new learning in revised syllabi and lesson plans.

One limited Teaching in the Learning College cohort study (Nellis, 2004) has indicated that adjunct faculty graduates are more successful with their students than they were prior to taking the course, resulting in an 8% average increase in students passing their courses with a grade of C or better.

During the 2003–2004 academic year, 135 participants completed ScenariosOnline courses. Post-course surveys of participants in the spring and summer 2004 sessions (n = 66) showed:

- 97% agree that they can "define and demonstrate learning-centered approaches to instruction"

- 94% agree that "this online seminar was helpful to me in improving my classroom performance"

- 95% agree that they can "truthfully tell other colleagues that I enjoyed being part of this online seminar"

Another evaluation method is the use of Teaching in the Learning College alumni surveys every two years. This is an effort to see how much learning has been retained and incorporated into classroom instruction. The results from respondents to the most recent (May 2006) survey indicate:

- 100% have made changes to their syllabus to make it more learning centered

- 100% have incorporated active or collaborative learning strategies in their courses

- 91% are using Classroom Assessment Techniques (CATS) in their courses

- 100% are engaging students in discussions around subjects that relate to life development activities (educational, vocational, social, etc.)

- 77% have begun to incorporate technology (student email, web assignments, group discussion boards, etc.) in their courses

In evaluations of ScenariosOnline courses, Valencia is not looking for or claiming to have found some new law of human behavior. It has collected a great deal of information on these courses, holding them to a high level of scrutiny because of their critical role in the adjunct development program (and in part because they are online, which is still considered to be a new and somewhat suspect method). Valencia believes that the assessment of these courses makes a strong case for its effectiveness with adjunct faculty. The college does not feel that the test of its merit lies solely with statistical significance. In any case, setting up a controlled study in this environment is not feasible at this point. This type of program has to be evaluated differently from the manner in which one would evaluate the effect of a drug in clinical trials before it goes to market.

Adjunct faculty are not the only participants in ScenariosOnline courses. The following comment from a senior science professor who was a participant and is now a facilitator captures the feelings about the value of this approach to faculty learning:

Teaching is not a science, it is an art, and as such is always changing, always evolving, assuming different guises each semester. Classes have personalities of their own and we need to know how to take their pulse and like a chameleon adapt to that environment in order to survive. That is what Scenarios presented.

The Next Steps

Although Valencia is getting very promising results with its adjunct faculty, there is still a long way to go. Central to Valencia's work over the next three years is a process designed to expand engagement of adjunct faculty in best practices for creating highly engaged learning environments and to complete efforts to assess learning throughout the college.

The first step in expanding adjunct faculty engagement will involve further development of the online faculty development curriculum. The second will be in the face-to-face realm where discipline-based development programs will be expanded. A third step will be to more closely align the online and face-to-face components of the adjunct faculty development program. This can be done by highlighting the content presented online through the face-to-face meeting venues, thus reinforcing the foundations of good teaching first presented in Teaching in the Learning College and other ScenariosOnline courses. Another strategy for reaching this goal is to recruit for ScenariosOnline courses from the face-to-face participants, and vice versa, ensuring that more adjunct faculty have a solid grounding in good teaching techniques. All of these steps will depend on partnerships, with academic leadership as well as adjunct and full-time faculty in steps one and three, and with academic deans in step two.

The assessment process will become more closely related to adjunct faculty engagement. When the Learning Evidence Team has established learning outcomes and shared assessment methods for the key "front door" courses, the adjunct programming can support transmission of those outcomes and assessment goals to the college prep adjunct faculty (and associate faculty) via a new online course and face-to-face seminars.

As of June 2006, Valencia has certified 128 adjunct instructors as associate faculty. Fifty more were expected to achieve that status in the fall. The goal is to have 500 associate faculty as partners in learning during the 2008–2009 academic year.

As Valencia moves forward, there is considerable enthusiasm about the new work with adjunct faculty. It is gratifying to see faculty development that was begun with small innovations and grant funding become a part of the college's operational budget. With the addition of the online components, the college is now reaching the instructors of a large number of course sections and having a positive impact on the learning experience of students. As the college grows even more dependent on the services of adjunct faculty, it is imperative to continue to expand efforts to draw them into the community of practice and the culture of teaching for learning. The associate faculty are valued through the step in pay and the change of status. They are connected to the academic community through the support of the faculty development programs, and their good work is becoming more visible through the Digital Dossier teaching portfolios, among other things. The progress so far has been very rewarding, and now Valencia is bringing the innovations to scale.

References

Bosley, M. (2004). *Professional development activities and satisfaction among community college adjunct faculty.* Unpublished doctoral dissertation, University of Central Florida.

Braxton, J. M., Bray, N. J., & Berger, J. B. (2000, March/April). Faculty teaching skills and their influence on the college student departure process. *Journal of College Student Development, 41*(2), 215–227.

Gappa, J. M., & Leslie, D. W. (1993). *The invisible faculty: Improving the status of part-timers in higher education.* San Francisco, CA: Jossey-Bass.

Grubb, W. N. & Associates (1999). *Honored but invisible: An inside look at teaching in community colleges.* New York, NY: Routledge.

Marquardt, M. J. (1999). *Action learning in action: Transforming problems for world-class organizational learning.* Palo Alto, CA: Davies-Black.

Nellis, P., Clarke, H., DiMartino, J., & Hosman, D. (2001). Preparing today's faculty for tomorrow's students: One college's faculty development solution. In D. Lieberman & C. Wehlburg (Eds.), *To improve the academy: Vol. 19. Resources for faculty, instructional, and organizational development* (pp. 149–168). Bolton, MA: Anker.

Nellis, P., Hosman, D., King, J. M., & Armstead, C. (2002). Web-based faculty development using time-revealed scenarios. In G. E. Watts (Ed.), *New directions for community colleges: No. 120. Enhancing community colleges through professional development* (pp. 27–35). San Francisco, CA: Jossey-Bass.

Nellis, P. (2004, March). *Faculty development program evaluation and ROI.* Paper presented at the annual meeting of the Chair Academy International Conference, Reston, VA.

O'Banion, T. (1997). *A learning college for the 21st century.* Phoenix, AZ: American Council on Education/Oryx Press.

Office of College and Community Relations. (2005). *Workshop evaluation statistics from Leadership Valencia program, 2003–2005.* Unpublished data, Valencia Community College.

Office of Institutional Research. (2004a). *Collegewide summary full- to part-time ratio for fall 2004.* Unpublished data, Valencia Community College.

Office of Institutional Research. (2004b). *Learning indicators resport* (Rep. No. IR2004-14). Orlando, FL: Valencia Community College.

Siegel, M. A. (2005). *Interactive narrative tools to generate insight within a collaborative work team.* Mahwah, NJ: Lawrence Erlbaum Associates.

Siegel, M. A., Ellis, S. E., & Lewis, M. B. (2004, January). *Designing for deep conversation in a scenarios-based e-learning environment.* Paper presented at the annual meeting of the Hawaii International Conference on System Sciences, Waikloloa, HI.

Wallin, D. (Ed.). (2005). *Adjunct faculty in community colleges: An academic administrator's guide to recruiting, supporting, and retaining great teachers.* Bolton, MA: Anker.

APPENDIX 4.1

ScenariosOnline Course Structure and Screen Shots

Figure 1. *Scenarios Structure*

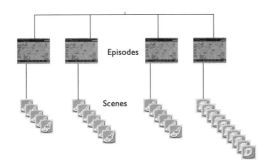

Figure 2. *Episode With Characters, Scenes, and Resources*

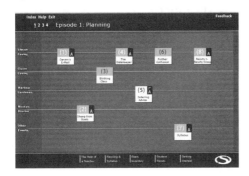

Figure 3. *Scene With Narrative, Activities, and Conversation Space*

5 MENTORING ADJUNCT INSTRUCTORS: FOSTERING BONDS THAT STRENGTHEN TEACHING AND LEARNING

Cynthia Zutter

Faculty mentoring programs are perhaps one of the best ways to create collegiality across disciplines and build community among instructors at postsecondary institutions. Mentoring between senior and junior full-time faculty is a time-honored tradition within higher education, but it is generally not as common between part-time and full-time faculty. At MacEwan College in Alberta, Canada, this mutually rewarding tool of professional development has been employed with adjunct faculty and, in the process, has fostered a connectedness within the faculty that mitigates the sense of isolation that part-timers often report, while contributing to deeper learning for students.

As an all-encompassing professional development activity, dyads consisting of adjunct and continuing faculty not only have the potential to enhance instructional techniques, but also to create bonds that support and empower all instructors. The following quotation from an adjunct faculty participant, which appeared in the final report of the Faculty Mentoring Program, illustrates this point: "By making us aware that we faced similar teaching challenges even though we were from different disciplines, the program increased our confidence and resilience [as instructors]" (Headley-Smith & Spronk, 2005).

MacEwan College is one of the largest postsecondary institutions in the province of Alberta, Canada, with more than 40,000 full- and part-time students. Offering bachelor of arts degrees, university transfer for bachelor of science and nursing, as well as diplomas in holistic health, police and security, or voluntary sector management, the programs at the college offer a wide breadth of choices for potential students and thus require the employment of a diverse group of instructors, including approximately 600 adjunct faculty. Established in 1971 by philanthropist and environmentalist Dr. G. M. MacEwan, the college "inspires and enables individuals to succeed in life through career and university studies" (MacEwan College, 2006a, ¶ 1).

Faculty development opportunities were first launched at MacEwan College in the 1970s, and have grown to be extensive in scope and depth. They include classroom instructional assistance through Instructional Skills Workshops (ISWs), research funds for attending professional conferences, and on-campus seminars to support faculty members' integrating technology into their teaching. Adjunct instructors have been included in all programming from the outset.

THE DESIGN AND IMPLEMENTATION OF THE PROGRAM

Perhaps one of the most influential faculty development programs, however, is the Faculty Mentoring Program. As one of the few structured faculty-to-faculty mentoring programs in a Canadian postsecondary institute, the MacEwan program is a unique, inclusive instructional development activity that focuses on improving student learning. The program was initiated in 2002 as part of a provincial government-sponsored initiative to assist postsecondary institutions with succession planning. Acknowledging the potential loss of instructional expertise and college history as many instructors were reaching retirement age, the vice president academic at MacEwan decided to investigate the potential benefits of a mentoring program. As a first step in creating the program, a coordinator (the writer of this chapter) was selected and provided with release time to conduct a preliminary survey of chairs and deans across all sectors of the college. The survey sought to gather information on informal mentoring processes and practices already in place at the college.

The survey results indicated that most chairs and deans were responsive to informal mentoring occurring in their areas and supported a facilitated program of mentoring to promote collegiality and rejuvenation of senior and newer instructors. Subsequent to the survey, a Faculty Mentoring Program committee was formed with representation from the four main instructional sectors of the college (i.e., arts/science, health and community studies, business, and the Centre for the Arts) in addition to the program coordinator. The initial goal of the committee was to formulate the program's mission statement: "The mentoring program is committed to the development of excellence in teaching through the facilitation of a collegial learning process between newer and more experienced faculty" (MacEwan College, 2006b,

¶2). In addition, the program's guiding principles, application process, and expected learning outcomes (see Table 5.1) were developed.

The central theme of mentoring at MacEwan is to promote lifelong learning among its faculty, who in turn model that behavior in the classroom. Embodying the MacEwan spirit of community, all faculty members are invited to apply to the program. The dyads are often cross-disciplinary in nature, creating a focus on instructional process, philosophy, and methods, rather than discipline-specific, content-related issues. A highly positive result of these cross-disciplinary pairings has been the marked increase in collegiality at MacEwan, a college that has three separate campuses and more than 800 instructors. The participants repeatedly express in their final reports that they have benefited from connecting with instructors from other areas of the college and established a long-term relationship with someone they may never have met if not for the mentoring program.

RATIONALE FOR A FACILITATED MENTORING PROGRAM

Newer faculty must overcome many challenges during their early years of instructing. Some of these include time pressures to get everything accomplished, preparation for new classes, dealing with difficult students, determining priorities, and feeling insecure about the evaluation of their teaching methods. Adjunct instructors must deal with the added challenges of teaching at remote times and places and feeling less attached to the college culture and its resources. MacEwan College is committed to providing newer faculty with quality guidance to maintain a focus on student-centered education with small classes and individualized instruction.

A unique feature of mentoring at MacEwan is that all faculty members at the college, including adjunct instructors, are invited to participate in this program through a voluntary application process. Mentors and mentees apply separately. Mentors are required to provide information regarding their strengths and abilities as instructors and mentors. Mentees list their needs and the goals that they hope to achieve through the program. The Mentoring Program Committee then selects the dyads based on the stated needs of the mentee applicants. In a few cases, preestablished mentor/mentee dyads have been granted for specific learning goals (i.e., online course development); however, preselected dyad applications are not encouraged. Every

Table 5.1. *Mentoring Program Process/Guiding Principles/Learning Outcomes*

Application/Participation	Guiding Principles	Learning Outcomes
Mentors and mentees complete and submit applications to the mentoring coordinator.	The mentoring relationship is egalitarian and voluntary.	Participants are interested in lifelong learning and growth.
Program committee reviews applications and establishes dyads.	The program facilitates matching the expressed needs of the mentees and mentors.	Participants form a bond with another faculty member who may serve as a confidant.
Dyads are commonly cross-disciplinary in nature.	There is increased awareness of the college, its mission, and its goals.	Participants develop a sense of collegiality within the college.
Mentors must have taught an equivalent of three years at the college. Mentees must have taught a minimum of four courses at the college.	The program is designed to welcome and support newer faculty and foster a deeper commitment to the organizational community.	Participants utilize key resources and people within the college to function effectively as a member of the college faculty.
Separate orientations are provided for mentors and mentees.	Mentors and mentees are introduced to the mentoring process.	Participants engage in the mentoring process as a form of lifelong learning.
Mentors and mentees are introduced to the reflective process and are provided with journals.	The program will value critical reflection as a core aspect of teaching and learning.	Participants demonstrate improved instructional skills.

Table 5.1 (continued). *Mentoring Program Process/Guiding Principles/Learning Outcomes*

Application/Participation	Guiding Principles	Learning Outcomes
Mentoring Partnership Agreements are created, including schedule of weekly meetings/classroom visitations.	The mentoring relationship is facilitative of long-term growth and teaching effectiveness.	Participants discriminate between various teaching methodologies and value the effect of learning styles on student learning.
A midyear summative evaluation meeting of all participants is held.	The program provides a framework within which both the mentor and mentee are accountable.	Participants assist in the functioning and evolution of the program.
End-of-year final reports from each dyad are submitted to the coordinator.	The program provides a framework within which both the mentor and mentee are accountable.	Participants reflect and reiterate their growth as learners in the program.

participant in the program is awarded a course release for the year to provide each member the time needed for weekly meetings and classroom visitations, thus enabling each party to derive full value from participating in the program. The program has support for eight dyads (16 instructors) and there are generally two or three applicants (mentors and mentees) who are not selected annually because their needs could not be met. Those not selected are encouraged to apply in the subsequent year and are generally given priority for selection.

To be eligible to serve as a mentor in the program, one must have taught a minimum of 30 course equivalents (i.e., three years of full-time equivalent instruction) and must have demonstrated a commitment to excellence in teaching. Further skills that are useful as a mentor include strong interpersonal skills and a fairly in-depth knowledge of MacEwan College resources and organization. A mentee must have taught at least four course equivalents at the postsecondary level and express a desire to participate. Having proven itself successful with full-time faculty, the Faculty Mentoring Program was extended to include adjunct instructors in 2003. Unlike full-timers who are provided release time, adjunct instructors are offered monetary compensation equivalent to their salary for teaching one course ($\approx$\$3,500–\$4,500CAD depending on their experience and level of education) for their participation in the ten-month program.

In late August, a week before the new academic year commences, the coordinator facilitates separate orientation sessions for incoming mentors and mentees to introduce the participants to the program. As part of the mentor orientation session, mentors complete an assessment of their mentoring skills and are introduced to the various stages of the mentoring partnership to assist them in anticipating the dynamics of the relationship. These stages include the initial trust building and informative phases followed by the mentor being a facilitator and motivator for the mentee. The final stage involves the mentees using their own initiative to accomplish the goals they set out to achieve. In the mentee orientation session, mentees are provided with guidelines to enhance their goal-setting skills and are encouraged to reflect on what they hope to achieve while in the program. Following their orientation sessions, an introductory dinner meeting is held to bring the dyads together in a relaxed social setting. The initial task for each dyad is to create a Mentoring Partnership Agreement that must be submitted to the coordinator by the end of September. Dyads are provided with a partnership template to complete that includes a list of goals, meeting and classroom visitation schedules, personal boundaries of their relationship, and any other issues the dyad has agreed to pursue (e.g., mental and physical enrichment). The mentor and mentee both sign and date the partnership agreement. A sample copy of the agreement is in Appendix 5.1.

Throughout the academic year, the dyads are required to meet at least once a week, preferably in person, although email or telephone conversations are widely used as well. The dyads also commit to visiting two of each other's classes each term to enhance the dialogue regarding teaching and practice. Further important responsibilities of the dyads include creating and submitting to the coordinator both a midprogram formative review and an end of year summative report. The coordinator is responsible for collecting, cataloguing, and distributing the summative reports to the deans and chairs. Blank journals are given to each participant to promote self-reflection and document their mentoring journey during the year. Journaling is optional, but general guidelines regarding the reflection process are provided to each participant, and at the end of the year, individuals retain these journals as a personal record of their journey in the mentoring process.

Although applications from the continuing faculty members were more numerous in the first year of the program—perhaps reflecting a pent-up demand—recent applications represent a more balanced ratio with 40% from continuing and 60% from adjunct faculty. An interesting trend noted in the applications from 2006 was that all of the chosen mentees were adjunct instructors and two of the mentors were also adjunct faculty. As expressed in their final report and summative evaluation of the program, the adjunct faculty members appreciate the benefits that mentoring can provide to their instructional careers. This program creates a collegial bond between adjunct and full-time faculty that is otherwise difficult to facilitate in such a large college community. One-to-one interaction between these instructors allows for dialogue and discussion focused on teaching while building awareness regarding adjunct faculty-specific issues, such as future employment opportunities and professional advancement (i.e., acquiring a continuing appointment). For example, various dyads have cotaught classes, copresented at professional conferences, and engaged in research together.

Since its inception, more than 35 adjunct instructors have participated in the Faculty Mentoring Program. Recent dyads have extended the traditional scope of their relationships to focus on e-learning processes and techniques. In the process, adjunct instructors have been able to explore interests beyond traditional teaching, and the college has expanded its cohort of online instructors. Partnerships that have grown from mentoring relationships between adjunct and continuing instructors in the social work program and the English department have led to adjunct instructors creating and teaching web-based courses.

Each mentor and mentee who is chosen for the mentoring dyad is provided with a release from teaching responsibilities (approximately 45 hours) or payment in lieu of a course for adjunct faculty to enable them to meet, reflect, and exchange dialogue about instructional processes. Time is essential and central to the success of the journeys of the dyads (Figure 5.1). As stated in a final report, "Time and ability to reflect about our meeting discussions are essential for the continuation of productive dialogue between mentor and mentee" (Symbulak & Davis, 2006).

Figure 5.1. *Time as the Interface for Successful Mentoring*

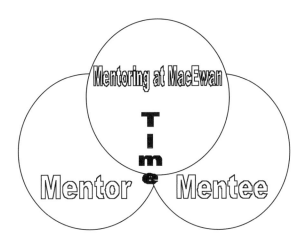

To document the performance of the program, annual summative surveys of the participants are conducted. Since its inception, more than 95% of the participants have rated the program as extremely worthwhile and claimed that it was an extremely effective method of improving instructional skills. Written comments repeatedly express that the most valuable aspect of the program was interaction with mentors/mentees, illustrating the community-building outcomes of the program. Numerous participants also state that it is the best professional development program at the college. Suggestions by participants are used to improve the program to meet the ever-changing needs of instructors at the college. In 2004 chairs and deans were also included in the evaluative process. Results of these surveys completed by the administration reflect an extremely successful program with more than 80% of the chairs supporting or strongly supporting its continuation as an important aspect of faculty growth and promotion of collegiality.

Perhaps the best measure of the program's success is reflected in the stories of the past participants and their willingness to express their own personal journeys. Participants in the program have presented their experiences in the program at three separate professional meetings; in 2003 and 2006 at the Alberta College and Institutes Faculty Association (ACIFA) meetings in Kananaskis and Jasper, Alberta, and in 2005 at the Leadership Academy meetings in Fort Lauderdale, Florida. In all cases the presentations received overwhelmingly positive reviews and the program was recognized for being inclusive of all faculty—adjunct and continuing.

Further accolades of the program are found in the following quotations from final reports that represent the personal and professional benefits collated from a variety of adjunct faculty who have participated in the program:

> I not only have a mentor, I gained a friend. . . . This program provided the opportunity to be evaluated by a well meaning and sincere colleague who gave a professional, unbiased opinion. The mentoring program has indeed been a worthwhile experience for me in its entirety. Through the different activities, I have engaged in another level of introspection regarding myself as a teacher.
> —Adenike Yesufu 2004–2005

> The program provided a collegial, stimulating, nourishing, and effective environment for those who wish to learn from experience and to improve for the future.
> —Sen Lin 2003–2004

> Perhaps the best part [of the mentoring program] has been my mentor's attitude towards guiding me to learning new things for myself, rather than just throwing information at me. They say that giving a person a fish will feed the person for a day, but teaching a person to fish will feed them for a lifetime. My mentor has given me a shiny new fishing rod and I am doing my best to use it every day.
> —Trudi Kwong 2005–2006

BENEFITS TO THE COLLEGE AND INDIVIDUAL PARTICIPANTS

The Faculty Mentoring Program at MacEwan builds community and promotes lifelong learning among the entire teaching faculty, adjunct and continuing. It enhances the instructional abilities and exemplifies cooperative learning strategies among the faculty, ensuring that students will receive the highest possible level of instruction. Mentoring at MacEwan creates increased collegiality and team building among faculty, as well as a sense of renewal and rejuvenation for more seasoned instructors. In its entirety, the mentorship program serves all levels of instructors, from recent Ph.D.s to 25-year veterans, in a cross-disciplinary manner, bringing together a very large and diverse college community. As one of the continuing members noted in his final report, "If there is any hope of continuing a sense of 'community' within the college, it will be through the connections we make with each other" (Taylor, 2004).

Mentoring is a valuable tool for helping adjunct instructors develop their teaching and classroom management skills, as well as their sense of connectedness to their institution. It also provides a valuable resource during challenging times, providing deeper understanding of college policies and procedures, insights into students' paradigms, and tips for preventing or correcting common mistakes. In addition, mentors often provide an advocate for the high-achieving adjunct instructor and introduction to key resources on campus.

For the mentor, the relationship with a mentee provides a sense of professional pride and accomplishment, ideas for integrating new practices and technology into their teaching, help with special projects, and sometimes a valued guest speaker or substitute for times when the veteran must be absent from campus. A carefully crafted mentoring agreement increases the chances that the mentor will feel rewarded and will therefore want to engage in a second or third mentoring relationship.

For several reasons, the MacEwan Faculty Mentoring Program requires that all mentees have taught at least four courses prior to being accepted into the program. This requirement typically eliminates the chance that mentees will ask too many elementary questions that mentors will get frustrated over answering repeatedly, delaying the onset of the deeper relationships that are the goal of the program. If mentoring is used with totally new adjunct instructors, it is critical to require the completion of a training course or series of workshops prior to, or at least concurrent with, the mentee's entry into the mentoring program.

Some degree of facilitation, orientation, and coordination is required if such a mentoring initiative is going to achieve its full potential. At the same time, the coordinator of such a program must be careful not to impose so many guidelines or rules that the process loses its spontaneity and personalized character. The MacEwan program has sought to balance this loose/tight dimension, achieving an environment that is both effective and personally fulfilling to its participants.

References

Headley-Smith, R., & Spronk, T. (2005). *Year end report—Faculty mentoring program.* Unpublished manuscript, MacEwan College, Edmonton, Alberta.

MacEwan College. (2006a). *About MacEwan.* Retrieved December 27, 2006, from: www.macewan.ca/web/home/DetailsPage.cfm?ID=503

MacEwan College. (2006b). *Grant MacEwan facilitated mentoring program.* Retrieved December 27, 2006, from: www.facultydevelopment.macewan.ca/metorDescription.html

Symbulak, D., & Davis, R. (2006). *Year end report—Faculty mentoring program.* Unpublished manuscript, MacEwan College, Edmonton, Alberta.

Taylor, P. (2004). *Year end report—Faculty mentoring program.* Unpublished manuscript, MacEwan College, Edmonton, Alberta.

APPENDIX 5.1

Mentoring Partnership Agreement

We have agreed to the following goals and objectives as the focus for this mentoring relationship:

- Helping MENTEE to deal with dominant students in the classroom

- Increasing MENTEE'S confidence level in dealing with evaluation (e.g., handing back exams, dealing with students' questions)

- Increasing MENTEE'S repertoire of teaching strategies to include experiential learning and inquiry/problem-based learning

We have discussed the protocols by which we will work together, develop, and in that spirit of partnership, collaborate on the development of a work plan. In order to ensure that our relationship is a mutually rewarding and satisfying experience for both us, we agree to:

1. *Meet regularly*
   Our specific schedule of contact and meetings are as followed:

   - Mondays (or Wednesdays) at 2:30 – 3:30 PM
     (adjusting times weekly as necessary, pre-arranged by both Mentor/Mentee)

   - E-mail or phone contact as needed
     MENTEE'S contact information:
     MENTOR'S contact information:

2. *Look for multiple opportunities and experiences to enhance the mentee's learning*
   We have identified, and will commit to, the following opportunities and venues for learning:

   - Looking into new technologies for the classroom (e.g., CPS-Classroom Performance System)

   - Attend a workshop offered by Faculty Development (e.g., Coping with Classroom Incivilities: Nanny 9-1-1 for the Professor)

3. *Maintain confidentiality of our relationship*
   Confidentiality for us means keeping the information discussed in our meetings private. This means not discussing each other's challenges with colleagues or friends.

4. *Honor the ground rules we have developed for the relationship*
   Our ground rules will be:

   - Being open and honest

   - Respecting each other's privacy

   - Attending meetings on time, and if we are going to be late or cannot attend, to contact the other individual as soon as possible

   - When attending each other's classes, to be constructive in feedback and to be sure to discuss strengths

5. *Provide regular feedback to each other and evaluate progress*

We will accomplish this by having weekly meetings and touching base via e-mail. If something is not working for one member of the team, he or she will bring it up and openly discuss it with the other team member.

We agree to meet regularly until we accomplish our predefined goals or for a maximum of 8 months. At the end of this period of time, we will review this agreement, evaluate our progress, and reach a teaching and learning conclusion. The relationship will then be considered complete. If we choose to continue our mentoring partnership, we may negotiate a basis for continuation, so long as we have stipulated mutually agreed on goals

In the event one of us believes it is no longer productive for us to continue or the learning situation is compromised, we may decide to seek outside intervention or conclude the relationship. In this event, we agree to use closure as a learning opportunity.

_____   _____
Mentor's Signature and Date   Mentee's Signature and Date

A MENTORING NETWORK FOR ADJUNCT FACULTY: FROM PROPOSAL TO PILOT TO FIVE-YEAR PLAN

Gayle Nolan, Cynthia Siegrist, Nancy Richard

SETTING THE SCENE

August 15, 1985. It was 5:00 on a Friday afternoon, and I was preparing to close the optometrist's office for the weekend. After working for the doctor for about seven months, I had applied in July for a part-time teaching position at Delgado Community College. I had always loved teaching in high school; no other job had been as satisfying to me as teaching, but with three children still in grade school, I needed a job that would allow me to be home by 3:00 every day. Glancing at the class schedule for Delgado Community College that had arrived by mail at my home, I had suddenly realized that, as a part-time teacher, I could do what I loved doing and still be at home when my children arrived from school in the afternoon. Because I knew there would not be time to process my application, call me in for an interview, and give me an orientation before classes began in August, I assumed that the fall semester would begin without me, and then I might be processed for the following semester, giving me lots of time to look through textbooks, prepare a syllabus, and plan teaching activities.

I was turning off the lights and preparing to lock the doors to the doctor's office when the phone rang. Technically, I did not have to answer it, but I decided to pick it up anyway.

"Is this Gayle?" asked the person on the other end. "I'm looking at your application to teach part-time. Can you start at 8:00 Monday morning?"

"Start what?" I asked in shock.

"Start teaching," replied the voice on the other end of the line.

"But what will I teach?" I asked, still not believing this was a real conversation, imagining myself to have fallen down the rabbit hole in *Alice in Wonderland* where the Mad Hatter talks without ever making sense. "I don't even have a textbook," I cried, bewildered about the potential of a Monday 8:00 a.m. entrance into a class without even a clue as to what material should be covered during the semester. Suppose a student asked a simple question about the college or about the course. I had never even set foot on the campus and would probably be more clueless than even a first semester student, who probably would have a catalog, at the very least.

"I know," laughed the voice on the other end. "The way we do things isn't always the best. But we had more students registered for developmental English than we expected this semester, and we need more teachers. Just come up the front steps to the second floor and turn right, go through the double doors, and I'll meet you in my office with your books at 7:30 Monday. We'll meet after your first class, and I'll fill you in then."

So went my entrance to Delgado Community College as a part-time teacher. Indeed, I did somehow struggle through that first class, and I was subsequently given a short orientation to teaching developmental English at Delgado. But left to my own devices after that, I quickly forgot some critical information about final grades given to me at the initial information session. Fortunately, since I did not have another job (I left the doctor's office), as most adjunct faculty do, I was free to sit in on grading sessions, faculty meetings, and lunch groups, where I picked up information and was able to ask questions on a daily basis. In addition, I picked up a contract for several hours of tutoring in the writing lab per week, a job that was to pay benefits far beyond the $7 per hour contract. It was in the lab that I learned firsthand what students do not know, what they do not understand, and how the more experienced teachers approach teaching and learning. In short, I learned on the job the "best practices" of teaching in the community college. Although I had been teaching for ten years previous to my community college experience, the students I had taught at the all-girls' college prep school were vastly different from those I met at Delgado. The major difference I discovered was that the students I now taught did not know how to learn, and I did not know how to teach them. I learned firsthand that teachers with a master's degree in specialized fields need to know much more than their subject matter if they want to teach at a community college; at least as important as content is knowing the students and knowing how one's students are different from oneself in life experience and responsibilities, as well as in attitudes towards school and learning.

In *Teaching at Its Best*, Linda Nilson (2003) states:

> Teaching well at the college level starts with becoming familiar with your institutional environment. Instructors, especially new ones, need to realize that they cannot and should not try to handle all the many challenges of their jobs single-handedly. Every college and university is a large, multilayered organization—a few rivaling small cities in size and complexity—each with its own unique subculture, norms and values, official power structure, informal power networks, and infrastructure of services and support units. Even seasoned faculty in a new institution feel unsettled as they anticipate unfamiliar policies, forms, procedures, expectations, and types of students. (p. 3)

Unfortunately, in 1985—and perhaps still today—most colleges left even their new full-time faculty to unravel the labyrinthine mysteries of college teaching for themselves, assuming that after three years or so, the new teacher would be ready for his or her first promotion process, having somehow caught on to the culture of the institution, the power structures, the norms and values, and the vagaries of student learning.

For adjunct instructors, the situation was even worse. As a daytime adjunct instructor in 1985 at Delgado Community College, I regularly (probably once a week) had to go in search of my purse, which I carried from class to class along with my books and student papers, because there was no office space for adjunct faculty, no desk at which to grade papers or confer with students, and no place to hang a raincoat or put down an umbrella. Full-time faculty members would allow me to use their desks or office cubicles when they were in class, but that meant coordinating teaching and office hours, leaving office doors unlocked, and other logistical difficulties. Nighttime adjunct faculty were slightly more fortunate, as there was a night dean on site who provided one room with a table and a photocopying machine for the use of all adjunct instructors. What I lacked in space and accommodations was compensated by my daily contact with full-time faculty who could answer questions and share their knowledge of the values and norms of the institution. What the night adjunct instructors gained in accommodations was lost in their isolation from contact with experienced teachers in their own disciplines—a supporting network of colleagues who could share teaching tales and offer some measure of emotional support.

Perhaps if we had worked at a smaller institution, the almost total aban-donment of adjunct teachers would not have been such a problem. The research on institutional support for new faculty members indicates that "feelings of isolation seem to be greatest at large institutions or institutions located in urban environments" (Walker & Hale, 1999, p. 229). However, as it turned out, the same factors that created the neglect of adjunct instruc-tors at Delgado Community College in 1985 in the long run became the impetus for change beginning in 1995.

For a ten-year span from 1979 to 1989, there had not been a single full-time teacher hired in the English Department at Delgado. Mostly, the college relied on adjunct faculty to support the minor variations in enrollment for those ten years. Because there was no hard and fast policy on the number of classes an adjunct instructor could teach, some part-time instructors taught five classes a semester, a *full course load*, for $700 a class. Without benefits.

For the college, the next five years marked a period of record growth. Between fall 1987 and spring 1992, Delgado more than doubled its enroll-ment from 7,093 full-time students to 15,065. A downturn in the economy had sent more of the New Orleans population back to school at the same time that the four-year colleges were tightening enrollment requirements. Moreover, in 1990, Delgado Community College merged with Charity School of Nursing, resulting in a concomitant demand for general education teachers to support the undergraduate applicants to the nursing school. Suddenly, Delgado could no longer support student enrollment by hiring and letting go significant numbers of adjunct faculty each semester; the col-lege began hiring full-time teachers, nearly doubling their numbers from 1987 to 1992. With a change of leadership in 1987 had also come a change in policy: Now adjunct faculty could no longer teach more than three class-es per semester.

As a result, the English Department increased its number of full-time faculty members from 25 to 50 within a space of five years, and the number of adjunct faculty continued to grow for the next ten years. Because the col-lege was desperate for classrooms and office space, the adjunct faculty were last in line for consideration of either physical or emotional support.

Although the college employed a night dean to support its evening adjunct faculty, the English department, in order to address the needs of daytime adjunct faculty members, created a buddy system between its full-time and adjunct faculty. In this informal system, a full-time faculty member volunteered to pair up with an adjunct instructor. The full-time faculty member was supposed to serve as a kind of mentor to the adjunct instructor, supplying information about college processes and classroom strategies, as well as completing the classroom observation form each semester. However, the entire process was more or less hit or miss, depending upon the interest, dedication, energy, and schedule of either or both partners in the system. Some adjunct instructors received guidance and encouragement; some did not.

At the time, even new full-time faculty received little support or direction other than a quick orientation to college policies and procedures. They were required to learn on the job and on their own when it came to classroom instruction. New full-time faculty were annually evaluated on classroom practice along with service to the college and community involvement, but it was up to each supervisor to define good teaching, and the new faculty member either knew how to do it or didn't.

In 1995 in the midst of a Southern Association of Colleges and Schools (SACS) self-study, the college leadership realized that its faculty evaluation policy would become an issue, because it differed in application from campus to campus and division to division. One year before the site visit, the Faculty Evaluation and Improvement of Instruction Committee, consisting of 25 members representing all segments of the college, was established to revise the policy and to standardize evaluation practice. As the committee began its study, it quickly came to realize that any summative "evaluation" process was all but useless in promoting instructional improvement. If the stated and primary purpose of evaluation was to improve teaching as the policy indicated, then the evaluative process had to be one of providing support and resources for teachers as they engaged in their own awareness, reflection, and growth in what constituted good teaching in their own disciplines.

A year later, the committee addressed its focus on the needs of the first-year teacher, developing a solid Mentoring Program for instructors new to Delgado Community College. The intention of the program was to create an environment wherein the first-year teacher at the college could network with other teachers, learn in an ordered and systematic way what the college expected and what it valued in its teachers, and find support for growing toward excellence in teaching in a community college.

THE PROPOSAL

Because adjunct faculty would not be included in the new evaluation system for full-time faculty or the Mentoring Program, part-time teachers were still left without systematic, comprehensive, college-wide support. What they did have at this time, however, was a confluence of people and events that moved them closer to this goal. While the full-time faculty evaluation system was being developed, the assistant dean of the evening and weekend division for City Park Campus was creating and implementing a paid, *mandatory* orientation for adjunct faculty. Furthermore, her "Adjunct Faculty Handbook" familiarized adjunct faculty with the policies and procedures of the college. She also created "Nuts and Bolts," a manual on the theory of teaching and learning and the practical applications to the classroom and provided all night adjunct faculty with *A Guide to Classroom Instruction for Adjunct Faculty* (2002, American Chemical Society). She regularly observed and surveyed her faculty, set up a workplace with three computer stations, and posted a web site for adjunct faculty.

Meanwhile, English faculty member Nancy Richard had been a vocal advocate for addressing the needs of adjunct faculty within her department. She had watched the number of adjunct faculty grow each year, and with that growth she noted with dismay that supervision of her part-time colleagues had become increasingly difficult. Many were teaching courses at no fewer than three different institutions, juggling dissimilar policies, expectations, and deadlines, as well as varied levels of student preparedness and collegial engagement. The English department's buddy system for managing classroom evaluations soon became unwieldy; the system was largely voluntary, and soon those who had been all too willing to mentor one part-time colleague found themselves juggling their own five-course loads and regular meetings with two or three adjunct instructors.

When the communication division saw a change in leadership, the new associate dean, the top-ranking administrator in the division, announced a new policy: each full-time faculty member was now required to mentor one adjunct instructor. At this point, two senior colleagues complained to the Faculty Senate that the burden was unfair, that adjunct mentoring was in fact not a part of their required responsibilities. The associate dean rescinded the ill-fated policy, and the number of available mentors dwindled. At the same time, the number of errors in matters of roster maintenance, grade inflation, and the posting of grades increased, thereby making life more difficult for the adjunct faculty and those who supervised them. Unfortunately, conscientious adjunct instructors and their overstretched department heads were often rebuked for adjunct instructors' errors made simply for lack of proper training and support. An unfortunate consequence was that part-time faculty became easy scapegoats: Every lapse in procedure, every student complaint could be attributed to the always culpable, nameless adjunct instructor. That was the fall semester of 2003, when Nancy Richard and the coordinator for faculty development met informally on occasion to chat about Richard's concerns. It was, in fact, during this semester that for the first time the number of part-time faculty in the English department outnumbered full-time faculty. They had reached critical mass.

In the meantime, the coordinator for faculty development approached the vice chancellor with the pressing concerns of the English department. In December 2003 she called Nancy Richard with news that the vice chancellor was ready to consider a proposal for an adjunct faculty mentoring position and asked her to compile a list of duties for such a position in two weeks' time. Richard recalled thinking, "After years of nagging and complaining, I could hardly refuse. Together with my department chair and division associate dean, I drafted a rationale and an initial list of duties." (See Appendix 6.1.)

By the time the spring 2004 semester began, administration had granted approval for a two-semester pilot of the position that was to be called adjunct mentoring coordinator. Because temporary full-time faculty were generally new to the college, the English department chair assigned their mentoring to the new coordinator as well. Given the number of part-time and full-time temporary faculty to be mentored, evaluated, and provided workshops (30, a number which would grow to 36), the division chair granted the coordinator three course releases for these duties.

THE PILOT

At midterm, Richard, who had been selected to fill the position of adjunct mentoring coordinator for English and developmental composition, submitted a progress report to the division associate dean and to the City Park Campus provost. By the end of the spring 2004 semester, the new chancellor had revised the organizational chart; the communication dvision was now part of a larger, merged liberal arts division with a new dean who requested an end-of-semester report on the pilot. (See Appendix 6.2.)

With the approval of the dean, we moved forward with the second semester pilot of the adjunct mentoring coordinator position in fall 2004. By this time the science and math division and business studies division had learned of our success and appointed their own adjunct mentoring coordinators. Richard met with both of them and corresponded by email on occasion to share the list of duties, classroom observation form, schedule of conferences, and the upward evaluation form. (Appendix 6.3 contains a copy of the form and summaries of adjunct instructors' responses to the upward evaluation in spring and fall 2004 and spring 2005.)

At the end of each of our first three semesters, Richard reviewed our adjunct instructors' responses. Their comments and concerns were critical in planning for the next semester's work. For example, a number of adjunct faculty requested either a handbook or packet of information early in the semester. Consequently, in collaboration with the associate dean of the evening and weekend division, the orientation and the "Nuts and Bolts" handbook were made available to both daytime and nighttime faculty. In addition to the handbook, part-time faculty received a folder of basic information about college policies and deadlines, provided by the associate dean, and a packet of important discipline-specific information from the English department.

Another concern of our adjunct faculty was the lack of designated work space and availability of computers and phones. At the end of the spring 2005 semester, when full-time faculty were moving into newly created offices, the dean of liberal arts offered the new coordinator a room to be used as office space for part-time faculty. The room would house four to six computers, work tables and chairs for conferencing with students, locking file cabinets, bookcases, a telephone, and two printers. By August 2005 Richard had drafted a list of 22 full-time English and developmental composition faculty who had volunteered to be observed by their part-time colleagues. After just three semesters of the new adjunct mentoring position, everyone—full-time colleagues, administrators, and adjunct faculty—remained positive that we had made a critical change in the culture of our college's academic environment. In fact, positive word of mouth spread, and by spring 2005, the total number of assigned mentors rose to six when the deans of the

Charity School of Nursing and West Bank campuses added assistant deans of the evening and weekend division.

THE PLAN

While we were piloting the position of adjunct mentoring coordinator, the Faculty Evaluation and Improvement of Instruction Committee prepared to address yet another issue. Having recently completed the implementation of the new faculty evaluation system for full-time teachers, the committee was finally able to turn its attention to part-time faculty. In fall 2005 the committee announced that it was their goal to develop and propose a comprehensive, college-wide plan for the support of adjunct faculty.

To educate themselves on the research, best practices, and issues related to part-time faculty, committee members were given a copy of *Success Strategies for Adjunct Faculty* by Dr. Richard Lyons (2004). Each member was then responsible for briefly presenting one chapter of the book to the rest of the committee, many of whom reported gaining a new appreciation and insight into the nature, role, and contributions of adjunct faculty. Experienced teachers on the committee found that the material in the book helped them to enhance their own classroom instruction as well. After reading and discussing Lyons's book, the committee began advocating for the creation of adjunct mentoring coordinator positions in each division, college wide, and decided to examine some of the other best practices that were being employed by or on behalf of adjunct faculty throughout the college. In affirmation of Nancy Richard's letter to the dean of liberal arts (see Appendix 6.2, #2), the committee's first recommendation was that the appropriate coordinators be included on search committees formed to fill full-time teaching positions.

Academic deans and coordinators on all of our campuses were invited to present to the committee what was being done to support adjunct faculty in each of their areas. It quickly became evident that there were many successful strategies and pockets of innovation going on independently of one another. Those assigned to mentor adjunct instructors began meeting together to see what methods, information, and resources could be shared to enhance adjunct faculty support while making it more consistent across the board.

Then, in April 2005, the Faculty Evaluation and Improvement of Instruction Committee and the Office of Faculty and Staff Development invited an outside consultant to Delgado for a two-day visit. On the first day, he hosted one focus group for those who were supervising adjunct faculty and another for adjunct faculty themselves. (See Appendix 6.4 for summary of adjunct participants' responses.)

On the second day, the consultant facilitated a two-hour workshop for all interested faculty and academic leaders in which participants devised an outline for a comprehensive college-wide plan for adjunct faculty support. Subsequent to his visit and the compilation of focus group and workshop discussions, the Office of Faculty and Staff Development and the Faculty Evaluation and Improvement of Instruction Committee produced the following five-year plan.

FIVE-YEAR SUCCESS PLAN FOR PART-TIME FACULTY AT DELGADO COMMUNITY COLLEGE (MARCH 2005)

Goals

1. Part-time faculty will indicate that the institution recognizes and appreciates the impact part-time faculty have on student success, recruiting, and retention.

2. Part-time faculty will indicate that they feel valued, supported, and included. They will indicate a sense of "belonging."

3. Part-time faculty will be provided with a space of their own and access to the classrooms in which they teach.

4. Part-time faculty will be provided with a college-wide (with some customization when required by individual sites or campuses) orientation and will indicate that this orientation meets their needs.

5. Part-time faculty will receive training and exhibit familiarity with administrative policy and procedures.

6. Part-time faculty will be provided with learning-centered, instructional enhancement activities and will apply some learning-centered teaching strategies to their courses.

7. Part-time faculty will be provided with opportunities to interact with other part- and full-time faculty.

8. The college will provide recognition and/or events that demonstrate appreciation and recognition of the contributions of part-time faculty.

(*Note:* This is an initial, organic plan that may be modified in the future. For example, the focus group expressed a strong desire/need to interact with both their part- and full-time colleagues. So far, the plan does not address this.)

Year I

1. Advocate for the continuation or creation of the position of adjunct mentoring coordinator in each division.

2. Develop and implement a college-wide orientation for all part-time faculty that prepares them for the reality of teaching at the community college and includes basic information that addresses both the administrative and academic (instructional) aspects of the job. (It was suggested that campus and building maps be included.)

3. Develop a college-wide part-time faculty handbook.

4. Include information from other campuses and sites in the existing adjunct faculty web page, developed by the associate dean of the evening and weekend division.

5. Link to appropriate, existing Faculty Development Associates' web pages or Docushare sites (e.g., www.developfaculty.com).

6. Work toward placement of part-time faculty on "faculty/staff" email distribution list immediately after the date of hire.

7. Work on the development of electronic portfolios for part-time faculty that would acknowledge participation in extra professional development activities.

Years II–III

1. Develop an online orientation.

2. Develop and launch a course for adjunct (new faculty?) development that includes the following:
   • Managing or launching the first class
   • Preparing the first test/midterm
   • Learning styles
   • Bringing a class to closure

Years IV–V

1. Develop and launch an interactive online course for part-time (and new ?) faculty that includes what is mentioned above as well as a greeting from the chancellor.

2. Provide adequate space for adjunct faculty.

3. Provide a program of part-time faculty recognition.

Shortly after the consultant's visit, the results of the focus group and the draft of the proposed five-year plan were distributed to all faculty and academic administrators via faculty/staff email. Also, following procedures outlined in its charter, the Faculty Evaluation and Improvement of Instruction Committee submitted a recommendation to accept and implement the proposed college-wide five-year plan to the vice chancellor of Learning and Student Development and the Office for Institutional Effectiveness at the end of spring 2005. Immediate feedback from the faculty/staff email was primarily positive. As mentioned earlier in this chapter, some deans and coordinators started meeting in order to craft a more standardized adjunct orientation, and adjunct faculty members were thankful to be heard and have their issues recognized. One serendipitous outcome from the focus on adjunct faculty by the Faculty Evaluation and Improvement of Instruction Committee and the Office of Faculty and Staff Development was that it sparked an increased appreciation, awareness of, and advocacy for adjunct faculty issues college wide.

One committee member reported the following:

I had always thought of adjuncts as full-time "wannabes" or somehow "less than" full-time faculty. What this experience has taught me is that a large percentage of adjuncts have chosen this lifestyle because they are engaged in other meaningful work or want to share their expertise with the community at large. Sitting in on the adjunct focus group was especially eye-opening to me. As adjuncts answered the questions posed, they talked passionately, insightfully, empathetically, and compassionately about their students and consistently put student needs before their own. As the session progressed, their level of experience, professionalism, commitment, dedication and enthusiasm bowled me over. Clearly, the other full-time faculty and I would greatly benefit from exposure to our part-time colleagues, at least as much as the other way around. In short, it was an honor and an inspiration to sit with this group.

Negative feedback to the faculty/staff email from some deans included a certain reluctance to be directed by a mandated college-wide plan. Some of the fears expressed were that the proposed five-year plan was yet another document to which they would be held accountable, and that a standardized plan would not address the inherent and defining differences of each division or campus. Aware of its obligation to respond to the diverse needs of the entire college community, the committee recognized that its plan must be flexible enough to accommodate those differences. As such, the plan will remain a dynamic document, subject to occasional emendation as necessary.

By the end of the spring semester, the committee had not yet received an official response from the Office of the Vice Chancellor or the Office for Institutional Effectiveness, so the group determined to follow up in fall 2005. At that time, the proposed five-year plan, still in its infancy, could be reviewed, reworked, and initiated under the coordination and/or facilitation of the Office of Faculty and Staff Development. This much could be accomplished even without a response from the higher offices, because all those who would be responsible for implementing the plan were familiar with it and had collaborated on its creation.

On Monday, August 29, two weeks after the beginning of the fall 2005 semester, Hurricane Katrina forever changed our lives and our collective sense of familiarity and security. The storm and the levee breaches in its wake took the lives of about 1,500 people in the New Orleans area. Homes, neighborhoods, communities, ways of life, and workplaces were utterly devastated, Delgado Community College among them. Virtually all of the college's locations suffered storm-related damage. The main campus (City Park) had critical flooding with up to eight feet of water. An estimated 60% of its facilities were significantly damaged, including the administration building, several state-of-the-art labs, central utilities, library, IT center, and scores of classrooms. The eight-story Delgado Charity School of Nursing Building, located one block from the Superdome, had four to five feet of water in the basement, incapacitating the electrical system and elevators. The West Bank campus had some roof damage to its main building, and the Slidell Learning Center, inundated with eight feet of floodwaters, was declared a total loss.

The storm's impact on the college community was profound. Students and faculty, like all other residents of the city, remained under mandatory evacuation for at least two months while waters that had covered 80% of the metro area receded and basic municipal services were restored. With the Delgado population in exile as far away as Alaska, the college heroically salvaged the fall 2005 semester by initiating 210 online courses. This represented a 233% increase over the fall 2004 online enrollment of 63. Then, the state slashed the college's budget by 17%, almost $6 million, resulting in agonizingly deliberated furloughs and layoffs of staff and faculty.

When the spring semester began in January 2006, the college had an enrollment of 10,002 students, down from the fall semester's all-time high of 17,400 registered students. With enrollment down by 40%, part-time and full-time temporary faculty were most vulnerable to staffing cuts. In fact, Richard reported that of the 82 sections of developmental and freshman composition offered by the English department in the spring 2006 semester, only one night class was covered by an adjunct instructor. In contrast, at the beginning of the interrupted fall semester, 22 part-time and three full-time temporary faculty had been scheduled to teach. In the meantime, released time for adjunct mentoring coordinators has been suspended until the need for part-time faculty increases.

Because of the immediate demands of recovery, the urgent need to develop faculty in distance education, and the dramatic decrease in the number of adjunct faculty employed by the college, the proposed five-year plan has been delayed but not forgotten. During the fall semester, the Office of

Faculty and Staff Development ordered Scenarios, an online development tool for adjunct faculty that features real-life simulations and case studies. Additionally, the office proposed that adjunct faculty who complete this training receive a $500 increase in salary. But, perhaps most hopeful of all, two weeks into our summer 2006 semester, Nancy Richard dropped by the faculty development office to say how joyful it made her feel when summer's first (and only) adjunct instructor stopped by her office to ask for some help.

In the face of what at times seem to be insurmountable challenges, Delgado Community College remains committed to its mission and to its rebuilding. There is no quick fix for the recovery and restoration of our hurricane-ravaged community or our campuses. When Hurricane Katrina struck, it had been 20 years, practically to the day, since Gayle Nolan first joined the Delgado faculty as an adjunct instructor. In those 20 years, the college saw its enrollment increase from about 7,500 to a record 17,400. We had made great strides in faculty development opportunities, in faculty and administrative pay increases, in building facilities, and in providing resources for part-time faculty. How then do we make sense of so much loss? A local writer and columnist for *The Times-Picayune* was invited to deliver the commencement address at a local all-girls Catholic school. Here is what Chris Rose (2006) had to say to the spring 2006 class of Ursuline Academy:

Like it or not, this storm, these circumstances, have marked you. My belief is that your generation and those who come after you in this town will be extraordinarily resilient. That is a good quality to carry with you. You have seen and suffered loss. (p. D-5)

We are indeed a resilient lot whose resolve is unshaken. Delgado Community College will maintain its focus on the creation of a working, learning, growing environment that nurtures the entire college community. New Orleans is still here, and so are we.

References

Lyons, R. E. (2004). *Success strategies for adjunct faculty.* Boston, MA: Allyn & Bacon.

Nilson, L. B. (2003). *Teaching at its best: A research-based resource for college instructors* (2nd ed.). Bolton, MA: Anker.

Rose, C. (2006, May 14). Children of the storm, it's time to represent. *The Times-Picayune,* pp. D-1, D-5.

Walker, C. J., & Hale, N. M. (1999). Faculty well-being and vitality. In R. J. Menges & Associates, *Faculty in new jobs: A guide to settling in, becoming established, and building institutional support* (pp. 216–239). San Francisco, CA: Jossey-Bass.

APPENDIX 6.1

December 16, 2003

Gayle Nolan
Coordinator of Faculty Development

Dear Gayle,

Enclosed is a list of duties to be performed by an adjunct coordinator assigned to the English department. [The associate dean], [the department chair], and I have met on three occasions and are satisfied at this point that we have covered the major issues. We are aware, however, that some fine-tuning will be necessary once the position is piloted.*

To follow up on our conversation about the recent shift in the English department, [the department chair] tells me that this semester has marked the transition from majority full-time to majority adjunct: 29 full-time positions—this figure includes four temporary—and 32 adjunct instructors. The supervision of so many part-time instructors has become prohibitive for someone in [her] position as department chair with teaching duties. As you can see from the enclosed list, our part-time instructors require supervision at a number of levels to ensure that our students are getting the quality of instruction they deserve. Given the nation-wide trend, our expectation is that the balance will shift even more toward reliance on part-time faculty. Before we lose control of the quality of instruction we have worked so hard to maintain at Delgado, we should seize the opportunity now to pilot an adjunct coordinator position.

Position: Adjunct Coordinator/English and Developmental Composition

1.   Hold three to four meetings of adjunct instructors per semester, arranged to accommodate the schedules of adjuncts who teach only daytime/night-time/Saturday. These meetings shall include workshops in syllabus construction, exit exam grading, developmental composition grading policies, training and norming for respective courses, etc.

2. Review syllabi of adjunct instructors for conformity with division policies.

3. Devise an evaluation instrument/checklist for use with adjunct faculty only.

4. Observe all adjuncts and use a specific evaluative form (cf. #2) developed for use with adjunct faculty only.

    - First-year adjunct instructors will be subject to at least one formal, planned observation each semester. The coordinator will make additional unplanned visits to any adjunct classrooms on a regular basis, especially if there have been student complaints.

    - Second-year adjunct instructors will be observed and evaluated at least once per academic year.

5. Compile a checklist of information adjuncts must have, i.e., deadlines, timelines, etc.

6. Require all adjuncts to phone/email the coordinator on a regular basis.

7. Work with hiring committee to provide feedback/recommendations for regular/full-time openings.

8. Work with department chair to interview/hire adjuncts, to coordinate submission of and review of credentials.

9. Review student evaluations of adjunct instructors and work with department chair to make determinations about rehiring.

10. Monitor adjunct instructors' usage of labs and other support services.

11. Monitor attendance of adjuncts at exit exam grading sessions.

12. Monitor pass rates of adjuncts' students on English 101 exit exam.

13. Monitor adjuncts' timeliness in posting midterm and final grades.

14. Draft an upward evaluation form to be completed by adjunct instructors at the end of the Spring semester.

15. Submit copy of final report to department chair.

Note: This academic year marks a significant shift in the balance of our English department: Statistics for fall semester 2003 indicate our department functioned with 32 adjunct instructors and 29 full-time instructors. For the new spring semester 2004, the English department will have hired 34 adjunct instructors (including seven full-time temporary), one more than the number of full-time regular instructors.

*The above list represents the first complete list of duties for the proposed position of adjunct mentoring coordinator. However, over the initial two (pilot) semesters, Richard made minor changes to the list when she did not find it necessary to *require* regular contact from adjunct faculty, or to monitor their students' usage of labs and other support services.

APPENDIX 6.2

July 29, 2004

To: Dr._____
       Dean, Liberal Arts

From: Nancy Richard
         Adjunct Mentoring Coordinator
English and Developmental Composition

Re: End-of-semester report/Spring 2004

Dear Dr. _____,

Per your request, I have compiled a number of documents relevant to our first semester pilot of the adjunct mentoring coordinator position in our division in spring 2004. Included are the following:

- A copy of my mid-term report, FYI

- Copies of my observation/evaluation forms for all thirty-four adjuncts

- Copies of our division adjuncts' upward evaluation of their mentoring coordinator

If I were to offer a rationale for supporting the position of adjunct mentoring coordinator, without a doubt my primary argument would be the issue of accountability. When adjunct faculty are accountable to a single coordinator whose job is their mentoring, they are more responsible employees and colleagues. When they have available in the coordinator a discipline-specific resource and source of support, they become more effective teachers. The following represent what I consider to be the most important issues we face with respect to the management and mentoring of our growing numbers of adjunct faculty:

1. It is a SACS standard that *all* faculty are evaluated annually, regardless of status or tenure. Prior to spring 2004 our division relied upon the goodwill volunteering of senior faculty to mentor/observe/evaluate our adjuncts. That pool has been diminishing, and even those few who continued to volunteer found it increasingly difficult to manage their own course loads and committee assignments around tracking down and meeting with their assigned adjuncts. With 34 adjuncts in two departments alone, the task had become unmanageable.

2. Further, there was no consistency in the feedback from volunteer mentors. On the basis of one or two meetings and a classroom observation, senior faculty are loathe to put into writing anything negative about another instructor. Consequently, the department chair had little reliable information with which to make decisions about rehiring. When one individual is responsible for mentoring, observing, and evaluating, the department chair has consistent, reliable, objective information and someone to assist, not only with rehiring, but with the screening and interviewing of new adjuncts. Surely we owe it to our students to hire their instructors with careful, due consideration of credentials, experience, and effectiveness in the classroom.

3. Aside from SACS-required evaluations, there are many other issues that are time intensive: When I assumed the responsibility at the beginning of spring 2004, I set up a schedule of 16 initial, individual meetings with new (i.e., first-year) adjuncts, 34 classroom observations, and 34 post-observation conferences to discuss their evaluations. In all, I held 50 individual, scheduled conferences during the spring semester. Additionally, I reviewed graded papers from all adjuncts and either met with them or corresponded by memo about their grading. I didn't keep track of the impromptu meetings to discuss classroom issues, to offer resources, or to provide assistance with posting grades.

4. I'd been concerned for some time that our part-time evening developmental and English composition faculty were isolated from their division colleagues. Though they were getting fine support from the evening division staff in matters of college policies and deadlines, there was no support network for discussions about the teaching of composition. To make myself available to evening faculty, I arranged my office hours so that I would be in my office at least two evenings a week. For each of several weeks when I was observing classes, I worked three to four 12-hour days. With even one class to teach and my duties on the SACS Team, the three course releases for adjunct mentoring were minimally adequate. I make this point because before we

launched this new project, very little mentoring of adjunct faculty was accomplished. There was simply no one, however willing, with the time to give them the support they needed in order to be effective teachers and responsible colleagues.

5. What was the impact of the project on our division? For the first time (in years? ever?), not one adjunct instructor was late submitting midterm and final grades. Once the exit exam grading schedule was posted, I sent out a memo, with an RSVP that adjuncts contact me to verify their receipt of the schedule and to make necessary changes. In response to my memo, adjuncts contacted me when they had scheduling problems; we made changes via email or phone, and avoided understaffed, overworked sessions. As a result, adjunct attendance at grading sessions was markedly more responsible, with not a single no-show at any of the 11 sessions.

6. What is the impact on our students? Again, I think the overriding issue is accountability. In two cases, we received complaints from students about their adjunct instructors. I was able to respond with visits to their classrooms, both of them in the evening, and to have follow-up conversations with both instructors. A volunteer colleague/mentor simply doesn't have the authority, the time, or the willingness to address student concerns. Also, because I required adjuncts to share with me a set of graded papers, I was able to check on grade inflation, inadequate focus on exit preparation, or a lack of emphasis on sentence mechanics. When we give our adjuncts the support they need, we can stand behind the quality of instruction in their classrooms, and we can stand behind our commitment to the college's mission statement.

7. What has been the response of our adjunct faculty? I enclose their upward evaluations. They are positive, and if these instructors indicate any misgivings, it is that they want *more* support.

Even as I imagined such a coordinator position and planned for its first-semester implementation, I didn't foresee how time-consuming such a job could become. Even so, I'm more convinced than ever of its necessity. Given the college's increasing dependence upon adjunct faculty, in the interest of our commitment to Delgado's students, we must in all good faith provide our students' instructors with consistent support in mentoring, in the providing of resources, and in assuring accountability. I am grateful for your support and your encouragement. Should you require any additional information, please do contact me at any time.

APPENDIX 6.3

Semester _____ Year _____
Evaluation of Adjunct Coordinator

To: Adjunct Faculty/English and Developmental Composition

From: Nancy Richard
       Adjunct Mentoring Coordinator

Date:

Please complete the following brief evaluation and return it to the Reception Desk in either the Evening Division Office or the Liberal Arts Office before you leave for the semester. You may type your comments if you prefer, and of course your signature is not required. Your honest responses will help me to serve you more effectively.

All good cheer,

1. What additional help or resources would you like your Adjunct Coordinator to provide?

2. What resources did you find
    (a) most helpful?

    (b) least helpful?

Additional comments: _____

_____

_____

Upward Evaluations of Adjunct Mentoring Coordinator Summary: Concerns, Suggestions, Requests

(Spring 2004)

1. I would have been lost without the coordinator as a resource. Because I taught at night, I had no chance to fraternize with my faculty colleagues nor to ask the dozens of questions about everything from bureaucracy to pedagogy that allow a new teacher to survive in a wholly new setting. I doubt very much that I could have made it through the semester without the exceptional support and generosity of the adjunct coordinator and the English department chair.

2. I would have liked to have an adjunct handbook. I think that there are a few things that still seem to fall through the cracks and don't surface until the deadline is upon us. I'd be willing to help put such a handbook together. I appreciated the grading session workshops; they really helped me understand what an English 101 student must be able to accomplish to be successful in English 102. Having a mentor that I can go to with my concerns and questions has made a world of difference.

3. I would have liked earlier feedback on my grading and a packet of specific information at the beginning of the semester: exit exam details, info on the writing lab, etc.

4. Perhaps someone could compile a "new hire" packet for all those little forms and bits of information which new hires don't always know about. The most helpful resource was the pool of experienced instructors who were always willing to answer questions.

5. I found most helpful the coordinator's undivided attention, her willingness to listen and to give advice about individual students, and her encouragement within the "bigger picture."

Fall 2004

1. My only concern is that adjunct instructors are like nomads—no office, no phone, not even a place to store the stacks of handouts we often prepare for our students. It would be nice if we had a room with a table and chairs and perhaps a file cabinet and a phone, even if it meant all adjunct instructors shared that same room. Having somewhere quiet and nondistracting to meet students or prepare lessons would be wonderful. When it's necessary to call students by phone, especially during exit exam time, it is very awkward to have to either make the calls from someone else's office or from my own home or cell phone. Finally, having a file cabinet to store handouts in would be great; I've been hauling around all my class materials from building to building this semester and it can be quite tiring.

2. Email! I did not have a functioning email account this semester.

3. Nuts and bolts info about procedure. (I know there is some.)

Spring 2005

1. Perhaps a meeting with the librarians prior to the semester would be an auspicious beginning for any adjunct instructor.

2. A grading workshop in the beginning of the semester would be wonderful. The exit exam grading sessions are useful, but they come so late in the semester that I felt like I would've been more aware of what I was looking for if the session had been earlier. . . . In the fall, a lot of people seemed to not know or were unsure of the 061 grammar component. Perhaps that could be avoided.

3. Perhaps, for new instructors, a rubric/sample packet of various graded papers might be helpful. . . . I think to relieve anxiety and to offer slightly earlier input, if possible, the observation could occur before the midterm.

4. Organizing a faculty and adjunct "get-to-know-you" meeting/party would be nice. I still know only a few of my colleagues here. [The adjunct mentoring coordinator] is best situated to foster ties between us as working scholars.

5. A phone, or at least voicemail access would be nice. . . . Re: the Orientation: For future first-time adjunct faculty, I think they would appreciate having that wealth of info before the semester begins. It would be more proactive, I believe, and the adjunct faculty would be able to do a better job of planning, as well as spend more time concentrating on teaching. I'm aware that this isn't always possible, but any

attempt to do so would be greatly appreciated. Perhaps a packet containing the materials we were given at orientation could be mailed to the adjunct faculty, or given to them when they are given their textbooks and other supplies. Just a suggestion; as I said, I know it's not always possible.

6. It would have been helpful in teaching 061 had I seen the departmental exam at the first of the semester.

7. A raise would be nice, but I realize that adjunct pay is low on the food chain around here. Otherwise, another copy machine would be a Godsend. . . . This semester, there weren't enough relevant essays in the reader.

APPENDIX **6.4**

Notes on Focus Group of Adjunct Faculty
Facilitated by Outside Consultant
March 21, 2005

Number of *participants*: approximately 17
- Freelancers   2
- Career enders   0
- Professional experts   7
- Aspiring academics   6
- Participants had either been with DCC a very long time or not long at all

What do you like about teaching at DCC?

Students, students, students!
- Participants found that our students did not match their preconceptions. They found students to be mature, capable, and willing to grow and develop. (Discussion on student attributes)

Academic freedom and the ability to manage the classroom as they choose
- K–12 teachers are not allowed this freedom.

Department chair
- Participant noted her chair was available and "stopped what she was doing" to provide help or resources. She gives adjuncts freedom, support, and confidence.

Adjunct coordinators
- Good resources; lots of experience
- Nancy Richard: positive, reinforcing, been in the trenches, understanding ear, respectful
- Dr. Pat Cox: a "dream;" got access to the classroom after many semesters
- Mercedes Munster and new night dean on West Bank campus: very supportive

People at DCC are nice
Don't feel a distinction between part- and full-time faculty/feel valued

As you think about teaching here, what is the significant challenge?

- Students' perceptions of themselves: have come to see themselves negatively—teacher must build confidence
- Teaching students about a good work ethic
- Motivating students (Adjuncts very cognizant and accepting of responsibility to motivate students and "teach" them how to learn, be good students; "acclimate them on how to be a good student;" "important to teach them how college works;" teaching adults how to balance work, kids, and school;" "management of their own lives;" "It's a lot more than teaching the course.")
- Last minute schedule changes; not knowing what you're going to teach until the day before

What could DCC do to better prepare you?

- Orientation for all
- Nighttime faculty need same kind of "curriculum discussion" as daytime faculty. Night faculty don't get a chance to interact, discuss academic issues, *share their own knowledge* with daytime faculty. Curricular decisions made during day at meetings in which adjuncts have no input.
- Night faculty don't know what daytime people do.
- Adjuncts would like to get the same information that students do during their orientation so they know what services are available to students and can refer students to these services.
- Eight adjuncts reported the experience of being given a syllabus, a book, and starting the next day.
- They want to know, "Who do I contact if I have a problem?"
- How do I put in my grades?
- No expectations communicated (West Bank campus)

- Would like an adjunct web site or faculty web site
- Seven reported that they had no adjunct orientation
- Provide adjunct coordinators and tenured faculty as mentors
- It would be helpful if adjuncts participated in planning and delivery of adjunct orientation
- A common master syllabus helps. Binders provided with supplementary materials for a particular course would be helpful.
- Classes like Blackboard and other technological training are appreciated.
- A "personal day" built into the schedule. Adjuncts reported being docked in pay for absences due to sickness.
- Need adequate advanced notice
- One adjunct reported that there is no interaction between adjuncts, even ones teaching the same course. "Am I over-teaching? Am I under-teaching?"

What could DCC integrate systematically?

- A directory of who's teaching what by course/subject matter
- Time for a faculty meeting that would allow face-to-face interaction, opportunity to discuss common concerns, divisional debriefing at the end of a semester
- An office
- A quiet place to meet with students
- Voicemail
- Keys
- A shelf
- Access to a copy machine
- "I feel like I'm not supposed to be here, except when I'm in the classroom."
- We're expected to meet with students and hold office hours but we don't have a place to do so.
- Daytime adjuncts would like to have access to nighttime space
- Higher pay
- Access to same info students get in their orientation
- Opportunity to meet and talk with advisors

"Many people that I have talked to have problems getting paid. In fact, it took me two months to get paid on time. The payroll staff (although working hard to make sure lots of people are getting paid on time) are not willing to do anything to help those who are having problems with their check. I had to borrow money from my family to pay my bills."

7 | A Consortium Approach to Supporting Part-Time Faculty

Helen Burnstad, Ben Hayes, Cindy Hoss, Ann-Marie West

Few people would argue that effective teaching is part art and part skill, which requires an environment of regular insights and supported practice to rise to a craft. In developing programming that enables adjunct instructors to gain an understanding of these complex factors, most colleges and universities choose to "go it alone." Whether this is a conscious decision grounded in perceptions of unique mission and culture, or a need to control content and costs, or the inability to see past outmoded paradigms is difficult to say.

In 1994 a group of faculty developers within the metropolitan Kansas City area approached their organizational needs in another way by leveraging an existing collaboration called the Kansas City Regional Council for Higher Education (KCRCHE). Formed years earlier to provide its 19 member colleges and universities increased efficiencies through collective purchasing, conference sponsorship, and staff development programs, KCRCHE was from its outset administered through a central office with its own staff funded by member institutions. As costs of supporting KCRCHE increased and consortium advantages declined in the perception of some institutional administrations, the served colleges and universities dissolved KCRCHE. Although the dissolution made sense to most stakeholders, it presented a dilemma to a core group of faculty and staff developers who had been working together to sponsor programming.

Having developed strong relationships with faculty developers from member institutions and being highly pleased with their achieved results, the group decided to pursue the continuation of their relationship without a central office. They sought the support of interested colleagues who could gain financial support from their presidents through extending a call to all former KCRCHE member institutions. For a variety of reasons, some members declined. But those from eight schools recognized the opportunity to build upon the synergies that had already been demonstrated. Staff and faculty developers from these diverse institutions met to develop a plan of action that resulted in an initial meeting with the respective presidents or designees. The group proposed a mission, goals, annual institutional membership fee of $5,000, and organizational structure for a new collaboration to be known as the Kansas City Professional Development Council (KCPDC). The response to the proposal was overwhelming, and a vote was taken to support the proposal, adding a guarantee of ongoing support from each school over time.

Following that meeting, staff and faculty development representatives met several times to establish the details of a unified governing council and to develop an initial program of activities. Members agreed to create a relationship in which each institution enjoyed the same status regardless of size or type designation of higher education institution; where all employees of all institutions could participate in professional development to meet their needs; where the governance structure would include a chair, a part-time support person, and would rotate between two-year and four-year institutions; where the council would maintain fiscal responsibility within the membership budget; and where the consortium would grow and change as the needs indicated over time. Since 1994 membership has remained static, with seven institutions currently members. One founding institution, Central Missouri State University (CMSU) withdrew support upon an administrative change, and the University of Missouri–Kansas City (UMKC) became a replacement member.

EVOLUTION

KCPDC is a unique consortium that includes members from two- and four-year institutions, public and private institutions, as well as a proprietary university. Current membership includes: Baker University, DeVry University, Johnson County Community College, Kansas City Kansas Community College, the Metropolitan Community College system (four colleges), Park University, and the University of Missouri–Kansas City. Membership crosses the state line within the greater Kansas City area to include organizations located in both Kansas and Missouri. Faculty and staff from other area schools are invited to participate in the Saturday workshops or major events.

Participants have attended from Avila College, Donnelly College, CMSU, and various public schools.

ORGANIZATION AND MANAGEMENT

The consortium is led by a board comprised of two representatives from each member institution. Typically one representative focuses on the wants/needs of faculty and the other is concerned with issues of all other staff members. Titles range from vice president of academic affairs to director of human resources to director of staff and faculty development. Each member has an equal voice and equal decision-making power. Each school continues to pay the annual membership fee, which is now $5,500. The council chair serves a two-year term supported by a paid part-time support person for 10–20 hours per week. The chair rotates every two years between a community college representative and a university representative. The budget is housed at the institution of the chair and managed by the support person. The incoming chair is a council colleague who has previously served on the board and is trained and mentored by the outgoing chair as necessary. Likewise the new support person is trained by the outgoing support person and the new chair.

The council meets six times a year. Five regular meetings cover the ongoing business of the consortium, evaluating the quality of program offerings, recruiting facilitators, and determining future consortium direction as well as sharing of programs at individual colleges. The last meeting of the academic year is a planning retreat held in late spring. Board members evaluate council financial statements, allocate funds, and determine the programming schedule and course offerings for the next academic year.

A web site is maintained by the consortium (see www.kcpdc.org). In addition, marketing of programs and events is handled on the individual campuses by the staff development program there. Registrations are taken by the support person for the consortium who then provides the participant list to the session facilitator. Evaluation sheets are provided to the facilitator at the scheduled school. As soon as both the participant list and evaluation sheets are returned to the support person, payment is generated for the facilitator.

SERVICES PROVIDED TO MEMBER ORGANIZATIONS

A comprehensive program of activities is offered to all faculty and staff from the member schools. These include:

- *Needs Assessment:* Conducted for three groups: full- and part-time faculty; clerical and support staff; and supervisory and managerial staff. Each school gathers its data and submits it to the council for tabulation. Each school receives its data and the whole is tabulated to govern the decision-making on programs for all employees of all member colleges. The needs assessment is completed every three years, which provides member organizations with current data for their programming as well as data that meets the consortium's needs.

- *Supervisor Development Program:* An ongoing certificate program for first-line supervisors or those who aspire to supervisory positions.

- *Enhancing Teaching and Learning Conference:* Held annually to focus on effective teaching strategies, it includes presentations by full- and part-time faculty from member institutions.

- *Master Faculty Workshop:* An annual weekend retreat that explores good teaching and finding solutions to issues that arise throughout the teaching/learning process.

- *Celebrate, Learn, and Build Workshop (CLB):* An annual retreat for office professionals and technicians to explore effective practices and seek solutions to workplace problems/concerns.

- *Peer Exchange Program (PEP):* An exchange opportunity for clerical staff and technicians to visit another school and job shadow for a day.

- *Workplace Issues:* A series of seminars designed to respond to current issues identified by the needs assessments.

- *Faculty Certification Program:* Twenty-four hours of programming to provide both full- and part-time faculty with tools and resources to enhance classroom effectiveness.

- *On-Campus Presentations:* Two presentations per year may be delivered to member institutions. A resource guide lists employees of the consortium schools who are willing and prepared to present topics of their choice.

- *Featured Guests or Scholar-in-Residence:* Identified national experts spend an extended period in the area, rotating between member colleges.

- *Invitations:* Invitations are extended to presenters and programs held on member campuses.

SERVICES FOR PART-TIME FACULTY

In 1999 the KCPDC board Council recognized that the growing population of part-time faculty members was underserved by existing programming. In discussing this issue, the council realized that a significant number of part-timers were teaching at more than one member institution. The decision was made to include all faculty who work at member schools in faculty development programs. The following year, the consortium designed and began delivering a program to prepare part-time faculty in the following six core areas.

Instructional Strategies

This course is an advanced offering in instructional design. Participants are challenged to view their instructional strategies from a new perspective. Instructors assess their current teaching strategies to ensure a match with their expectations of what students will know or be able to do. This course relies on interaction and participation from class members. Small groups, discussion questions, and practice application are mainstays of this course. This course is taught by a full-time staff member from Baker University.

Evaluating Student Achievement Through Testing and Writing

This class is designed to answer frequently asked questions by faculty members who have had little or no experience evaluating student achievement by testing or writing assignments. The content guides participants through developing a test using a variety of questions and formats and evaluating the results of tests. Guidelines are shared for using writing assignments to promote critical thinking. Practical information is shared and supplemented with extensive handouts to serve as good resources for use after class. This course is taught by a full-time faculty member from the Metropolitan Community Colleges.

The Impact of Learning Styles

There is now a greater awareness of basic learning styles, but instructors are often not aware of the differences in learning preferences related to personality type. This course addresses how learning styles and personality types are related to our teaching preferences and how our students prefer to learn. Different learning styles, types of intelligence, and personality types (i.e., Myers-Briggs) are discussed, and related teaching strategies are addressed. Upon completing this session, participants gain an awareness of the diversity of learning styles and are better equipped to facilitate classroom activities that have the potential to reach all students. This course is taught by a part-time faculty member from the Metropolitan Community Colleges.

Educational Equity Seminar

This course provides an introduction to multicultural education aims and methods as well as a look at the relevance of local history. Participants are exposed to concrete methods of studying race, class, and gender inequalities. They probe these issues as coinvestigators and share their own best practices. This course is taught by a full-time faculty member from Kansas City Kansas Community College.

Legal Issues/Sexual Harassment Prevention

This workshop provides training that is both didactic and participative. Small working groups consider several scenarios and discuss within buzz groups. These buzz groups are then reorganized to field comments and questions. This course is taught by a full-time faculty member from Central Missouri State University (CMSU), a nonmember institution.

Writing Across the Curriculum (WAC)

This course familiarizes adjunct instructors with writing across the curriculum theory and techniques that can be used immediately in any course. Using WAC strategies enables students to learn and cement new concepts more deeply. After this workshop, instructors will be able to develop writing assignments to help them know if students have mastered the process of learning as well as course content. This course is taught by a part-time instructor from the Metropolitan Community Colleges.

Electives

In addition to the core courses, participants must complete two of the following electives:

- CATs in the Classroom (Classroom Assessment Techniques; Angelo & Cross, 1993)

- Active Learning

- Effective Communication

- Adult Learning Characteristics

- Community-Based Learning

These elective courses are also taught by full- or part-time faculty members from member institutions. The facilitators rotate for these courses more than on the core courses.

Upon completion of eight modules, the participant is recognized with a certificate of completion of the program by KCPDC. Individual schools further recognize participants. For example, Kansas City Kansas Community College awards the certificate to the part-time faculty member at the end-of-year retirement dinner and celebration. The recognition is appreciated by faculty members and their guests at the dinner. The consortium has considered suggesting to member schools that they may want to require completion of the program as a prerequisite for employment as a part-time faculty member at one or more of the colleges. To date the requirement has not been implemented.

EVALUATION OF THE CONSORTIUM

In addition to the quality of programming evaluation undertaken for the KCPDC board, member institutions are charged with designing their own evaluation system. Statistics are collected on participation in programs, use of services by colleges, number of participants for each activity, and cost of each program. Some schools have used focus groups for feedback and evaluation or held directed conversations about the outcomes participants gained from completing a certificate program. Some have gone to the next step of requiring a program such as the supervisor development program and then asking for evaluation from the supervisor of the participants. For some colleges, evaluation of consortium membership includes a return-on-investment (ROI) analysis.

LESSONS LEARNED

KCPDC has taught us some very important lessons that may help other colleges and universities;

- Look for like-minded colleagues. Be creative in designing a consortium.

- Extend the scope of members. The membership of KCPDC is enriched by the variety of colleges and universities who are members. If institutions start a consortium, invite all postsecondary education institutions in your immediate area.

- Use the expertise available. Some schools will have dedicated offices to support staff and/or faculty development. Others may have a decentralized system where the support is provided by an administrator, such as a vice president for academic affairs, who is responsible for all faculty development. Therefore, learn from each other.

- Time is involved to make a consortium work. Every member institution must select representatives to the council and dedicate the time needed for meetings and hosting activities. KCPDC requires approximately 40 hours per year per member.

- Willingness to take on leadership roles. KCPDC rotates the chair of the council every two years with one term being held by a community college representative and the next held by a university member. The support person rotates with the chair and is usually a part-time employee of the chair's school.

- Listening is a very important skill for members of the board. The issues have been identified through the needs assessment, but the programming and scheduling must be mutually agreed upon. Openness to differences is important.

- Fiscal responsibility is mandatory. The board manages the KCPDC annual budget. Careful financial management has resulted in cost savings from year to year. Surpluses have been previously used to fund major events or prominent keynote speakers. Such major events have been subsidized by individual colleges if the presenter will be used for a professional development activity on their campus.

- The focus on part-time faculty members has paid off in that some have now been hired as full-time faculty at the same or another school. Part-timers are more confident and willing to share their experiences in teaching and learning.

- Establish equality regardless of type of institution or size. All members have access to the same activities, which have been planned cooperatively.

- Make your consortium dynamic. You must be willing to change as the needs change. Some programs will need more nurturing than others, but in the end, all schools will benefit.

ADVANTAGES OF A CONSORTIUM

KCPDC has allowed the member institutions to offer programs that would not have otherwise been possible. A good example of this is the supervisor development program, which is offered every semester. The program requires six core courses and two electives. By combining resources and participant populations, this program can be offered in a cost-effective manner.

The membership is very cost effective. If you weigh the annual fee against the depth and breadth of programs available, it becomes very attractive as a way to enhance the programming that is done on each of the campuses.

For members of the council, it is nice to be able to share issues—both successes and difficulties—with like-minded colleagues. The camaraderie is energizing despite the work that is involved with the council.

A priceless outcome of consortium activities is the sharing of knowledge, skills, and attitudes among employees of the seven member schools. Classroom strategies have been shared and adopted between community colleges and universities; individual systems have been changed by support staff who learned a very different method from another college; employees are more effectively supervised due to the training supervisors have received; college programs have been enriched by the resources discovered in other colleges; and the council members have enjoyed their colleagues on the council. A major outcome of the consortium is an enhanced working relationship across various types of higher education institutions.

Consortium activities have provided wonderful outlets for the training and development of staff members. The people who have taken leadership for the support staff retreat have learned to work collaboratively, facilitate effective meetings and retreats, and design creative projects.

As evidenced by surveys conducted by member institutions, part-time faculty members have become more engaged in their teaching and the learning process of their students. They have grown significantly through their participation in the certificate program. There is further evidence that part-time faculty have also learned strategies to enhance teaching from their colleagues from different types of institutions. Specifically, one part-time faculty member reported that she was surprised to learn of all the interesting getting-acquainted activities used by faculty at community colleges. She had only taught at a university and had not been encouraged to spend the time to get to know her students. She was thrilled by the change in her classroom the following semester after she implemented some of the climate-building ideas shared during the elective module on Active Learning. Such unsolicited feedback is very rewarding to the consortium members.

The advantage of a consortium was effectively summarized by Ann-Marie West, Park University Training Manager, when she said, "Collaborative learning across all levels is what the consortium means to members of the council as well as its member institutions." Each member institution has achieved a greater scope of programming to meet the needs of all employees of their college. The council members have been rewarded by the feedback from participants, their supervisors, and the students who have noticed changes in their classrooms, which can be linked to the training and development of their part-time instructors. Members have also discovered the comprehensive development of their adjunct faculty members to be an invaluable tool for their retention within their institutions (Burnstad & Gadberry, 2005). A consortium works for all involved. Try one and you will be rewarded as have the members in the greater Kansas City area.

Reference

Angelo, T. A., & Cross, K. P. (1993). *Classroom assessment techniques: A handbook for college teachers* (2nd ed.). San Francisco, CA: Jossey-Bass.

Burnstad, H., & Gadberry, J. (2005). Retention of part-time faculty. In D. L. Wallin (Ed.), *Adjunct faculty in community colleges:* An academic administrator's guide to recruiting, supporting, and retaining great teachers (pp. 113–126). Bolton, MA: Anker.

8 | AN APPLIED COURSE IN TEACHING THAT SERVES THE HOME AND NEIGHBORING INSTITUTIONS

Thomas Lux

Located some 30 miles south of Chicago, Governors State University (GSU) plays a special role among the plethora of higher education institutions in the metropolitan area. Rooted at its inception in 1969 in an optimistic vision, GSU took a deliberate step away from the establishment and forged opportunity through experimentation. With its emphasis on inclusion, its mission focused on serving a growing population of recent community college graduates and working adults who sought a higher education to advance their careers.

In 1999 after 26 years in the corporate world, I returned to GSU to complete my bachelor's degree, then stayed on to pursue a master's in communications. Like many graduate students, I was mentored by a senior professor—in my case, Dr. Michael Purdy. Dr. Purdy's research interests include dynamics of effective listening, philosophy of communication, and communication technology, while his teaching interests include communication theory, interpersonal communication, philosophy of communication, listening, communication technology, speaking, and debate. Following my teaching of a communications course and in the spirit of experimentation that is at the core of GSU, Dr. Purdy invited me to develop and then to teach a graduate course titled Applied Communications: Community College Teaching. Dr. Purdy's vision was that the course would help prepare graduate students in the communication program for teaching positions in nearby community colleges. The class was to fill a gap in the curriculum and provide skill development for graduate students who wanted to teach college. This chapter details the research, planning, implementation, evaluation, and revisions made in the course.

Prior to the development of the course, the master's degree in communications provided graduates the credential they needed to be hired as adjunct instructors at community colleges, but little in the way of learning to teach. The research required to support the new course in sound theory was conducted over a three-month period. Much of my research was done through visiting the community colleges that are the feeder institutions to the university. Interviews were conducted with human resources directors, deans of instruction, deans of academic services, and instructors themselves, many of whom would later serve as guest speakers after the course was implemented. During my research, I discovered that a few community colleges had developed their own programs to improve the skills of their faculty members—both full- and part-time. Those involved in such programs displayed a keen interest in GSU developing programming that would complement their own. I gathered information about their processes for hiring new part-time instructors and found that reviews of applicants' resumes or vitae, personal interviews, and teaching demonstrations—some to an entire committee—were standard.

While pursuing a master's degree, I had written a paper on public speaking anxiety and concluded that there was a parallel between fear of public speaking and first-time teaching. I drew upon that research as the course was developed, and I included the field experiences focused specifically upon approaches that might be utilized in the new course. While monitoring the first offering of an online speech class at Moraine Valley Community College (MVCC), I was allowed to participate as if I were a student. My paradigm on public speaking instruction was shaped by an extensive background in sales and marketing and as a motivational speaker for the sales industry, and the online format challenged my preconceptions. However, while monitoring the chat room of the online class, I gained an insight that would have a profound effect upon the course that would be developed. In a forum labeled Stage Fright, students discussed their fears on the upcoming required speeches, and the learning environment came alive. The anonymity of the Internet encouraged participants to admit their fears openly. Many did—in very emotional ways. The poignancy of that exchange was unprecedented in any of the face-to-face public speaking classes that I had previously taught. Adult students who deal with the public all day long spoke of their horror about standing up in front of a group to speak. I wondered how widespread and deep this fear runs and especially what teachers can do to help students overcome their fears. In my work as a sales trainer, I had many times taught a seminar to aspiring salespeople on overcoming their fear of approaching and communicating during cold calls. It was reassuring to hear the same principles I had used being utilized by the online facilitator to help these students overcome their fears. It was also helpful to gain insights into techniques that might be used within the developing course, most notably visualization methods, systematic desensitization, skills training, and cognitive modification.

Upon reflection, important parallels between statements made by students in the online course and participants in the course for potential adjunct instructors became evident. Such factors as familiarity with the audience, the outcomes generated by a preceding speaker (instructor), the congeniality of the audience, and the connection to planning became issues that I realized my course would need to include if it were to be truly effective. I also realized there were strong connections between such generalized public anxieties as adaptation to an unfamiliar role, making mistakes in front of the audience and its resulting humiliation, and negative feedback—both verbal and nonverbal—received from the audience. Especially interesting was the fact that the instructor's announcement of an upcoming speaking assignment evoked the second highest level of anxiety, while in-class preparation of public speaking assignments produced the lowest level of anticipatory state and trait anxiety.

Seeing a parallel between my speech research on the fear of public speaking and first-time teaching, I designed the course to provide opportunities for participants to teach in a safe environment in which a sense of community and mutual acceptance had been fostered. Realizing that new adjunct instructors would learn best by doing, I became committed to providing multiple opportunities for each to teach and be evaluated by the course instructor and by their peers. In addition, course participants would be required to submit a reaction paper to each of their in-class teaching assignments, learning at a deeper level through the process of reflection upon feedback received and developing their own solutions to the suggestions provided.

In developing participants' specific teaching assignments for the GSU course, I took two from the focus questions found in chapters of the textbook that had been selected for the course, *Success Strategies for Adjunct Faculty* by Richard E. Lyons (2004). In each case, those topics had been previously assigned and addressed in class. Two other teaching assignment topics were chosen by the students from topics listed on the faculty development web site of Honolulu Community College, which include developing students' critical thinking skills, assessment of student learning, feeling good about teaching, and many others. The final teaching assignment was discipline specific, and was designed to mirror the type of teaching demonstration often required by hiring committees.

In each case, the participants proved to learn effective techniques not only by delivering and reflecting upon their own presentations, but also by experiencing the successes and shortcomings of their peers. The anxiety displayed by participants could be seen to decline from the first teaching assignment through each succeeding one as each student acquired new insights and skills and changed the way they thought about teaching. "Learn by doing" is a mantra used in the business world in which I am grounded, as well as in the most effective public speaking classes. It is self-evident that it would work well to develop new adjunct instructors.

One of the students, who has gone on to teach as an adjunct instructor at several community colleges, responded to my follow-up inquiry with the following:

> Having given numerous presentations throughout my A.A., B.A., and both M.A.s, this was different: This was an individual choice of the subject and that means a lot when considering the task of college instructor. He or she must be comfortable presenting the information for the class (being taught by someone who has a genuine enthusiasm for the subject, hence the master's degree). Most of the college presentation work focuses on "teach a chapter" and not pick your *own* topic; I think a central strength of the course was found in the ability to teach absolutely anything for the demo. The smaller, weekly presentations were great precursors for what was to come, but the demo seals the deal. In fact, I would suggest that the syllabus embrace two separate presentations of the same caliber: one at the beginning and one at the end of the term, along with a written assignment to be included in the portfolio regarding the difference in experience.
>
> When asked how a student could improve his or her speaking skills in any of my classes at Joliet Junior College or MVCC, my answer is always the same: do it! The more a student—and this is especially true for all prospective college instructors—is put in a position to present in front of

a group, the more comfortable he or she becomes. This skill, the ability to practice, and, in essence, persevere, is one that all adjunct faculty must work on mastering when preparing to set foot in the classroom.

As stated earlier, much of the research that led to the development of the course was done by visiting the community colleges that are the feeder institutions to the university. The input provided by instructional leaders at those colleges at the time, and later when some served as guest speakers within the course, contributed to the development of a network for both GSU and the course participants. Participants' questions were answered promptly by email and telephone, enabling participants to gain clarity on key issues, make applications in the real world, and establish contacts for seeking teaching assignments. The network enabled GSU to recruit participants for subsequent sections of the course more efficiently and build the reputation of the course.

From the outset of offering the GSU course, each participant was required to interview a community college instructor of his or her choice, using a standard interview guide that was provided. However, participants were encouraged to expand the interview to include questions in which they had a particular interest and include those answers in the written reports of their experience. This assignment further expanded their growing network and also encouraged them to ask for help and experience the quantity and quality of feedback others were willing to provide. They were free to go back to favorite teachers from the past or venture out to new teachers or new schools more relevant to their current and future interests. Although only one interview was required, students were encouraged to use this interview assignment to do multiple interviews at multiple schools as a strategy for further expanding their personal networks.

Built into the original course design, another very rewarding course component was a group email protocol. Email was used by the instructor to provide handouts that could be conveniently stored for future reference and materials that reinforced or supplemented lessons after being presented. In addition, biographies of upcoming guest speakers were provided in advance with encouragement for participants to send thank you messages via email to guest speakers. PowerPoint presentations of those used in class and the scripts of several seminar presentations on such topics as learning styles, the

Myers-Briggs Type Indicator, and multiple intelligences were also provided. With the permission of the writer, exceptional participant papers and research were shared with the entire class as an email attachment. Participants were encouraged to email useful insights on teaching and learning to each other, which besides its informational value also served to deepen the bond between them. I heard from participants that they valued the opportunity to communicate with each other—collectively and individually—and that those communications were an especially safe and rewarding resource.

Their frequent communication individually with the instructor—on any issue they deemed relevant—was also encouraged, and most students took full advantage of the invitation. This free-flow of communications continued even after the class ended as evidenced by reports of being hired, attending job fairs, sharing position openings, and expressions of caring about each other. Students were encouraged to subscribe to *Tomorrow's Professor* listserv (established by Stanford University) and were provided with subscription information on how to receive this ongoing faculty development tool, at their desktops, throughout the academic year.

Besides the adopted course text, *Success Strategies for Adjunct Faculty* (Lyons, 2004), participants were also required to read Parker J. Palmer's (1998) *The Courage to Teach*. A video based on this book, which was viewed in class, featured a group of teachers discussing their experiences and feelings about teaching. Quoted below is an excerpt from a paper written by one of the course participants, Courtney O'Leary, that flowed from the class discussion that followed.:

> Parker J. Palmer's *The Courage to Teach* at one point focuses on an issue that I deem to be extraordinarily important: the teacher's fearful heart. Palmer points out that teachers are faced with many fears: having the hard work go unappreciated, being inadequately rewarded, discovering that the wrong profession was chosen, spending lives on trivia, and ending up with feelings of fraudulence. Teachers walk into classrooms and look into a sea of younger faces that seem to signal blatant disinterest, a lack of confidence in the teacher's ability, a lack of desire to even be in the classroom or college itself, a lack of motivation to learn anything at all about the given subject, and so forth.

Yet the signals of disdain that many teachers assume to be the underlying student emotion are usually misread—the signals are usually those of fear.

When a teacher is fearful, he or she tends to stagnate (as described by Erik Erikson) [and distance] him or herself from the students. Palmer explains that the gap between students and teachers (whether it's an issue of age, experience, and the like) can serve to bond the student/teacher relationship rather than divide. Clear-sightedness is a key issue; a focus on the positive elements of fear can only encourage an individual to maintain strong teaching behaviors.

Further assignments for the course required participants to prepare a personalized syllabus on a course they would likely be assigned to teach, which employed the model provided in the text. Syllabi were graded on completeness and clarity of required elements. Participants were provided the opportunity to correct mistakes and resubmit a revised syllabi for an improved grade, thus deepening the learning from the exercise.

Near the conclusion of each course section, participants were required to submit their portfolios with resumes/vitae and cover letters applying for teaching positions. Students were encouraged to retain all their work electronically for future revision, updating, and use.

The GSU course was initially delivered as an 800-level graduate course that met weekly throughout the semester. Since then, it has been offered as a 500-level course, open to undergraduates as well as graduate students. Based upon feedback from the initial group completing the course, the class now meets six Saturdays from 9:00 a.m. to 5:00 p.m., which reduces the inconvenience to those who must drive an extended distance and also requires a lunch hour that provides participants with additional bonding time. Appendix 8.1 includes some participants' comments generated through a follow-up done several months after the class conclusion, and Appendix 8.2 includes a syllabus of the revised COMS505.

What appears to be the end of this story is only the beginning. Future classes add to the networking possibilities of our new adjunct professors. The willingness to share and interact as a community serves our educational system well as we enter a period of retiring teachers and growing enrollment.

The class will continue to evolve to address the changing needs of the colleges and their students.

References

Lyons, R. E. (2004). *Success strategies for adjunct faculty.* Boston, MA: Allyn & Bacon.

Palmer, P. J. (1998). *The courage to teach: Exploring the inner landscape of a teacher's life.* San Francisco, CA: Jossey-Bass.

APPENDIX 8.1.

Comments From the Computing Course Students

The instructor requested via email:

> Hi Group, I want to put out an update of the class of COMS861. Please respond with any information you have so I can compile an update of the class's experiences with employment in teaching since the class was completed.

Replies indicated job opportunities that existed for those who had not yet finished their master's degree. Several replies are quoted here. Some of these replies indicate the results of the class from the perspective of the student.

> Hi Everyone, I'm taking a break to send you all a friendly update, as many of you may remember I began a new job at The Joliet Job Corp. Center as one of the Vocational Training Managers. The job would be challenging had I not gained so much insight from you all in the COMS 861 course. I am responsible for helping 146 of the 280 students on center obtain their high school diploma or GED as well as a trade. To date since starting in April, 85 have obtained both. WOW I ROCK!!!!!
>
> —V. A.

> Hi everyone, I hope this summer has been relaxing for you . . .
> I had been working, after my internship, at Prairie State College. I taught a few computer courses and then did their Kids@College program with four classes. It was over at the end of July and I immediately

began to work at KCC . . . I am an Academic Advisor (in training) and I will teach 3 Speech classes this year as a part of that contract with Kankakee Community College. So I am officially an Academic Advisor/Speech Instructor. That entire application, meetings, interviewing, teaching demo etc. process was an absolute breeze. The class we had [was] so helpful to me. I was not nervous about how to present myself and I felt completely prepared for all of them. My portfolio must have wowed a few folks at KCC because I have received a number of compliments on it; I changed the contents a bit from my "for a grade" submitted version.

—O. S.

As for practical experience, I'm teaching two classes at Moraine Valley this summer (the term concludes on Thursday, so I'm almost done). Both courses are COM 103 (speech fundamentals/public speaking) and I absolutely love my work as an instructor. I'll be teaching one speech course at MVCC again this upcoming fall, and I'm really looking forward to it. Additionally, I was offered an adjunct position at Joliet Junior College for the fall 2004 term. I've gladly accepted it, and will be teaching three composition/rhetoric classes at the main campus. I can't believe how natural it feels to be in the front of a classroom. There's no nervousness or angst, just energy and excitement. I'm excited at the prospects of what's to come, and I wish you all continued success and happiness.

—C.F.

I am currently working at Governors State University in the Board of Governors program. I am the Student Service Coordinator. I work on evaluating non-traditional credit. I coordinate the portfolio process, evaluate military transcripts and attend college fairs promoting the Board of Governors program and GSU in general. Within the next few semesters, I plan on teaching ENGL 302—Introduction to Writing a Portfolio which is an online course offered to our BOG students. I have had plenty of opportunities to practice and increase the skills that I learned from your class and it has been helpful using those techniques in recruiting students. Thanks!

—J. Y.

My next career will definitely be in the drug/alcohol counseling field and teaching GED at night. Governors State gave me the tools and they won't be wasted!

—B. E.

I got a new job at Robert Morris College at the Chicago Branch in the Career Services Department. I am a Career Services Advisor helping Bachelor level student[s] with their job search in Business Administration. I am also on the Business Advisory Board, which helps bridge the gap between employers and teaching administration—basically, they give us feedback on what they are looking for in a candidate when they are hiring. I am also the Career Services chair for the Institute Effectiveness Committee—they see how the students and community perceive Robert Morris College. Also, I am a member of the Premier Placement Committee—this is a program offered by the college to help students prepare themselves for job searches and interviews. Once I finish my classes towards my Masters, I have been offered an adjunct position with the college for basic speech com in Chicago and Orland Park. So...things are great. Thanks to everyone in class for motivating me to push hard in my teaching demo. And thanks to Tom for introducing me to the idea that I can teach. Hope you all are doing well and I'll be talking to you soon.

—C. F.

I wanted to tell you how much I enjoyed your course. You put a lot of effort into it, and I appreciate that. Of all the classes I've taken at GSU, I think yours is my favorite. I have taken many courses where at the end of the term, I look into my course folder and all I see are the syllabus and papers I've written.

Looking into my course folder now I see that it is full of useful information you provided, and I've also got an email folder full of links and various resources that I can use in the future.

I discovered that I really looked forward to each of the teaching demonstration[s] in the class, and that has opened my eyes. In the course of the past few months, I have rethought my teaching plans. I am changing directions to pursue an opportunity at the community college/college level. I feel better prepared as a result of things I've learned in 861.

—P.C.

Appendix B

Governors State University
Communication Program, LIBA
College of Arts & Sciences

Syllabus
Communication Studies COMS505
Applied Communication—Community College Teaching
Spring/Summer Trimester 2006
Tom Lux, phone 708/977-4243
t.lux@att.net

Credit Hours:	3.0
Catalog Description:	The class will explore teaching at the Community College from many aspects. There will be guest speakers from human resources, dean of instruction, dean of academic services, and teachers. There will be lectures as well as student presentations and papers. There will be an interview format for contacting teachers at community colleges at the school and in the subject area of your interest.
Prerequisites:	Some computer skills are desirable, but not mandatory.
Rationale:	This class will explore and help students learn about teaching in the community college. Students will learn by developing their own syllabus, lesson plans, teaching demonstration, resume, and portfolio. Students can elect to work as individuals or teams. Students will lecture as well as present papers. An interview format will be provided to contact teachers at community colleges in the school and subject area of the student's interest.
Intended Audience:	COMS505 is an elective for all undergraduate and graduate students. The class may be of interest to students of communication, psychology, education, management, and other disciplines wanting to prepare for teaching in the community colleges.

Disability Statement: Students who have a disability or special needs and require accommodation in order to have equal access to the classroom must register with the designated staff member in the Division of Student Development. Please go to Rm. B1201 or call (708) 534-4090 and ask for the coordinator of Disability Services. Students will be required to provide documentation of a disability when an accommodation is requested.

Expected Student Outcomes/Course Objectives:

This class will enable students to:
- Consider the community college history and understand its mission today
- Describe the factors that impact the success of today's community college students
- Discuss and consider students as clients
- Prepare a lesson plan
- Design an effective course
- Identify possible instructional resources
- Develop a syllabus
- Infuse technology into teaching
- Adhere to ethical codes in teaching
- Conduct an effective first class meeting
- Demonstrate a variety of instructional methodologies
- Compare and contrast test formats
- Use alternative methods of assessing student learning
- Conduct formal and informal student evaluations
- Develop your teaching career

Instructional Modalities:
Lecture, discussion, interview, group/team project work

Evaluation methods:
Class attendance and class/team participation:	10 pts
A personal syllabus with required elements:	10 pts
Four one-page reports with oral presentations:	20 pts (5 pts each)
Teaching demonstration:	20 pts
Interview report with a teacher in your field:	20 pts
Portfolio including resume and cover letter:	20 pts

Grading:
90–100 pts = A
80–89 pts = B
70–79 pts = C
60–69 pts = D
Less than 60 pts = F

Attendance:
Consistent attendance and active participation in the class are essential for the successful completion of the course. The number of absences will affect the final grade.

Perfect attendance earns	10 points.
One absence, subtract	5 points.
Second absence, subtract	10 points.
No additional absences	

Course completion requirement
Students are required to complete all work by the last class period. Only if a student has participated and turned in work for more than half of the class will an "I" be given.

Class Schedule
This class will have a flexible schedule. We will address the objectives of the class over the course of the trimester. As a team we will all carry out common tasks such as reading and research. We will plan, design, develop and carry out our projects before the end of the term.

Essentially each class session will consist of the following general agenda:
- Guest speaker when appropriate
- Set up/review goals and objectives for study and implementation
- Student teaching presentations
- Students will also share their research on a weekly basis
- Go into project team mode to discuss projects as needed

Text required:
Lyons, R. E. (2004). *Success strategies for adjunct faculty.* Boston, MA: Allen & Bacon.

You can preview the book at:
The Faculty Development Associates web site: www.developfaculty.com/online/index.html

Other readings:
Assigned materials will be handed out in class.

Student resource web sites:
Class web sites about college teaching.

> Honolulu Community College Faculty Development:
> http://honolulu.hawaii.edu/intranet/committees/FacDevCom/

> Faculty Development Associates:
> www.developfaculty.com/online/index.html

> What you need to know about education—Community College, University,
> Adult Education: www.about.com/education/

> Link to Tom Lux's web site
> http://webserve.govst.edu/users/gslux/

I. Class organization — Critical Elements of the Class
- Get acquainted
- Form a supportive community
- Get everyone connected via email
- Everyone is expected to contribute in some way to each week's class team meeting
- As a class/team member everyone is expected to pull her/his own weight
- Other operating principles can be established by the team as needed

Important:
- Where do we go? We set the direction for the class, within course parameters.
- What are our goals? What do we want to accomplish?
- How do we get there? Who does what? How do we manage our projects?

Some of the Things We Will Do:
- Everyone works on his or her class project from day one.
- Collect and share research and helpful website information via mail group.

II. Weekly Syllabus of Material Covered
- We will work our way through the textbook chapter-by-chapter.
- Students are expected to be ready each week to review and discuss problems in class.
- Schedule for each class will be provided.

Schedule is subject to change. Instructor will announce changes.
The contents will be subject to change or amendments as needed.

THE ASSOCIATE PROGRAM: A FOUNDATION FOR PROFESSIONAL GROWTH IN ADJUNCT FACULTY

Russell Richardson

They wander our hallways with a ghost-like presence, familiar apparitions lingering on the edge of our campus consciousness. Gradually we recognize their faces and their habits and come to know them as colleagues in the vague way that we recognize the neighbors six doors down on our street. However, most administrators and faculty have a hazy, some might say an intentionally unclear, notion of who these strangers are and the lives they lead within our institutions.

They are our part-time or adjunct faculty members, and colleges could scarcely function without their willingness to assume their critical role. Although we may know very few of them as individuals, we have come to understand how collectively crucial they are to the education of our students. And, when we think about it, we know how important their teaching skills must be to the quality of the education that our colleges are providing. The sheer number of class sections assigned to adjunct instructors makes a powerful argument that responsible colleges should invest in their teaching lives.

The program described in this chapter is a cornerstone of that effort at College of the Canyons (COC) in Santa Clarita, California. It addresses an array of faculty development goals through one program that focuses on enhancing the teaching and classroom management skills of adjunct faculty. The Associate Program at COC has provided a variety of teaching improvement activities at a reasonable cost and a minimum of bureaucracy while strengthening the ties between adjunct instructors and the institution. The effectiveness of the program is based on the provision of practical teaching-improvement activities, concrete incentives for faculty involvement, and the ability of the program to accommodate the schedules of adjunct instructors.

College of the Canyons, a medium-sized community college in northern Los Angeles County, employs about 375 part-time faculty and about 175 full-timers. When planning the Associate Program before its launch in 1989, a committee of faculty members decided that four major conditions related to adjunct instruction could be addressed under one umbrella: 1) a weak sense of connection and commitment to the institution for most part-time faculty; 2) very little interaction between part-time faculty and other faculty members; 3) a dearth of professional development opportunities for part-time faculty; 4) an absence of incentives and rewards for pursuing professional improvement.

The Associate Program was conceptualized as an umbrella that addresses these concerns in a series of teaching-related activities, each enhancing an adjunct faculty member's knowledge of basic teaching practices while building new links to the institution and other faculty members. The program requires adjunct instructors to complete professional development activities in three successive semesters. Participants volunteer for the program and work in cooperation with full-time faculty members. Completion of the program results in the granting of associate adjunct status, which is linked to an increase in pay for each course taught.

PROGRAM DESCRIPTION

The Associate Program includes three phases, all of which are directly related to teaching improvement. The first phase focuses on a specific set of instructional skills, which are the basis for planning and implementing any successful lesson. The program creates opportunities for faculty members to practice and develop these specific skills. The second phase introduces participants to broader teaching topics that go beyond the planning of an individual lesson. These topics affect the planning of an entire course or propose the introduction of an entirely new approach or teaching practice throughout a course. The third phase is a teaching demonstration in which the adjunct instructor, working with a mentor who is a veteran full-time or part-time instructor and facilitator in the program, plans and delivers a lesson in a real-world classroom. This phase emphasizes reflective practice and culminates with a reflective paper written by the adjunct faculty member.

The first phase is called the Teaching Skills Workshop (TSW) and is based on "microteaching" practices used nationally. Microteaching essentially requires teachers to teach 15-minute lessons to each other in a small-group setting. The workshop focuses on helping the adjunct instructor understand the structure of a lesson and how it can be successfully presented. One facilitator works with a group of four workshop participants. The lesson presenter receives immediate verbal feedback as well as more detailed written feedback. The lesson is videotaped to give the presenter an additional opportunity to learn from the experience.

The structure of the lesson is very basic, yet it contains elements that are apparently not practiced by most teachers on a daily basis. For example, the practices of bridging into a lesson or providing objectives are sometimes new to even experienced teachers. During this 18-hour workshop, each participant presents two lessons and observes and provides feedback in six other lessons presented by other participants. The learning is highly experiential and, frequently, as much learning occurs while observing lessons as when presenting. Many teachers have forgotten what it is like to be a student, and the role reversal can be an eye-opening experience.

Facilitators are careful to create a comfortable atmosphere in which feedback is offered with care and thought. Participants receive feedback that is much more focused than might occur in a typical classroom observation/evaluation. Participants must then teach a second lesson on a new topic. This part of the workshop design promotes reflection and rapid improvement.

Ultimately, the experience is designed to prompt teachers to shift their focus from teaching to fostering student learning. The lesson structure used in the workshop places an emphasis on a "check for understanding" through which teachers gain a deeper understanding of the disconnect that frequently exists between teaching and learning.

Having been grounded in the basics of lesson presentation, participants move on to the second phase, called the Advanced Teaching Workshop (ATW). The ATW broadens the discussion of teaching and addresses topics that extend beyond the framework of an individual lesson. For example, the syllabus is a basic building block of course construction. Even experienced teachers seem to have issues related to the syllabus that they are interested in exploring with other teachers. Active learning, classroom assessment techniques, educational technology, and learning styles are other topics addressed in this 18-hour workshop. The workshop also includes time for participants to initiate discussion of challenges that they are experiencing in their own classrooms. In this way, the workshop is, in part, molded to the desires and predilections of the group.

According to a study done by the U.S. Department of Labor, employees learn as much about their jobs through informal discussions with colleagues as they do through formal training ("Employees Learn More," 1998). All of the Associate Program workshops are filled with opportunities for colleagues to converse informally, including a communal brown bag lunch. Facilitators regularly observe these exchanges leading to a meaningful discussion of teaching.

All the workshops are designed, as much as possible, to model the principles and techniques espoused by the program. Consequently, the participants continue to learn through the simple process of watching other teachers teach. Most of the workshops include an active learning component because the participants are adult learners who need to interact with the material and approach their learning pragmatically. Therefore, the workshops almost always require that the participants develop a plan for implementing the techniques that are being discussed.

The idea of applying the learning from the workshops extends directly into the third phase of the program where participants are challenged to practice and demonstrate their skills in the classroom. This phase, called the Reflection on Classroom Teaching (RCT), is designed to promote deeper reflection on one's application of the principles and techniques promoted by the program. Each participant is paired with a member of the facilitation team, who serves as a mentor. The mentor and mentee meet to discuss the planning of a lesson. The mentee produces a lesson plan, which is reviewed by the mentor and approved by the facilitation team.

The participant then gives the lesson in the classroom and is observed by the mentor. In contrast to a classroom evaluation, the process places the responsibility for analysis and learning squarely on the presenter. During the post-observation meeting, the presenter is challenged to analyze his or her own performance. The mentor provides feedback, but the mentee is asked to write a reflection paper in which the lesson is analyzed and the process of reflection is recorded. The paper is reviewed by the mentor and, usually, returned for revision. The mentor then submits the final reflection paper to the facilitation team for approval. The team seeks to ensure that sufficient and significant reflection has occurred. As has been emphasized, the learning is highly experiential and individualized, and no attempt is made to establish a universal bar over which everyone must leap. Completion of the three-phase program constitutes a prima facie case for advancement to associate adjunct status.

PROGRAM SELECTION PROCESS AND COSTS

The program selection process is weighted to favor instructors with the longest periods of employment with the college so that long-term employees have a greater opportunity to advance to higher pay and that the college is assured of investing in instructors who are most likely to remain with the institution. Participants are paid a small stipend for each of the workshops they attend, and associate adjuncts are permanently paid at an hourly rate 10% higher than other part-time instructors.

Although part-time faculty seem very eager for this type of training and report that a pay increase is not their prime motivation, the demand for the program and its long-term success are surely dependent on the fact that the college has been willing to offer a significant financial reward for participation. Every fall, the program forms a new cohort of 16 faculty who complete the three components of the program in two semesters. Since the TSW is designed for a ratio of one facilitator per four participants, the total number of participants is restricted by several factors. Each of the four groups of participants must have a room in which to present lessons and, even on weekends, college facilities can be limited. Every facilitator is paid a stipend and, therefore, the program budget limits the total number of participants.

In addition to the pay increase for adjunct instructors and the stipends for workshop facilitators, a faculty member is given reassigned time to coordinate the program and to serve as team leader. Because the ratio of facilitators to participants is necessarily low, the costs are somewhat higher than a more traditional professional development design in which one trainer makes a presentation to a room of 25–35 faculty members. The benefits of individualized and small-group feedback seem, from the feedback provided by participants, to be worth the extra costs. Granted, positive changes can occur when teachers simply listen to other teachers talk about teaching. However, having teachers teach to each other is a more powerful and direct route to teaching improvement. The difference in the quality of learning in a traditional workshop and that received from their small group and mentor design is the difference between coffee and espresso. The latter is richer, more full bodied, and much more likely to open one's eyes.

PROGRAM EVALUATION

A workshop evaluation is administered at the end of each day of the workshops, and a program evaluation is given at the end of the three phases. All the evaluations are anonymous, anecdotal, and simply ask the participants direct questions about their experiences in the program and about their teaching practices. The evaluations from the Teaching Skills Workshop have been extremely positive. Teachers are quick to see the power of the microteaching model and the value of practicing what they do. Through the evaluations, participants share with the workshop facilitators how they are making changes in their teaching practices within weeks of the workshop. A new appreciation for clarity in a presentation is frequently noted. Having been placed in the role of students, faculty members begin to see the potential pitfalls of muddled objectives and fuzzy content from the student's point of view. One participant said, "If I'm confused by another teacher's objectives, then it's likely that some of my students are confused by mine." When asked how the workshop is changing their teaching practices, participants are most likely to indicate the use of a "check for understanding." This response indicates a shift of attention to the learning side of the equation and the use of techniques that help the teacher to know if learning is occurring.

The Advanced Teaching Workshop allows for more "teaching talk," and the evaluations show that participants appreciate the opportunity to discuss specific issues in depth or to trade classroom experiences. A typical participant's response is, "It's great to find out how other teachers deal with these same problems." As is customary of adult learners, participants expect to see a practical application for their learning. Consequently, they are more interested in the nuts and bolts topics within teaching and learning. Because the group is always composed of teachers from a variety of teaching fields, it is inevitable that some workshop topics will appeal more to one participant than another. The evaluations sometimes indicate that the topic was well presented, but that some teachers simply could not identify the relevance for their own teaching situation.

To some extent, the facilitators are able to gauge program effectiveness, or lack of it, through observation. Working with teachers in groups of four and, eventually, one on one, a facilitator is able to observe changes in teaching practice, in some cases from week to week, but in nearly all cases over the two semesters of the program. One could argue that there is no better evidence of change than seeing it in action.

The summative program evaluations show a satisfaction rate of greater than 90%. Interestingly and importantly, one of the benefits most frequently noted is a new feeling of connectedness to the campus and the faculty. Adjunct instructors often say that they lead a lonely existence on campus. Through the program they meet colleagues from varied disciplines and begin to develop a greater appreciation for the college culture. Most participants are emotionally warmed and intellectually informed by the realization that they share a common classroom and common challenges. Many of the evaluations indicate an appreciation for the shift in consciousness that is promoted by the program, a new or renewed focus on learning, and an appreciation for the teacher's role in assuring that learning occurs. One respondent said, "I had no idea I was so focused on what 'I' was doing. This has given me a new way to 'see' my own students!"

The evaluations sometimes show that a small minority are dissatisfied with the timing or the format of the workshops. All the workshops are held on Saturdays because, after several years of trying different configurations, Saturdays have proven to be available to the largest number of participants. Regrettably, some potential participants are prevented from applying for the program because of commitments on Saturday. Other participants experience conflicts with family and professional duties as the workshops proceed. The workshops tend to be closely timed to assure that no workshop presenter is slighted and that the workshop never runs overly long. Sometimes a few participants prefer a more casual pace and feel that the schedule is overly restrictive.

The Teaching Skills Workshop, in particular, presents a structured approach. Lesson planning, a structured lesson, attention to timing, and checking on learning all require that a teacher be organized and thoughtful about presenting a lesson. One or two teachers each year have a negative reaction to these approaches and requirements. Some teachers apparently feel that structure and planning sap the necessary spontaneity out of teaching.

A COC study conducted in 1993 found that program completers exhibited a higher usage of good teaching practices than adjunct faculty in general, with the greatest positive correlation found between program participation and using a posttest or checking mechanism at the end of the lesson (Mattice & Richardson, 1993). The key program element for shifting attention to student learning is the check for understanding. Therefore, a change in this particular teaching practice is considered to be a significant success.

Throughout its existence, the program has remained popular, and demand for slots has always exceeded the supply. Since its inception, more than 230 part-time faculty have participated in the program. Of that number, more than 60 are still employed as associate adjunct faculty at the college, and 21 have become full-time faculty members at COC. One of the traditional barriers to professional development for adjunct instructors is an argument that because they are transient, the college will generate a low return on investment. However the results attained indicate a continuing benefit to the college, particularly when one considers the number of students positively affected by these instructors' improved performance. Many of the participants who have not remained at the college are known to be teaching at nearby institutions. Thus the program is contributing to a greater good, that is, benefiting students and supporting excellence in education. If other colleges were to accept a similar responsibility, everyone in the educational community would reap the benefits.

The Associate Program at the College of the Canyons has been recognized in a number of ways at the state and national levels. It was featured in *1001 Exemplary Practices in American Two-Year Colleges* by Roueche, Parnell, and Kuttler in 1994. In February 1999 the prestigious Hesburgh Awards, sponsored by TIAA-CREF, recognized the program with a certificate of excellence for teaching improvement and professional development—one of only three awards presented that year. In 2002 the program received an award for excellence in professional development sponsored by the California Community College League.

Program Support

The success of the program rests on two important factors. First, from its inception, COC administration has embraced the program and the underlying goal of providing significant professional development opportunities for adjunct faculty. The resources to increase adjunct pay and to support the facilitation team were, obviously, crucial, and COC administration was able to see beyond the short-term limitations and barriers that frequently block such programs. They understood the central role that adjunct instructors play in the education of students and were willing to make a long-term commitment to professional development for a class of instructors who are often marginalized at other institutions.

Second, the success of the program would not have been possible without the development of a group of dedicated, highly trained facilitators. There are currently nine team members, all of whom are full-time college faculty. In most years, exemplary adjunct instructors have also served on the team. As is to be expected, adjunct trainers are more likely to leave the team for a variety of reasons, but the program leadership is committed to keeping part-timers involved in the facilitation process.

Principally, facilitators must be trained in the techniques of microteaching. Many team members have participated in the Associate Program or other microteaching workshops and have experienced the process from the perspective of a learner. However, having this experience is not a requirement for becoming a facilitator. The program has used two methods of training. In some cases, training in microteaching techniques external to the COC campus has been available. Various groups in the U.S. and Canada provide such training. At times the program has provided in-house training through a process of mentoring. At College of the Canyons, a train-the-trainer program has been developed, which takes a trainee through a full TSW while simultaneously providing facilitator training.

Team members learn other aspects of the program through mentoring and observation. In addition, the program holds an annual training retreat. Every summer the team spends two days off campus reviewing the program, planning the following year, and developing and honing the skills of facilitation. Consequently, the program is under continual review and reassessment. These periods of extended time away from the distractions of campus life have been a boon to the program. Many of the most important changes and innovations that have been made in the workshop format have resulted from work done at the retreats.

NEW PROGRAM DEVELOPMENT

For other institutions considering the development of similar programs, several key factors are critical. First, the administration must buy in to the concept and be persuaded to firmly support the program from its inception. Some campuses have done the legwork necessary to start a program only to discover that the resources for supporting it were not available. Second, microteaching is at the core of the program. At least two faculty members must be trained in this technique to facilitate microteaching workshops. In most cases the program will have to start small, with four or eight adjunct instructors (four per facilitator), then grow as it proves itself to the administration and the participants. Eventually, recruiting a team of full-time faculty members who have excellent teaching skills and who are willing to make a long-term commitment to the program will become a key to providing an extensive, successful program.

Bringing adjunct instructors into the planning and execution of the program as early as possible is another critical strategy. Their insights into the life of an adjunct instructor on campus will be valuable, and they will become influential cheerleaders and successful recruiters in the early stages of the program. During those early stages, both full- and part-time faculty may not fully understand the program's objectives, and some may be skeptical—even suspicious—of its usefulness. Consequently, an emphasis should be placed on marketing the program during its first year. Opportunities to explain the program to college groups, from the board of trustees to the staff, must be proactively pursued. Typically, as was the case on the COC campus, such programs are introduced with less time than is needed to get them started. Ideally, a year of planning would precede the program, and a teaching survey of the entire faculty would be administered and analyzed before the program commences. Data about teaching practices will help the team to plan workshops and will serve as a useful baseline for making comparisons and evaluations in later years.

CONCLUSIONS

Proven knowledge and information about effective teaching practices should be at the core of any faculty development program. Programs that promote hollow theories using clichéd formats will not prosper. Moreover, programs that move beyond knowledge and information to provide teachers with worthwhile experiential learning will have the greatest success. The success experienced by the Associate Program rests largely on the use of the microteaching model and other experiential learning techniques. These approaches, along with a concomitant emphasis on the learning portion of the teaching and learning equation, quickly convince most participants that the program offers opportunities to look at teaching from new perspectives and that those perspectives will be shaped by their own experiences, not by the dictates of other faculty or the institution.

Admittedly, using the microteaching approach and one-on-one mentoring are not as cost effective as a traditional teaching workshop, which has a much higher presenter to participant ratio. Leaders of the Associate Program are convinced, however, that the benefits outweigh the increased costs. Through microteaching and one-on-one mentoring, improvements in the teaching practices of participants can be observed within a relatively short time period. Each college must decide if the professional lives of its adjunct instructors, and the increases in student learning, are worth a significant commitment in time and resources. In addition, faculty development for adjunct faculty members will not succeed unless sufficient incentives, including monetary ones, are provided for participation.

Faculty development cannot reconcile the many distinctions and divides that exist between full-time and part-time faculty, but it can create bridges for faculty members and for the institution. The Associate Program conveys to adjunct faculty that they are important to the institution and that their teaching is important. Participation in the program provides solid ground for building new links and relationships within the institution. As much as what they learn about teaching, adjunct faculty members appreciate the bonds of collegiality that accompany their participation. Such programs are just one way that colleges can begin to bring these valuable contributors out of the shadows and to acknowledge the significance of the role they will continue to play in the American educational system.

References

Employees learn more in informal talking, study finds. (1998, January 7). *L.A. Times,* p. D1, 13.

Mattice, N. J., & Richardson, R. C. (1993). *College of the Canyons survey of teaching practices.* Valencia, CA: College of the Canyons, Office of Institutional Development. (ERIC Document Reproduction Service No. ED357776)

Roueche, J., Parnell, D., & Kuttler, C. (1994). *1001 exemplary practices in American two-year colleges.* New York, NY: McGraw-Hill.

10 ADJUNCT FACULTY ASSOCIATES PROFESSIONAL DEVELOPMENT PROGRAM

Keith Barker, Dan Mercier

OVERALL PURPOSE AND OBJECTIVES

Many frontline instructors teaching lower division courses at large research universities are either teaching assistants or adjunct faculty. This has been the case for many years where the emphasis is on research productivity and funding for promotion and tenure. The University of Connecticut, in recognition of the responsibility it has to the undergraduate programs, provides a range of training, acclimatization, and culturalization opportunities for U.S. and international teaching assistants. However, the university has traditionally provided nothing specifically aimed at supporting its adjunct faculty. Historically, part-time faculty are mostly hired for a fee for service, paid poorly, given no medical benefits, provided with minimal physical facilities, and given little or no opportunities for personal and professional development. Many of the University of Connecticut's adjunct faculty are at the five regional campuses that are in a 100-mile radius of the main Storrs campus.

With that simplistic background, the Institute for Teaching and Learning (ITL) decided to create a program to provide professional development opportunities for a selected and willing group of adjunct faculty based at the regional campuses. The activity operates under the title Adjunct Faculty Associates Program. After some early challenges, the program now appears to be overwhelmingly achieving the degree of success envisioned by campus leaders.

Those initiating the program identified six objectives to guide the development of the program's features:

- To provide a faculty development program for suitable adjunct faculty candidates from the regional campuses

- To help develop strong pedagogies appropriate to the adjunct faculty's discipline

- To expose each adjunct faculty member to a range of technological opportunities for course and curriculum enhancement

- To encourage the creation of innovative or creative course materials

- To provide a comprehensive introduction to the facilities and personnel of the ITL

- To encourage the faculty associate to share gained expertise and ideas with the regional campus faculty and administration on a continuing basis

Beyond these objectives was an overriding goal of increasing the status of the adjunct faculty among all members of the university community. Because many adjunct instructors teach in a number of university and college programs across the state, there has been little cogent reason for any real relationships to be built, and with the casual approaches from some academic departments and their administration, there was no incentive to bond with the overall program or full-time faculty. Adjunct instructors do not typically have the assurance of continuing appointments, multiyear contracts, or the guarantee of repeat course offerings. Their status is low and, though they often make significant contributions to the university by successfully teaching what are often perceived as the undesirable courses at unsociable times, they are sometimes considered to be second-class citizens. Hence the goal is to improve their status.

Thus, in addition to the goals listed above, the Adjunct Faculty Associates Program provides adjunct instructors with an opportunity to document the processes of increasing their skills and knowledge. When shared with others, this evidence increases the status of adjunct faculty and the recognition they receive at all university campuses.

The regional campuses of the University of Connecticut are each headed by an academic director or associate vice provost. The adjunct faculty associates (AFAs) are nominated by these campus heads, who know the candidates well, recognize the longer term potential of the individual adjunct instructor, and are prepared to work in partnership with the Institute for Teaching and Learning to cultivate the talents and enthusiasm of those selected for the program.

Each nominated adjunct instructor is interviewed by the director of the institute and the director of the instructional design and development unit of the ITL. Because the candidates have been carefully screened before selection, the program has had 100% acceptance and subsequent success. The expectations and qualities that are sought include the following:

- A commitment to travel to the main (Storrs) campus to meet with the ITL staff roughly once per week (travel expenses are not reimbursed, but parking is covered)

- A course project that can be used as a vehicle for the application of good pedagogical practice and hence the creation of the course or instructional modules for use at the home regional campus, or

- A project that allows the development of significant educational technology involvement such as can be obtained by immersion in WebCT (Vista) or electronic portfolios

- Demonstrated expertise in using PowerPoint, Photoshop, Dreamweaver, or audio and video digitization software

- Instruction, development, and practice in the use of video distance learning course delivery

- The willingness to develop a teaching portfolio

- Attendance at the seminars and workshops offered by the ITL

In addition, there is a strong expectation that all AFAs will return to their respective campuses and support the curriculum and faculty development programs extant there.

For this list of expectations, the institute's promise is to use all of its appropriate resources to make the program as successful as possible, to provide the adjunct faculty with materials and staff time, and to provide a stipend equivalent to that paid for the delivery of a 3-credit course.

INITIAL REACTIONS

Upon completion of the Adjunct Faculty Associates Program, new colleagues were asked to assess its qualities. Comments included the following:

> The first thing that struck me and that continues to strike me, is just how much room for improvement there is in our teaching.
>
> —Lisa Zowada

> My first reaction: Someone is going to help me!?! And I am getting paid to get help!?! I have always wanted to formalize this type of curriculum, because it is not traditional academic teaching-learning.
>
> —Susana Helm

> Too often, I think, those of us who have taught for a long time assume that we know what we're doing, and that's that. We tend to reflect on the materials we are going to use, rather than the methods and the means we will use to achieve our goals and assess our success or failure in achieving those goals.
>
> —Paula Lennard

> I realized I was employing some good techniques without being consciously aware of why I was using them. When I had to think about what I did and why, it gave me a new perspective on teaching preparation. I use this as a reminder to focus not just on subject content but also to devote time to instructional planning and utilize various techniques. I also realized that my unconscious approach was also a weakness because I would sometimes [be] inconsistent with different classes.
>
> —John Long

INTEGRATION OF THE AFA PROGRAM
INTO THE INSTITUTE

The Institute for Teaching and Learning is comprised of eight units, details of which can be found at www.itl.uconn.edu. The institute is centrally funded, although some services are charged at cost. However, curriculum creation projects such as the AFA program are totally supported, thus enabling the ITL to utilize any and all relevant units within the institute. Perhaps two of the most useful of the units to the AFA program have been the Instructional Resource Center (IRC) and the Instructional Design and Development unit (IDD).

The IRC provides hardware advice, software training, and, most important, pedagogical directions for the use of computers for all faculty. It has been the practice for several of our AFAs to spend a considerable amount of time in the IRC developing their WebCT and other software and digitization skills with the aid of the IRC staff and working collegially together to develop their learning materials. This facility, together with the resources of Video Design Services and Graphics and Photo provides a horizontally structured, enabling environment that leaves nothing to be desired when support is needed.

INSTRUCTIONAL DESIGN WORK

While the IRC focuses on pedagogy from a technological standpoint, the Instructional Design and Development unit is devoted to working with faculty to improve their courses through a structured approach to course design. Using a student-centered learning approach, IDD works collaboratively with faculty members to design or redesign their courses, making sure to address such things as multiple learning styles, information literacy, and relevant use of technology. A rigorously constructed course is often the goal of the faculty member, while development of the faculty member is the goal of IDD. Applying this student-centered approach to faculty members wishing to design their courses is the process with which the ITL engages the adjunct faculty associates.

In addition to the design framework provided by IDD, each adjunct faculty member brings his or her own background, experiences, unique ideas, strengths, and areas of improvement to the process. The adjunct faculty often begin the process with an enthusiastic idea for a course design or redesign, but they lack a structure within which to frame and build their ideas. No matter the discipline, type of course, or experience of the instructor, each adjunct faculty member is engaged in the process of an intensive course design as facilitated by IDD staff and their formal design model.

The first few weeks of the program typically find the adjunct instructors working closely with an instructional developer, deconstructing and then reconstructing an existing course or, in some cases, creating a new one. Deconstruction or initial creation begins with an identification of the course's fundamental components, most notably the course goals and learning objectives, their corresponding assessments, and the activities used to help students obtain these objectives. Two AFAs commented on this process:

> Working with instructional design has kept me focused on the learning objectives for my courses and kept me honest when it comes to designing assignments and classroom activities to meet those objectives. Too often it's easy to think that, as long as you've identified objectives and put them in your syllabus, somehow, magically, your students will end the semester having achieved these goals.
>
> —Lisa Zowada

> Working with instructional design to identify specific educational goals, articulate measurable ways of determining whether those goals were achieved, and map an entire semester according to those parameters was both challenging and fun.
>
> —Paula Lennard

Having stated student learning objectives and identified how these objectives are going to be assessed, the adjunct instructor and designer collaborate to identify or modify existing activities or create new ones to support learning in the designed course. Many times these activities require integration of technology into the course. Together, the adjunct faculty and designer enlist the help of media developers in the IDD or staff members in the IRC to increase the adjunct faculty's proficiency with the technology, sometimes software based and sometimes hardware based. In addition, the fundamental pedagogical focus of the curriculum design can draw on Video Design Services, who can help the adjunct faculty when video or audio segments are needed for their coursework. Similarly, the Graphics and Photo unit can provide print and electronic images. Adjunct faculty reacted to being offered such services:

> The first time I met with members of the ITL staff, I was overjoyed with their commitment to, and passion for, their job. They have made teaching important again—or, more accurately, since it's always been important to me, you put the university's imprimatur on good teaching, validated my efforts to learn and improve my teaching, and provided warm and supportive positive reinforcement for doing so.
> —Paula Lennard

> I wanted to gain a new perspective through a different team approach of educators. I also wanted to have contact with the main campus and learn more about the technology available for faculty and students. At the regional campuses, we do get memos on technology but don't always have the opportunity to meet with people during the day in order to understand and use technology for our students.
> —John Long

The final piece of the design process involves evaluation of the course design itself. The members of the IDD unit work with the adjunct instructors to measure the overall design of their course and assess its success in fulfilling student learning objectives. This process is a fundamental design construction that the IDD has often found to be absent from faculty curriculum projects, but one that has provided the "aha" moment for both novice and mature faculty members.

The ITL's formal obligation to the adjunct faculty associates is for one year. However, because course design is an iterative process, IDD is committed to working with the adjunct instructors indefinitely. In fact, the AFAs are considered to be part of the instructional design team, and collaborative work is expected to continue with them after they return to their regional campuses:

> Instructional design has helped to develop and strengthen my skills in areas that will benefit the entire faculty at Avery Point [one of the five regional campuses]. I have also grown personally, both inside and outside the classroom. By providing the adjuncts with support, they feel that they are valued.
>
> —Julia Launer

> I'm learning how to incorporate new technologies while retaining academic standards. Students at the regional [campuses] need more flexibility than students residing in dorms on campus. Designing classes to use traditional classroom techniques mixed with individual work through technology makes the courses much more appealing. I think it will be a major advantage for the regional campuses to offer this style of instruction in the setting of small classes.
>
> —John Long

FUNDING AND SUPPORT FOR THE PROGRAM

The ITL is privileged to have a foundation account funded by a former faculty member and administrator at the university, Dorothy Goodwin, that is dedicated to professional development. This account allows the university to provide stipends for the adjunct faculty associates as an incentive to travel to the main campus, where the ITL is located, and to continue to attend meetings, workshops, and consultations on a weekly basis. All other costs, excluding travel but including software, are covered by the ITL.

For the participants in the AFA program, there is an expectation that continuous learning and development will take place beyond the weekly visits to the main campus. Most agree that with such a strong stimulus, either through the fresh instructional design philosophies or the introduction to new technologies, that a great deal of time is spent on developing their curriculum projects at home or in their regional campus settings. Leaders of the program believe that it has provided sufficient fiscal incentive, a friendly nonthreatening place to work, ample pedagogical and technical resources, talented and knowledgeable ITL colleagues, enormous encouragement, and the promise of continued support after their project is completed.

So, what aspects of the program did participants find most beneficial?

> The opportunity to rethink a course I had developed myself and taught for many years. I wanted to gain a new perspective through a different team approach of educators. I also wanted to have contact with the main campus and learn more about the technology available for faculty and students. At the regional campuses, we do get memos on technology but don't always have the opportunity to meet with people during the day in order to understand and use technology for our students.
>
> —John Long

> I was attracted to this program in part because the instructional design director made a great pitch for ITL when he came to speak at the faculty orientation a couple summers ago. He made the idea of working with ITL sound enjoyable, nonthreatening, worthwhile. Last semester, when I heard that there was an opportunity for adjuncts to work with the ITL staff, I wanted to know more about the program. I was attracted to the opportunity to improve my technological skills, to develop my teaching approaches, and to become a resource for the Waterbury campus.
>
> —Lisa Zowada

EVALUATION AND SATISFACTION

How is this program evaluated? Some of this is objective and some is subjective—in effect, anecdotal—but that is the nature of many efforts such as this. The main objectives of the program are to provide an opportunity for faculty development and to achieve a pedagogically sound product, usually a course or part thereof. However, this goal is used as a means to instill a structured and appropriate process for the faculty member.

There are a number of distinct successes, some of which the adjunct faculty have been able to express to us. From the affective side:

> The most fun was working with people who were totally involved with and excited about issues of effective course design and instruction. The university's focus on research, publishing, and presenting at conferences sometimes leaves one feeling that teaching doesn't matter. The first time I met with members of the instructional design staff, I was overjoyed with their commitment to, and passion for, their job. They were a wonderful antidote to that more typical Tier I Research University message, and I found the emphasis on teaching methods and course design exhilarating! What struck me most forcefully when I began this process was both their enthusiasm and a sense of possibility!
>
> —Paula Lennard

From the practical pragmatic angle:

> I have seen improvement in the peer group workshop activities I design. I have always liked the idea of students working with one another to understand difficult readings or to find ways to engage the texts in their own writing, but didn't always see those activities leading to better papers. Now I see tangible results in their writing. The students themselves have credited the activities with helping them revise their essays.
>
> —Lisa Zowada

> The main point is that learning objectives correspond to learning activities. There needs to be a clear link in my mind so that I articulate that link during class, office hours, etc. with students.
>
> —Susana Helm

From those of us who have organized and implemented the program:

In observing our six adjunct faculty associates over the past few years, I have seen them continuously engaged in a reflective process, one in which they challenge themselves and their teaching. They have addressed both pedagogical and technical aspects of their courses and made adjustments as appropriate and in the end have not only improved their courses but have developed themselves. The ultimate beneficiaries of their hard work are their students. However, those of us in ITL who have worked with them have been able to observe first hand, good teaching and have ourselves benefited a great deal. The AFAs will prove to be great resources for faculty at each of their respective campuses.

—Dan Mercier, director, IDD

Post-Program Benefits to the Regional Campuses

One of the ambitions of this program was to avoid the syndrome that removal of funding often creates—that of the inability and/or unwillingness to continue. In this area it has been gratifying that the development efforts are paying dividends. Having began the AFA program at the Avery Point campus four years ago, that site has been significantly encouraged to embrace the talents gained by their AFA and has incorporated her abilities within a growing learning resource center for students and an emerging faculty development program for all faculty.

In recognition of the need for technical and learning assistance, the Avery Point learning resource center provides day-to-day help for WebCT and other software needs as well as writing and quantitative support for the students.

However, the cultural change that was hoped for at the inception of the AFA program is now happening:

Our AFA has brought back to the campus a strong sense of the resources available to all university instructors, as well as some very valuable training in instructional technology as it supports good course design. She now provides regular workshops to faculty and staff at this campus. The obvious results include a stronger understanding of best practices in teaching and learning, but equally important to this campus has been the effect of our AFA bringing faculty and staff together to discuss common goals and interests, which has led to the creation of informal, supportive, and collegial learning communities.

—Susan Lyons, program director at Avery Point

On returning to Avery Point, what was not obvious to me immediately was that we seem to be creating a very different atmosphere at our campus, and I think that the creation of my position as a teaching resource associate has a lot to do with it. By offering many workshops (I offer two workshops every week), adjuncts are meeting on a regular basis and they are getting to know each other in a way that wasn't possible before. We discuss classroom and instructional problems and how technology might help solve some of them, but many times the discussions go in other directions. We seem to have a growing community of adjuncts that know each other's names, communicate, support each other and even socialize! Many adjuncts are beginning to feel more of a connection to the university and are no longer "unknowns" who come in, teach and leave. I am constantly told how much everyone appreciates everything I am doing and I feel that I have become an important part of the faculty, not just for my students, but for my friends and colleagues as well.

—Julia Launer

(Julia refers here to her position as a teaching resource associate. This position was created as a result of the continuing discussions between the ITL and the Avery Point campus administration and has continued since Julia's return from the program.)

The position itself is based on an acknowledgement of the excellence of the adjunct faculty member's teaching skills and the potential contribution the adjunct can make to enhancing the skills of other adjunct faculty. Informally, adjunct faculty look to our AFA as a model for their own work; also, the university has acknowledged the contributions of our AFA and is looking for ways to build the position into the structure of the academic programs at the regional campuses.

—Susan Lyons

The other regional campuses are not as far ahead as Avery Point, but each has played a part in developing adjunct instructors who are able to help start similar activities and to define the appropriate resources for students and faculty:

Other adjunct faculty have asked about the benefits of instructional design and ITL. I can see how difficult it is to get all adjuncts up to speed on technology like WebCT when they all have such different schedules. For the most part, faculty use WebCT for electronic reserves, no different than putting material on reserve at the library. Seeing beyond that usage requires a familiarity that comes through time they do not have. Students also have problems with WebCT because so many of them are accessing the material from home on a variety of computers, links, software, etc. They get discouraged when it does not work as smoothly as on campus. The need for a presence on regional campuses who can assist both faculty and students in utilizing these technologies is clear. I hope as I finish the program I can fulfill some part of those needs, but it will not be effective on a part-time basis and will require a larger commitment.

—John Long

I have extensive experience in student development, having been a study skills instructor and a writing/learning specialist. I would like to combine that expertise with what I am learning through the Adjunct Faculty Associates Program in order to be a resource for both students and faculty. I would like to assist students directly, but I would also like to assist them indirectly by sharing what I've learned in the program about instructional design with other faculty.

—Lisa Zowada

STATUS AND ACHIEVEMENT RECOGNITION

The AFA program has sought to affirm and support its participants, instructors, and their achievements. The regional campus directors and associate vice provosts have been continuously informed of their progress and achievements. In the spirit of collegiality and recognition, all of the AFAs have been presented with plaques of acknowledgment of their success at the ITL annual teaching excellence dinner each April. (It is also a pleasure to see the plaques on their office walls.) In addition each of the AFAs are photographed and have a special page on the ITL web site. One of the important factors is that the vice provost and the provost fully support the program, have met with each of the AFAs during their program time, and have recognized them publicly and formally whenever appropriate.

In several cases, the developed skills of the AFA participants are being used to further support the regional campus activities. The Avery Point campus employs Julia Launer to help in their developing student learning center and to offer workshops on WebCT for the faculty. Paula Lennard now works with the W (writing) center, and Lisa Zowada, at Waterbury, will be supporting the writing program and advising on their proposed learning center.

SUMMARY

The Adjunct Faculty Associates Program is a comprehensive initiative that is designed to achieve the objectives stated in this chapter. Like most innovative projects, it is a dynamic, living entity that evolves with each implementation. Each AFA has been slightly different, and it has been challenging for the ITL to adapt to each individual's needs. Each adjunct faculty's course has had a different realization as the modality of delivery has evolved. The faculty development aspect of the program has led the AFAs to an understanding of the need for individualized consideration of activities to support learning objectives and also a reminder that each class is different from the last.

The success of the AFA program has been so significant that a commitment has been made by the institute to continue the program as long as personnel and funds are available to do so. It has been extremely rewarding, and the university is seeing the continuing value as the AFAs return to their respective campuses.

SUPPORTING ADJUNCT FACULTY THROUGH ORIENTATION AND MENTORING INITIATIVES AND AN ONLINE PROFESSIONAL DEVELOPMENT COURSE

Jeanne C. Silliman

With the start of the 2005–2006 academic year, Ivy Tech Community College (ITCC) Southwest in Evansville, Indiana, launched a program of adjunct faculty development initiatives, developed with funding from the Lilly Endowment. These integrated initiatives were designed to develop, support, and retain part-time faculty—in the process improving their integration into the overall faculty community and enhancing student learning. ITCC Southwest formulated three strategies for this professional development initiative: enhanced orientation of faculty, a system of mentoring for newer faculty, and an online faculty development course called Teaching in the Learning College. The primary target of all initiatives was ITCC's adjunct faculty, but because the college wished to blur the lines between the communities of full-time and adjunct faculty and to foster collegiality and idea sharing, all programs would also be available for all faculty members.

BACKGROUND OF THE PROGRAM

Ivy Tech Community College Southwest is one of 14 regions of the Ivy Tech Community College system that serves the entire state of Indiana. In 2004 the statewide system submitted a grant proposal in response to the Lilly Endowment's Initiative to Recruit and Retain Intellectual Capital for Indiana Higher Education Institutions (Ivy Tech Community College, 2004). The ultimately successful proposal focused on two major strategies: strengthening its adjunct faculty base and expanding student development opportunities. The proposal sought to implement these strategies with initiatives developed and installed by each of its 14 regions as well as statewide. Like most community colleges, Ivy Tech relies heavily on its adjunct faculty. At the time of the grant proposal, almost 60% of all Ivy Tech courses statewide were taught by part-timers. Part-timers comprised 2,400 of

ITCC's total of 3,200 faculty members, and with the anticipated growth in enrollment, this number was certain to increase.

ITCC Southwest's initiatives grew out of the opportunity supplied by the three-year grant obtained from the Lilly Endowment. The grant proposed that major initiatives for strengthening the adjunct faculty base at the campus level would include programs "to improve compensation, to provide adequate permanent space and physical resources, and to expand professional development opportunities." The space and physical resources issue at the Evansville regional campus was addressed by the addition of a Faculty Resource Center (FRC) that houses computer workstations and lockable individual space for adjunct faculty to store materials. In close proximity to the offices of general education and business division full-time faculty, the center's location provides opportunities for collegiality between full- and part-time faculty and thus helps blur the lines between them. Year two of the grant will see the addition of a second FRC in another area of the campus. Beyond these physical resources, emphasis in the region for supporting adjunct faculty focused on the development of programs for orientation, training, and professional development.

Establishing Regional Goals for Adjunct Faculty Development Initiatives

Ivy Tech Community College Southwest saw the Lilly grant as an opportunity to expand its support for its large and growing population of adjunct faculty. Already in place was an active faculty development team. The team, comprised of full-time and adjunct faculty representatives from each of the college's academic divisions, sponsors adjunct faculty orientations, a spring inservice, and monthly brown bag "conversations about learning" on various topics. This team assisted the dean of instructional affairs in formulating a plan for implementation of the Lilly grant initiatives. The goals of the grant were threefold: to expand and enhance orientation for adjunct faculty members, to provide a system for mentoring of newer adjunct faculty, and to provide an online course called Teaching in the Learning College.

To ensure the accomplishment of these goals, a coordinator (the author of this chapter) was appointed. The coordinator was responsible for the development and implementation of the initiatives in consultation with the academic council (the dean of academic affairs and the division chairs), the faculty development team, and the faculty council.

THE DEVELOPMENT PHASE

The spring semester of 2005 was devoted to research and development for the three major initiatives. The coordinator recruited adjunct faculty volunteers from diverse academic divisions, as well as longtime part-timers who had recently been hired full-time, to serve on a focus group that would provide input into the development of the program. The initial meeting with this group identified several points that informed subsequent planning of the programs:

- An overriding interest among the adjunct faculty was the opportunity for collegiality among fellow faculty members.

- The group identified a need for additional information to be available online to supplement the information that was provided at the face-to-face orientation.

- They preferred the idea of a group of faculty in a mentored situation, rather than one-to-one mentoring, once again stressing the desire for optimum sharing and collegiality.

- The group expressed enthusiasm for an online professional development course that included topics such as the definition of a learning college, active learning strategies, diversity, and assessment.

- They appreciated and attended other inservice opportunities offered by the college through the faculty development team.

At the time, the faculty development team (FDT) offered an adjunct faculty orientation session at the beginning of each semester. The program consisted of break-out sessions on a variety of teaching topics for continuing faculty and a session called New Kids on the Block for adjunct faculty teaching at the college for the first time. The information presented included college resources, policies and procedures, Family Educational Rights and Privacy Act (FERPA) guidelines, and tips for getting started. Ample handouts with information on all these topics were provided. As might be expected, new adjunct faculty were happy for the information, but were somewhat overwhelmed by its scope. After consultation with the FDT, the focus group of adjunct faculty, and academic leaders in the college, it was decided that a good option would be to enhance the New Kids on the Block orientation session and to complement it with an online resource that would provide additional information that could be better assimilated. The Lilly grant coordinator worked with the instructional technologist to develop the online resource and sought information from all relevant areas of the college to include in the guide.

The goal of developing a mentoring program for newer faculty was substantially affected by input from the adjunct faculty focus group. These individuals felt strongly that they would be better served by working with a small group of colleagues under the guidance of an experienced faculty member. The focus group also felt that experienced adjunct faculty should be encouraged, along with full-time faculty, to take on the mentor, or team leader, role.

Under the leadership of a broad-based group of faculty and staff serving on the student-centered team, ITCC Southwest adopted the philosophical elements of the learning-centered college described by Barr and Tagg (1995), Terry O'Banion (1999), and others and exemplified through the Vanguard Colleges (League for Innovation in the Community College, 2006). To promote the instructional elements of this approach and to further improve and develop teaching excellence, the Teaching in the Learning College course was researched and developed. The research influenced the academic leaders and focus group to design a blended course that would be delivered through a combination of online and face-to-face content and activities.

Initiative One—Faculty Orientation and Resource Guide

The online *Faculty Orientation and Resource Guide* (Ivy Tech Community College, 2006–2007) developed through the grant initiatives is intended to answer those day-to-day questions faculty face as they attempt to perform duties related to their teaching. It does not supplant the faculty handbook, but instead its location on the college's web site places frequently needed information in a form that is more readily accessible. The guide includes such college information as campus directories, academic calendars, maps and directions, emergency procedures, faculty resources and organizations, and mailroom/copy center services and procedures. A particularly useful section of the guide organizes information in sections according to "What Faculty Should Know and Do: At the Beginning of the Semester, During the Semester, and at the End of the Semester." Frequently used forms are appended where appropriate, or information is provided about where they may be obtained.

The *Faculty Orientation and Resource Guide* was created as a Word document and contains a table of contents with hyperlinks to the pages listed. The document has also been converted to Adobe PDF format to take advantage of its bookmarking capabilities, thus assuring ease of navigation for the user. Currently, during the face-to-face adjunct faculty orientation that takes place at the beginning of the semester, new instructors can be referred to the online guide as part of the training, and they know that it will be available whenever they need to refer to it in the future.

INITIATIVE TWO—MENTORED TEACHING TEAMS

Research done during the development phase of the grant initiatives reinforced the value of the college's goal to provide mentoring for adjunct faculty. This goal was discussed at length with a focus group of adjunct faculty. The consensus of this group was that more value would be obtained through a team approach than from one-to-one mentoring. The group was very enthusiastic in their suggestions. Some felt that teams of faculty who teach in the same subject area would be most beneficial, while others preferred the shared ideas of cross-discipline teams. When asked if they preferred the team leader be a full-time faculty member or an experienced adjunct instructor, they decided that either would work. Their enthusiasm for the group approach stemmed from a desire for collegiality as well as the resources and information provided by a more experienced faculty leader. In addition, the team approach would recognize the experience and professionalism of all members while providing acclimation to the college for those who might be new to the institution but not to their profession or to instruction. The focus group was asked what characteristics they considered necessary in a team leader. Not surprisingly, the interpersonal skills necessary to encourage and support others were seen as the most valuable.

With focus group input, the Lilly coordinator proceeded to explore logistics like assigning team members to leaders, training participants, necessary instruction and resources for participants, recruitment, and program evaluation. The Teaching Team program was then developed and established with clearly defined goals, and information about the program was disseminated to all faculty members with an invitation to participate.

Goals and Description of the Program

The goals of the Teaching Team program are:

- To help new faculty become acclimated to the college

- To increase support for new faculty so that they will enjoy their experience with Ivy Tech and wish to continue teaching at the college

- To improve teaching and learning through discussion, research, projects, and mutual support and inspiration

- To encourage professional development for Ivy Tech faculty

- To promote collegiality and collaboration among Ivy Tech faculty

Teaching teams consist of three to four faculty members, one of whom is an experienced Ivy Tech instructor who serves as the team leader for two or three faculty members who are new to Ivy Tech. The team approach allows acclimation to the college for the new faculty and a built-in cohort for sharing of teaching experiences. The teaching team forms and continues for one semester.

At the beginning of each semester, new faculty members, or continuing faculty members requesting the experience, are assigned to a team leader who serves as a resource for the newer faculty members and takes a lead role in arranging meetings among the members of the team. The initial meeting takes place at the general Teaching Team Orientation held at the beginning of each semester. At that time, the team leader arranges for meetings with team members to become further acquainted and to establish goals for the semester. Further meetings are decided by the team and are dictated by their own goals and needs. Teaching development goals may be generated between the team leader and an individual member or among all members of the team, depending on individual needs and interests.

The Team Leader and Team Members

The Teaching Team leader applies for the position and, upon approval from his or her division chair, becomes a part of the pool of team leaders. Leaders are assigned by the Lilly grant coordinator in consultation with the academic cabinet to new faculty members or others who wish to be a part of a teaching team. Team leaders must meet the following requirements:

- Full-time or adjunct faculty member with substantial Ivy Tech teaching experience

- Demonstrated interest in teaching growth and improvement

- Excellent communication skills and the desire to assist other teaching professionals

- Knowledgeable about Ivy Tech and available to provide information, advocacy, and networking opportunities for newer faculty members

- Willing to devote approximately 10–20 hours per semester to the teaching team process

Teaching Team members apply for membership on a team and are assigned at the beginning of the semester to a team leader by the Lilly grant coordinator in consultation with the academic council. Team members must meet the following requirements:

- New adjunct or full-time faculty member, *or*

- Continuing adjunct or full-time faculty who wish to participate to further their knowledge of the college (e.g., faculty who have worked for only a year or who have taught only one or two courses) or to further develop teaching skills in a collegial setting (e.g., a transition to teaching online or teaching in a new discipline)

- Willing to work with other faculty to learn more about the college and to further develop teaching skills

- Willing to devote approximately 10–20 hours per semester to the teaching team process

Application and Assignment Process

Adjunct or full-time faculty members who are interested in participating on a Teaching Team complete the application for team member (see Appendix 11.1). New faculty members are informed about the Teaching Teams and are encouraged by program and division chairs to apply for membership. Applications are submitted to the Lilly grant coordinator, who forwards copies to appropriate division and program chairs.

Experienced faculty members complete the application form for team leader (see Appendix 11.2) and submit it to their division chair. The division chair decides on the suitability of each applicant based on the criteria for team leadership, keeping in mind that accessibility, availability, and communication skills are essential for team leaders. Approved applications are forwarded to the Lilly grant coordinator.

Approved applicants are added to the list of available Teaching Team leaders for assignment to team members. Assignment of team members to team leaders is made on the basis of application information by the Lilly grant coordinator in consultation with the academic council.

Teaching Teams are designed to be collegial and an opportunity for acclimation and growth and are not intended to be evaluative or supervisory. For this reason, a team member is assigned to a team leader who is not his or her supervisor. Exceptions are made with the permission of the dean of academic affairs.

Some team members prefer to work with a team leader from their academic discipline, and others want the perspective of a team leader from a different discipline or have no preference. Every effort is made to honor the preferences stated on the application.

If for any reason or at any time during the semester a team member or team leader is not comfortable with his or her assignment, reassignment is made without question or recrimination.

Orientation and Stipends

Team leaders and members are oriented to the program at a general session early in the semester and plan subsequent activities among the team. At the conclusion of the semester, participants evaluate the experience to provide input into future planning and improvement of the program. All Teaching Team participants are provided a small stipend in recognition of their willingness to grow as instructors and to nourish the growth of their colleagues.

Year One Participation

The Teaching Team project kicked off fall semester 2005. All new and continuing faculty were notified of the opportunity and encouraged to apply as appropriate. Program chairs were encouraged to refer new adjunct faculty as they were hired. During the fall semester, 31 faculty members—24 adjunct faculty, and seven full-time—faculty applied for Teaching Teams. Nine teams consisting of two to five members were formed. Each participant completed an application, and team placement was based on the interests and needs indicated on the application. Team leaders and members met at the beginning of the term for an orientation meeting and were given suggestions and guidelines for team activities. At the conclusion of the semester, all participants were required to fill out a confidential evaluation of the experience before receiving certification and a stipend. Interestingly, several of the teams requested the opportunity to continue through the next semester because they had found the experience useful and positive and wished to develop further as a team. The spring semester saw the participation of 28 faculty members—22 adjunct faculty, and six full-time faculty on seven teams. Fifteen of these individuals were continuing from fall semester. Teams reported meeting formally and informally, on campus, in restaurants, and in members' homes. Many arranged guest speakers on topics of concern to the members such as financial aid, computing resources, and information about areas and programs of the college other than those of the members. Teams reported meeting from three to seven times throughout the semester. In addition, some teams communicated online using eLearning (Blackboard) or via email.

In response to interest from participants, an organization was set up on the college's eLearning platform with discussion boards, links to teaching/learning web sites, and shared resources for and from participants. Although participants were encouraged to observe each other's classrooms and were provided with a nonevaluative observation instrument, only one participant was observed. Several participants indicated that they would like to observe or be observed at a later time.

Evaluation of Teaching Team Program

Evaluations completed by team leaders and members were tied to the stated objectives of the program and included a Likert rating and opportunity for open-ended comments. A compilation of the responses from fall and spring shows strong satisfaction among the participants that the goals of the experience were met. Tables 11.1 and 11.2 compile the 16 responses of team leaders and 42 responses of team members from the two semesters.

Program participants offered numerous comments about the evaluation items and about the program in general. Comments were overwhelmingly positive, with the largest expressed area of concern being the issue of finding mutually convenient meeting times for the group members. Many expressed positive comments about the support, collegiality, and informational aspects of the experience. Representative comments include the following:

- It was wonderful to know I have someone to go to regarding questions and concerns.

- I was already acclimated, but talking with other instructors helps me as an adjunct.

- Nice to have people outside your department know who you are.

- Compared fair ways to handle grading and discipline issues, which was a big help.

- I received many valuable and useful hints.

- This is the first time I have felt like I knew my faculty peers well enough to have a dialogue.

- Exchange of handouts. Exchange of ideas on teaching. Sharing PowerPoint presentations.

- Shared teaching strategies, discussed our major classroom challenges and shared ideas about learning centered college.

Table 11.1. *Team Leader Evaluation of Teaching Team Experience*

Fall 2005 & Spring 2006						
Do you feel that your Teaching Team experience:	1 Not at All	2	3	4	5 Greatly	Avg.
Helped the members become better acclimated to the college	0	0	1	10	5	4.31
Provided support to enhance team members' teaching experience at the college	0	0	2	8	6	4.25
Provided an opportunity for collegiality and collaboration with fellow faculty members	0	2	2	2	10	4.25
Provided members with useful teaching ideas	0	1	3	5	7	4.13
Met the goals and expectations established by the team at the beginning of the semester	0	1	4	5	6	4.00
Overall, was the Teaching Team experience positive for you?	0	1	0	6	9	4.44

Table 11.2. *Team Member Evaluation of Teaching Team Experience*

Fall 2005 & Spring 2006						
Do you feel that your Teaching Team experience:	1 Not at All	2	3	4	5 Greatly	Avg.
Helped you become better acclimated to the college	0	1	12	14	15	4.02
Provided support to enhance your teaching experience at the college	0	1	5	20	15	4.12
Provided an opportunity for collegiality and collaboration with fellow faculty members	1	1	4	7	29	4.48
Provided you with ideas you could use in your teaching	1	1	6	13	21	4.24
Met the goals and expectations established by the team at the beginning of the semester	0	2	5	18	16	4.17
Overall, was the Teaching Team experience useful for you?	0	1	3	11	26	4.51

- It helped me feel a part of the academic community at Ivy Tech and a feeling of belonging there, as opposed to slipping in to teach a class and no one other than the students knew I was there.

- I felt relieved that some of the problems I faced as a first-time teacher were not uncommon and had resolutions to them.

- As an evening adjunct, I have never felt very connected, professionally, to my colleagues. This experience helped!

Suggestions from participants indicated that they would appreciate more formalized use of online resources to compensate for the difficulty of finding mutually convenient face-to-face meeting times. In addition, several participants expressed an interest in another gathering of all Teaching Team participants during or toward the end of the semester for additional sharing of ideas. These suggestions will be implemented as the program goes forward. (See Appendix 11.3 for possible Team Teaching activities.)

INITIATIVE THREE: TEACHING IN THE LEARNING COLLEGE COURSE

When planning programs for adjunct faculty development and inclusion, the idea of a teaching and learning course was a high priority. From the start, regional goals under the Lilly grant included the development of a course called Teaching in the Learning College (see Appendix 11.4 for the course syllabus). The title reflected the region's desire to incorporate learning college principles into its academic programs. With certain principles in mind, the course was not intended only for new faculty, but was designed for all faculty. In addition to its learning college focus, it would prioritize the involvement of adjunct faculty, but be available to full-time faculty as well—thus reinforcing an emphasis on *one* faculty and allowing for maximum collegiality and sharing of ideas. Delivery would be flexible in terms of time, content, and delivery method. Course content and delivery would involve a variety of key figures in the college as guest facilitators. The course would also model active learning-centered techniques and principles.

To provide maximum flexibility, developers decided on a hybrid format, delivering course content online for six weeks with two face-to-face meetings during that period. Major course objectives included the following:

- Identify the characteristics of learning-centered teaching and incorporate its principles in the classroom.

- Identify personal learning styles and use tools to assist students in knowing and using their learning styles.

- Define characteristics of adult learners and formulate classroom activities and environments that motivate these learners.

- Use a variety of active learning strategies to promote student responsibility for learning.

- Use classroom assessment, testing techniques, and rubrics to evaluate teaching and learning.

- Promote and use diversity to enable and enrich the learning experience.

Course Content and Delivery

Each week participants are given required course content, including readings on the week's topic, PowerPoint presentations, and discussion boards. In addition, each weekly module includes an "I Want to Know More" section containing a wealth of information and references on the topic being covered that week.

Included in course delivery are a variety of active learning strategies, including a face-to-face session in week two on the 4-MAT learning type measure and its model and cycle for instructional delivery (McCarthy, 1996). Additionally, in week four participants are divided into small groups to explore various active learning strategies. They are provided with online communication tools and may meet face to face if they choose. The small groups select content to post online for the class as a whole and prepare presentations to be delivered during the face-to-face session in week six. Throughout the course, participants respond to online content in interactive discussion boards.

Guest facilitators are a key element of the course. The 4-MAT session is presented by the business division chair, who is a trained 4-MAT facilitator. In addition, guest facilitators include the dean of academic affairs and the dean of student affairs discussing the learning college principles, the special needs coordinator discussing diversity, and the director of student success and development discussing student rights and responsibilities and discipline issues. A faculty member with extensive research experience on generational differences provides content for the discussion of characteristics of the adult learner. In addition to the expertise provided by these guest facilitators, their involvement provides the opportunity for participants to become acquainted and interact with key figures in the college.

Because all faculty in the region are encouraged to use eLearning (Blackboard) to support their face-to-face classes, and all online classes are offered on this platform, an additional benefit provided by the hybrid format of the course is the opportunity to model strategies for the use of the online platform. Faculty who have not yet used eLearning become better acquainted with it, and those who have used it in the past have a chance to see it from the perspective of the student.

Four cohorts of faculty completed the six-week course during the fall and spring terms 2005–2006; 33 were adjunct faculty and 18 were full-time. Adjunct faculty who completed the course were paid a stipend through the Lilly grant. All participants received a certificate of completion, and full-time faculty counted the course toward their ongoing professional development requirement.

Course Evaluation

All participants were asked, as a requirement for completion, to evaluate the course. Evaluation data from four cohorts who completed the course during the fall and spring semesters 2005–2006 indicated that the goal relating to faculty interaction and collegiality was met. In addition, participants indicated that they had obtained many ideas for teaching strategies and found the course to be a worthwhile professional development activity. At the request of many of the participants, the online content was made available beyond the duration of the course so that it would be accessible as a continuing resource.

The course evaluation measured achievement of course objectives on a Likert scale and provided opportunity for open-ended comments. A compilation of evaluation data from Cohorts I through IV is shown in Table 11.3.

When asked if they use or plan to use any of the ideas or content from the course in their classrooms, 42 of the 51 participants indicated that they plan to use content in the classroom, and 32 of them gave specific examples of their planned use. When asked if they would recommend the course to colleagues, 48 of the 51 participants replied with strongly positive responses. Typical responses to, "What did you like best about the course?" included:

- The wealth of resources available.

- The course reenergized me. I struggled with how I could get students more enthused during class lecture sessions and how I could get more enthused with lecturing. Teaching in the Learning College has given me concrete information that I will put to use. I feel I have a new outlook on classroom presentation, assessment, and evaluation.

- Discussion board. I learned quite a bit from others.

- It gave me a wider point of view of good techniques.

- It was very flexible. I could log-on whenever I had time in my schedule.

- I was getting a little stale, and this course has revived my creative thinking.

- I am so glad that I signed up for the class and feel that I have definitely expanded my options for enabling my students to learn.

Table 11.3. *Evaluation Compilation*

<table>
<tr><td colspan="8" align="center">Teaching in the Learning College
Cohorts I, II—Fall 2005, and III, IV—Spring 2006</td></tr>
<tr><td colspan="8">

Please check one:
__33___ Adjunct Faculty Member   __18___ Full-time Faculty Member

Overall Evaluation of the Course Objectives
Please respond on a scale of 1 to 5 how well the course will help you to better achieve the following objectives.

1 = Not at All, 5 = Very Much
</td></tr>
</table>

Course Objective	1	2	3	4	5	Avg.
Identify the characteristics of learning-centered teaching and incorporate its principles in the classroom.				9	13	4.46
Identify personal learning style and use tools to assist students in knowing and using their learning styles.			1	6	15	4.18
Define characteristics of adult learners and formulate classroom activities and environments that motivate these learners.			2	8	12	4.45
Use a variety of active learning strategies to promote student responsibility for learning.			2	6	14	4.55
Use classroom assessment, testing techniques, and rubrics to evaluate teaching and learning.		1	3	7	11	4.27
Promote and use diversity to enable and enrich the learning experience.			3	6	13	4.45

Table 11.3 (continued). *Evaluation Compilation*

Please respond about other aspects of the course on a scale of 1 to 5.						
1 = Not at All, 5 = Very Much						
Course Content and Delivery	1	2	3	4	5	Avg.
Overall, did you find the readings helpful to you as an instructor?		1	1	4	16	4.59
Overall, did you find the topics covered in the course to be relevant?			1	4	17	4.73
Overall, do you feel that the course provided resources that will assist you in being a better teacher?			1	4	17	4.68
Did you find the small-group activity to be a positive learning experience?	1			5	16	4.59
Did you find the discussion boards useful?				8	14	4.64
Did you find the face-to-face meetings helpful?			1	8	13	4.55
When you began the course, how familiar were you with using eLearning?	2		3	7	10	4.05
Did the course make you more comfortable or more skilled with eLearning?	2	2	3	2	13	4.00
Do you use eLearning for the classes you teach?	2		3	3	14	4.23
Are you likely to use it more as a result of this experience?		2	1	4	15	4.45

CONCLUSION

The overriding goals of the Lilly initiatives for adjunct faculty were to provide support for them, to integrate them into the college community, and to offer them the opportunity to expand and develop teaching skills. Comments on the evaluation of each component repeatedly included the participants' appreciation for the opportunity to interact with other faculty. Measured by voluntary participation in the initiatives, year one initiatives succeeded in meeting these goals. In fall semester 2005, Ivy Tech Evansville employed 184 adjunct faculty and in spring semester there were 188 adjunct faculty members. Many of those teaching in spring were returning from fall. Face-to-face adjunct orientation sessions offered at the beginning of each term drew 93 in the fall semester and 77 in the spring. Faculty were introduced to the online *Faculty Orientation and Resource Guide* at these sessions as well as by periodic fliers and newsletters. Twenty-four adjunct faculty participated on teaching teams in the fall and 22 in the spring. Thirty-four adjunct faculty completed the Teaching in the Learning College course during the academic year. The combined effect of the initiatives allowed the participating adjunct faculty to feel more a part of the academic community. Many commented on how much less isolated they felt and how idea sharing helped them to grow as instructors. In addition, interaction with full-time faculty in the programs helped the full-time faculty members to become better acquainted with their colleagues on the adjunct faculty. Participants in the Teaching in the Learning College course expressed an interest in additional courses on teaching and learning topics. Some of the adjunct faculty who participated as members of Teaching Teams indicated an interest in becoming team leaders in subsequent semesters. Adjunct faculty are utilizing the Faculty Resource Center, and their presence on campus increases the overall sense of community among faculty.

Ivy Tech's commitment to the Lilly Foundation is to continue its initiatives beyond the term of the grant. The region is working to strengthen and continue the initiatives begun in 2005 and to expand both physical and academic resources to support and develop one of its richest resources—its adjunct faculty.

References

Barr, R. B., & Tagg, J. (1995, November/December). From teaching to learning—A new paradigm for undergraduate education. *Change, 27*(6), 12–25.

Ivy Tech Community College. (2004). *A proposal in response to the Lilly Endowment's initiative to recruit and retain intellectual capital for Indiana higher education institutions.* Indianapolis, IN: Author.

Ivy Tech Community College. (2006–2007). *Faculty orientation and resource guide.* Retrieved January 2, 2007, from: www.ivytech.edu/evansville/fac_resources /faculty_orientation.doc

League for Innovation in the Community College. (2006). *Learning college project—Vanguard Colleges.* Retrieved January 2, 2007, from: www.league.org/league /projects/lcp/vanguard.htm

McCarthy, B. (1996). *About Learning.* Barrington, IL: Excel, Inc.

O'Banion, T.. (1999). *Launching a learning-centered college.* Mission Viejo, CA: League for Innovation in the Community College.

APPENDIX 11.1.

Teaching Teams: Application Form for Team Member

Teaching Teams at Ivy Tech Southwest are designed to connect new faculty members to one another under the guidance of a team leader who is an experienced member of the faculty. The goals of the Teaching Team are to acclimate and inform new faculty and to provide a cohort for sharing and development of teaching experiences.

The Teaching Team Member must meet the following criteria:
- New adjunct or full-time faculty member, *or*
- Continuing adjunct or full-time faculty who wish to participate to further their knowledge of the college (for example, faculty who have worked for only a year or who have taught only one or two courses) or to further develop teaching skills (for example, a transition to teaching online, teaching in a new discipline) in a collegial setting
- Willing to work with other faculty to learn more about the college and to further develop teaching skills

• Willing to devote 10–20 hours per semester to the teaching team process

Name_____Date_____

Division_____Program_____

Check one: _____ Full-time faculty _____ Adjunct faculty

Courses Taught _____

Phone Number_____email_____

Two to three new faculty members will be assigned to a team led by an experienced Ivy Tech faculty member. Do you have any preferences you would like us to know about in assigning you to a team leader (e.g., same or different academic discipline, teaching goals or style, full-time or adjunct etc.)?

Please briefly describe your primary teaching approaches (e.g., lab work, hands-on, lecture, small group, discussion, case studies, online, etc.).

Do you have any particular goals in mind for exploration or improvement in teaching?

Please submit completed form to Jeanne Silliman, Lilly Grant Coordinator, Ivy Tech Community College, 3501 First Ave., Evansville, IN 47710. jsillima@ivytech.edu Ph. 812-429-1416

For office use: Copy sent to Division Chair _____ Division Chair Initials_____

APPENDIX 11.2.

Teaching Teams: Application Form for Team Leader

Teaching Teams at Ivy Tech Southwest are designed to connect new faculty members to one another under the guidance of a team leader who is an experienced member of the faculty. The goals of the Teaching Team are to acclimate and inform new faculty and to provide a cohort for sharing and development of teaching experiences.

The Teaching Team Leader must meet the following criteria:
- Full-time or adjunct faculty member with substantial Ivy Tech teaching experience
- Demonstrated teaching excellence
- Demonstrated interest in teaching growth and improvement
- Excellent communication skills and the desire to assist other teaching professionals
- Knowledgeable about Ivy Tech and available to provide information, advocacy, and networking opportunities for new faculty members
- Willing to devote 10–20 hours per semester to the teaching team process

Name_____Date_____

Division_____Program_____

Check one: _____ Full-time faculty _____ Adjunct faculty

Courses Taught _____

Phone Number_____email_____

Two to three new faculty members will be assigned to your team. Do you have any preferences you would like us to know about in assigning team members (e.g., same or different academic discipline, teaching goals or style, etc.)?

Please briefly describe your primary teaching approaches (e.g., lab work, hands-on, lecture, small group, discussion, case studies, online, etc.).

Do you have any particular goals in mind for exploration or improvement in teaching?

Do you have any particular teaching skills you'd like to share with team members (e.g., online instruction or teaching with technology, classroom assessment or research, collaborative learning, etc.)?

Please submit this form to the Division Chair of your program area. Approved Team Leader applications will be forwarded to the Lilly Grant Coordinator for assignment of team members.

For Division Chair Use—Please initial: _____Approved _____Disapproved
(Include comments below or on back.)

APPENDIX 11.3.

Possible Activities for Teaching Teams

The Teaching Team is a partnership designed to provide assistance for new faculty members in becoming acquainted with the college, to provide a collegial resource for new faculty, and to encourage professional growth among all faculty. The actual activities of the team will be dictated by the needs, interests, and goals of its members. The following is a list of suggested activities that might assist team members in establishing and accomplishing the goals of the team. It is by no means exhaustive. The team will decide which activities they will pursue as part of their partnership.

A. Setting up the Team
1.   Exchange contact information.
2.   Decide on type (e.g., lunches, formal or informal meetings, online discussion) and frequency of meetings.
3.   Discuss the purpose of the team: help and advice about navigating the college, classroom issues, professional growth, a support system and a sounding board for team members.
4.   Identify expectations of new faculty members for support from the team leader—what would be too much, too little.
5.   Team leader—be available by phone, email or in person to answer questions or provide information.
6.   Negotiate a mutually agreeable set of expectations for the team partnership.
7.   Fill out the Teaching Team Information, Goals, and Expectations form to assist you in planning and make sure each person has a copy.
8.   Decide what each individual will do if the partnership is not working for any reason.

B. Basic Survival Training at Ivy Tech
(Note: While Teaching Teams are not intended to substitute for the general or division/program specific orientation processes, new faculty may have questions that Team Leaders will be able to address/assist with.)

1. Discuss college calendar, map, and the employee orientation web site at: www.ivytech.edu/evansville/fac_resources/faculty_orientation.doc
2. Visit the Faculty Resource Center, the Carter Library, and discuss other campus faculty resources.
3. Obtain college I.D.
4. Go on a walking tour of the campus.
5. Introduce new faculty member to division personnel, Pat Strouse, mailroom staff.
6. Make sure the new faculty member knows the location of various offices he or she may need to access—registrar, human resources, disability services, Ivy Tech library.
7. Provide an orientation to telephone, voice mail, and email (on and off campus access).
8. Discuss computing resources for faculty (eLearning, Campus Pipeline, Web4).
9. Discuss emergency procedures and evening services and personnel.
10. Discuss procedures for obtaining copies, supplies, forms.
11. Make sure new faculty members complete the paperwork to receive an ivytech.edu email address and understands how to access Ivy Tech email on and off campus.

C. More Information about Ivy Tech
1. Discuss the organizational structure and who's who in the region.
2. Discuss the statewide structure and history of the college.
3. Discuss instructional procedures and timelines: never attends, last date to drop, divisional policy on dropping for non-attendance, etc.
4. Discuss the college's teams and committees and the possibility of participation on them.
5. Visit the college's web site and Infonet and explore resources.
6. Discuss departmental/divisional procedures and practices.
7. Discuss departmental/divisional policies regarding finding replacements in the event of absences from class.
8. Discuss issues and options for students with special needs.
9. Discuss attendance policies and issues.

D. More Information about Faculty Resources at Ivy Tech State College
1. Discuss professional development opportunities—in-service events, Lilly reimbursement for professional development activity expenses, Teaching in the Learning College course.
2. Acquaint new faculty with the Faculty Resource Center and its equipment and teaching materials.
3. Acquaint new faculty with the teaching resources available through the Carter Library or their divisional area.
4. Encourage attendance at faculty meetings, in-services, and other training events.
5. Make new faculty aware of the possibility of taking Ivy Tech classes free.

E. Learning more about the classroom

1. Discuss components of a good syllabus, its preparation, and use.
2. Discuss student behavior issues and procedures for handling disruptive students.
3. Compare classroom successes, surprises, disappointments, thrills.
4. Visit each other's classrooms—with a clear understanding of objectives and an understanding that this is not evaluative.
5. Review each other's tests, writing assignments, projects, or rubrics and provide feedback.
6. Discuss attendance issues and techniques you've tried for promoting better attendance.
7. Discuss, prepare, research, and experiment with active learning strategies (e.g., group projects, games, learning circles, and other collaborative activities).
8. Discuss, prepare, research and experiment with classroom assessment techniques.
9. Consider ways to make instruction more learner-centered.
10. Explore the print and audiovisual materials on teaching and learning available in the Faculty Resource Center and the Carter Library.
11. Explore Ivy Tech's Virtual Library.
12. Participate in faculty development events together.
13. Attend faculty meetings together.
14. Explore the use of technology for teaching: eLearning, PowerPoint, classroom performance systems, etc.
15. Read an article and discuss teaching philosophy, classroom management, test construction, assessment techniques, first day activities, handling disruptive students, etc.

Source: Adapted from Parkland Center for Excellence in Teaching and Learning, *Possible Activities for Mentoring Partnerships:* www.parkland.edu/cetl/documents/Mentoring PacketFall06.pdf

Appendix 11.4.

Teaching in the Learning College: Course Syllabus

Description

Teaching in the Learning College is a six-week hybrid course offered for Ivy Tech Faculty. The course will introduce and discuss the concept of the learning college. It will focus on learner-centered teaching strategies and ways of assessing learning outcomes. In particular, learning theory will be examined as a means of strengthening practical classroom applications. The course is designed for instructors who are interested in enhancing their teaching skills.

Major Course Learning Objectives

Upon successful completion of this course the participant will be expected to:

1. Identify the characteristics of learning-centered teaching and incorporate its principles in the classroom.
2. Identify personal learning style and use tools to assist students in knowing and using their learning styles.
3. Define characteristics of adult learners and formulate classroom activities and environment that motivates these learners.
4. Use a variety of active learning strategies to promote student responsibility for learning.
5. Use classroom assessment, testing techniques, and rubrics to evaluate teaching and learning.
6. Promote and use diversity to enable and enrich the learning experience.

Course Content

Topical areas of study include: the learning college, learning styles and teaching styles, learning communities, characteristics of the adult learner, classroom management, motivation, active learning strategies, assessment, evaluation, rubrics, diversity in the learning college.

Methods of Instructional Delivery

The course consists of six weeks of online instruction and two face-to-face meetings during the six-week period. Participants will apply learning theory and strategies in their classrooms and will participate in a small group activity/presentation on an area of active learning.

Required Texts

Readings will be posted online or provided in printed form or on reserve in Carter Library.

Course Completion

Participants are expected to fully participate in online, face-to-face, and small-group activities. Upon successful completion, each participant will receive a certificate of completion. Adjunct faculty participants will receive a stipend from the Lilly foundation grant for adjunct faculty development initiatives. Successful completion for each weekly module will be posted in the eLearning grade book.

Weekly Schedule

Week One—The Learning College
Topics:
What is a Learning College?
What are its implications for instruction?

Application:

Reflect on your approaches in one or more of your courses.

Identify learning-centered strategies you are currently using.

Identify one area for improvement and a strategy you might use to implement that improvement.

Week Two—Learning Styles and Teaching Styles

Topics:

- The Learning Type Measure: What is your learning style?
- 4-MAT System of Delivering Instruction: How can you use what you know about learning styles in the classroom?
- Online Learning Styles Resources: Where can I find learning styles inventories online?

Face-to-face meeting:

- Learning Styles Theory and The 4-MAT System of Instruction.

Application:

- Evaluate and post response to learning styles—your own and others.
- Develop a lesson plan based on the 4-MAT system and post to eLearning.

Week Three—Learning Communities: Building a Learning Atmosphere

Topics:

- Generational Characteristics of Our Learners
- The Learning Environment
- Motivation for Learning
- Classroom Management
- Establishing Behavioral Rules
- Handling Problem Students

Application:

- Evaluate your current classroom management techniques for one class.
- Identify strengths and weaknesses and a strategy you might implement to strengthen one of the weaknesses.

Week Four—Learning Communities: Active Learning Strategies

Topics:

- Teamwork—Small groups, cooperative student projects, service learning
- Critical Analysis—Simulations, case studies, problem solving
- Experiential learning—Service-learning, internships, co-ops
- Lecture/Response—Questioning, discussion, lecture, writing and reading in the classroom

Application:

- Teams will examine one of the four areas and design a presentation on content and classroom applications to be delivered at face-to-face meeting in week six. Teams will also post online content during weeks four to six.

Week Five—Assessing Learning
Topics:
- Classroom Assessment
- Testing
- Rubrics

Application:
- Design and administer a new classroom assessment technique or rubric for one of your classes. Evaluate results and post comments.

Week Six—Diversity in the Learning College
Topics:
- Cultural, Ethnic, and Socioeconomic Diversity
- Diverse Learning Styles
- Diverse Approaches to Learning
- Diverse Intellectual Development Levels
- Diversity for Students with Disabilities

Application:
- Face-to-face Meeting—Small Group Reports on Active Learning Strategies

A Proven, Comprehensive Program for Preparing and Supporting Adjunct Faculty Members

Frank Harber, Richard E. Lyons

Typically, new faculty development initiatives begin on a modest scale. In most cases, this is a wise course of action because it enables the institution to focus on a single issue and achieve some success while using modest resources. When some positive outcomes are achieved, it can more easily attract additional support that enables it to expand or modify to further increase its effectiveness. Starting small also permits the initiative's leaders to manage the expectations of stakeholders and thus reduce the political risk of failure.

During the summer of 1996, Florida's Indian River Community College (IRCC) was ahead of most institutions in the degree of support that it was providing to its part-time faculty members. A handbook had been developed and distributed, and an annual meeting had been conducted for several years, which all adjunct instructors employed by the college were required to attend. Its agenda included a welcome by the college president, a review of major developments since the previous year, as well as changes in policies and leadership roles. An adjunct faculty committee had been appointed in 1994, which was developing improved ways of communicating with the adjunct faculty, including the publication of a quarterly newsletter. The instructional dean who coordinated the big picture of adjunct faculty provided excellent leadership for the committee and was supported in the work by other instructional administrators and department chairs, all of whom had volunteered for the assignment. Because IRCC employed nearly 1,000 adjunct instructors, all saw why it was critical to improve the status quo. All committee members were line supervisors of adjunct faculty, and each had invested valuable hours in putting out fires caused by uninformed or untrained part-time instructors.

The committee included one department chair, who was pursuing his doctoral degree at the time. He saw his studies as an opportunity to contribute to the committee's work while focusing his research into a literature review for his dissertation. The committee chair was especially invested in a research-driven approach that would identify the issues whose solutions would have the greatest impact on the long-term effectiveness of the committee's work. Soon after, the doctoral student shared his copy of the recently published *The Invisible Faculty* (Gappa & Leslie,1993), which had begun to make higher education leaders more aware of the dimensions of the part-time faculty situation throughout North America. Committee members fully embraced the call to arms of Gappa and Leslie:

> It is time to admit (because of budgetary and planning realities) that part-timers are a substantial and permanent part of the academic profession and should be treated as such. We do not foresee any real aggregate diminution in their use, and we advocate the adoption of fair and equitable policies that will help them play constructive roles in providing quality education. (p. 91)

RESEARCH AND ASSESSMENT

A subcommittee was subsequently appointed to develop a survey of the needs and perceptions of Indian River's adjunct faculty members. Their work was facilitated by a second national study, *Strangers in Their Own Land* (Roueche, Roueche, & Milliron, 1995), which was perceived to be even more compelling, because it focused solely on practices toward part-time faculty members within community and technical colleges. Its findings confirmed those in *The Invisible Faculty* (Gappa & Leslie, 1993) that little or no difference could be found between the teaching effectiveness of full- and part-time faculty, and that often part-timers were held to a higher standard of teaching performance than their full-time colleagues. These findings underscored the importance of developing a comprehensive set of strategies that supported and helped retain a resource that was being viewed with increasing respect.

The survey results suggested that IRCC's adjunct faculty was nearly evenly divided between those teaching academic transfer courses, occupational courses, and adult education programs such as General Educational Development (GED) and English as a Second Language (ESL), and was comprised nearly totally of the two profiles Gappa and Leslie (1993) identified as *specialist, expert* or *professionals,* and *career enders.* It included very few *aspiring academics,* of which so much had been written and was driving perceptions nationwide, or *freelancers*—individuals who by choice pursue several part-time jobs that include a regular college teaching assignment. These findings made sense given the fact that IRCC's four-county service district includes a significant population of upscale retirees and is not home to the primary campus of a major research university.

FINDINGS AND APPLICATION

The committee member's dissertation was designed as a qualitative study, employing face-to-face mentoring interviews with, and the journal writings of, 22 adjunct instructors from across the spectrum of disciplines. It also employed focus groups of additional adjunct instructors and interviews with instructional leaders to delve more deeply into the part-time teaching environment. The study found, among other things, that participants required a grounded foundation of teaching and classroom management skills, a more thorough orientation to the institution and their teaching assignments, social learning opportunities, and more accessible professional development resources. It concluded by recommending the implementation of a program to address these needs (Lyons, 1996).

In the fall of 1996, the dissertation's recommendations were implemented through the launch of a comprehensive initiative for all of the adjunct instructors within one of the college's larger instructional divisions. Its components included 1) a systematic orientation regimen designed to ensure an understanding of basic policies and procedures; 2) a course titled Instructor Effectiveness Training (see Appendix 12.1 for syllabus) that is required for all new adjunct instructors prior to, or concurrent with, their initial teaching assignment, which focused on basic teaching and classroom management concepts; 3) a mentoring program between new adjunct instructors and a veteran full- or part-time instructor designed to fill in the gaps of the course's curriculum and make applications to the instructor's specific course; 4) a series of meal meetings to remedy the widespread isolation perceived by adjunct faculty that was reported in the national studies, at which new and veteran full- and part-time faculty members could socialize, foster bonds, and participate in a professional development opportunity; and

5) a materials resource center that contained books and papers on key topics of interest to full- and part-time instructors.

Systematic Orientation

Adjunct instructors often report that their initial teaching assignment meeting sounded something like, "The class starts next Monday night. Here is the textbook and a previous syllabus. Call me if you need help." While darkly humorous, such orientations to part-time teaching are unfortunately all too common—setting the new adjunct instructor up for failure to achieve the level of success that we expect in the increasingly accountable environment of higher education. In planning a more effective and manageable orientation regimen, committee members and instructional leaders developed a protocol for addressing the range of issues affecting part-time teaching. It included two elements.

The first component was a group orientation that was piggybacked on the existing annual meeting. All new part-timers were scheduled to arrive an hour earlier than the annual meeting that included all adjunct faculty members. Following their receipt of a revised *Adjunct Faculty Handbook* and a copy of the college catalog and other publications, each document was reviewed for its most critical elements. An extended question and answer time completed the hour, at which time the veteran adjunct instructors entered the meeting room.

The second element was the implementation of a face-to-face orientation delivered in a one-on-one or small group setting by the department chair, which employed a checklist that had been designed by the committee and instructional leaders. Its topics were grouped into human resources issues that included instructor certification, instructional issues including available support resources, and department-specific issues. In a 2003 survey, more than 83% of the respondents, including those who began teaching prior to the implementation of the initiative, reported having received an orientation, and 86% of them said that it was well managed.

INSTRUCTOR EFFECTIVENESS TRAINING COURSE

From its inception, the cornerstone of the IRCC adjunct faculty program has been the Instructor Effectiveness Training course. Beginning a week or two before each fall and spring semester (depending upon the academic calendar), its four sessions of three and one-half hours each focus on course planning, managing the course effectively (with emphasis on student retention and program completion), strategies for delivering more effective instruction (including active learning), and evaluating student achievement and teaching effectiveness. Besides the achievement of those objectives, the 500 adjunct faculty members (and 50 full-timers) who have since completed the course have also fostered collegial relationships and identified valuable teaching resources that probably would not have been otherwise discovered. As instructional deans and department chairs received feedback on its effectiveness, participation widened until the program was subsequently required of all of IRCC's newly hired part-time instructors as a condition of their employment.

In addition to the critical information that the course imparts, it also provides its instructor with the opportunity to evaluate the critical thinking skills and attitudes of new instructors, thus enabling more effective course assignments. Its journaling assignment grounds participants' understanding in sound theory and best practices. Lastly, as demonstrated in research conducted by the lead author of this chapter in 2005, the course has improved the retention of students enrolled in the participants' course sections as well as the retention of the instructors themselves. In spite of the fact that the course is scheduled on four Saturday mornings, its textbook must be purchased by the participant, and no additional remuneration is provided for the time in class, 74% of the survey respondents completing the course indicated in a 2003 survey that it prepared them well to be a successful instructor.

In 2002 the course was adapted into three online versions for delivery to an increasingly time- and place-challenged adjunct faculty. One version focused on the needs of those who teach academic transfer courses, another on those delivering occupational-oriented courses, and the third for instructors who teach in adult education programs. The online courses enable acceleration of completion, are more convenient than the classroom-based course, and focus instructional content more tightly on the discipline area of the participant. The version that targets instructors who teach GED and ESL courses, for example, emphasizes mastery of the one-on-one strategies more common in that teaching environment. The success of the classroom-based course had generated the publication of a textbook (Lyons, Kysilka, & Pawlas, 1999) that the participants in the online and Saturday courses have found to be very effective. The downside of the online version includes greater attrition and a limited ability to contribute to the building of a community of learners within the college overall. Only 51% of the respondents who completed the online version reported that it prepared them well to be an effective instructor. The 2005 study indicated that the participants in the face-to-face version of the Instructor Effectiveness Training course displayed enhanced performance in seven areas over those completing the online version: respect and concern for students, pace of instruction, organization of instruction, use of a variety of teaching methods and materials, use of technology, encouragement of independent, creative, and critical thinking, and response to student questions.

Together these studies indicate that perhaps instructors who will teach a classroom-based course would benefit more from completing the face-to-face version of the Instructor Effectiveness Training course.

MENTORING COMPONENT

To provide completers of the course with support in applying its content and to reduce the sense of isolation that adjunct instructors commonly experience, a mentoring component was designed that would provide maximum flexibility. Unlike some programs in which new instructors are assigned mentors based upon factors considered significant by a program coordinator, the IRCC approach provides mentors and their mentees with opportunities for making their own partner matches at brown bag lunches, required college meetings, and other occasions. Full-time faculty members are encouraged to cite their involvement in their annual self-evaluation, which is required by college policy. One veteran full-time instructor got so caught up in the mentoring enthusiasm that he took it upon himself to mentor an entire cohort of instructors who delivered the same critical course—meeting with them each Friday for lunch and remaining until all issues related to delivery of that course were resolved. In addition, a number of mentoring relationships were initiated by a veteran adjunct instructor who recruited new part-timers from their place of employment or a civic or religious organization to which they belonged. The 2003 study found that 67% of respondents had been mentored by at least one person at IRCC, and of these, 82% found the experience to be effective.

SOCIAL ACTIVITIES AND RECOGNITION

Beginning with the initiative's launch in 1996, two regular social components have had a lasting impact on the success of the entire adjunct faculty support effort. The first has been a series of brown bag luncheons whose agendas are evenly divided between sharing a meal and a professional development activity for all faculty members within the instructional unit. Initially scheduled for the first Friday in each month, the brown bag approach has evolved into other time slots. Besides the introduction to a wide range of colleagues and the information sharing that has been engendered, the brown bag meal meetings (some are now breakfasts) have also provided opportunities for individuals to share teaching strategies and to deepen their relationships. Although schedule conflicts and driving distance limit these activities from achieving a consistently wide attendance, 38% of respondents in the 2003 survey reported having participated.

The second social event has been an annual spring reception that celebrates the contributions of the college's adjunct faculty members. Cosponsored by the IRCC chapter of the Florida Association of Community Colleges, each reception has featured a welcome from the IRCC president, serving to strongly reinforce the importance of the adjunct faculty in achieving the college's overall mission. The reception has grown in attendance and ambiance each year, and it was provided additional prestige in 2003 when it integrated the recognition of the first group of "Outstanding Adjunct Faculty Members." Award winners are encouraged to bring their spouses and children, which fosters an even more special environment filled with photo opportunities that live on in the culture of the institution.

RECOGNITION OF OUTSTANDING PERFORMERS

Earlier that academic year, the Adjunct Faculty Committee had focused its work exclusively on developing the Outstanding Adjunct Faculty Member award whose objectives were to recognize high performers, provide role models and mentors for future adjunct instructors, and to elevate the status of adjunct instruction. It invested meeting and additional time in formulating the award's eligibility criteria, nomination guidelines, and selection process in an effort to ensure award winners would be selected on merit. A major challenge was enabling all stakeholders, that is, adjunct instructors, department chairs, full-time faculty members, and students to have an opportunity to provide input into each step and to be kept appropriately informed of decisions in the design process. All parties seemed quite satisfied that this challenge was successfully managed when the first group of award winners represented a wide array of discipline areas and all five of the college's campuses.

In subsequent years, the award has gained prestige, serving as a high profile commitment by the college to the importance of part-time teaching. The implementation of the award has fostered a cadre of ambassadors to the community and a role model for other adjunct instructors to emulate. While impossible to measure, its press coverage has likely affected the pursuit of part-time teaching at the college by additional members of the community.

INFORMATION RESOURCES

The final component of the adjunct faculty professional development initiative was the creation of a professional development information resource that could be accessed by individuals as needed. A growing collection of books is housed in the campus library to provide greater access and convenience. The 2003 adjunct faculty survey indicated that a better effort needs to be made to promote awareness of this resource because only 28% of respondents had used it.

As the IRCC web site evolved, a professional development page was added that included links to online resources that would appeal to all instructors—new and veteran, full- and part-time. In addition, FAQs with hot links to key sections of the *Adjunct Faculty Handbook* and additional resources, especially for adjunct instructors, were posted and continue to be updated. The 2003 survey indicated that just over 60% of respondents had accessed the web page and that 76% of them found it to be useful. Making this resource even more inviting and valuable to adjunct instructors will have the additional benefit of encouraging the integration of technology into their own instructional practices.

CONCLUSION

Shortly after its inception, this low-cost initiative began to show significant improvements in the teaching and classroom management skills of its participants, and it began to foster a stronger sense of community among the division's faculty members. More than a decade after its inception, the initiative has become a part of the fabric of the institution with the results of the 2003 survey and 2005 study documenting its value to those who might have doubts. It has fostered complementary elements in some departments and instructional divisions that further strengthen its impact on institutional effectiveness. Opportunities for full- and part-time faculty to talk on a collegial level have expanded, and the bifurcation between full- and part-time faculty members that was cited so widely in *The Invisible Faculty* (Gappa & Leslie, 1993), and which had previously existed at IRCC, have eroded nearly totally. The disparaging remarks about "adjuncts" that had once been embarrassingly common have become increasingly rare. Adjunct instructors are increasingly visible on campus, more frequently stopping by their instructional departments to get updated on critical issues and discuss teaching and classroom management strategies with full-timers. The end-of-the-year reception has become an event that full-time faculty members and administrators look forward to attending and in which they have become more openly and genuinely engaged with their part-time colleagues. Increasingly, adjunct instructors are being recognized as a priceless resource that has enabled IRCC to serve its students more effectively, especially in the evening and weekend courses populated by adult learners. In the process, the reach and influence of the college have expanded (Lyons, 1999).

Today our colleges and universities are justly proud of their achievements—perhaps most notably of bringing in ever-larger numbers of first generation students upon whom our impact is especially significant (Rodriguez, 2001). For decades, adjunct faculty members have been increasingly employed to provide expertise in critical areas, mitigate fluctuations in enrollment, staff course sections at difficult times and places, and control costs (Gappa & Leslie, 1993). While some want to perceive a disparity in teaching quality between full- and part-time faculty members, research continues to find no significant differences (Leslie & Gappa, 2002). During the tight budget times expected to extend well into the future, our institutions will no doubt employ as many or more part-time instructors to staff their courses than before. In an age when legislators, students, their employers and parents, and financial aid providers are expecting increased instructional quality and accountability, all institutions owe it to their students and other stakeholders to provide sufficient, integrated professional development resources to their increasingly critical part-timers (Lyons, 2004).

In a 2003 comprehensive survey of IRCC's adjunct faculty members, the initiative to support their teaching demonstrated its effectiveness when nearly 70% reported feeling "like a true member of the IRCC faculty." The strategic plan, its tactical action steps, and the evaluative information that drove and explain this transformation have been well worth the effort of the many individuals—full- and part-time—who have been involved in the planning and delivery of the program's components. Having both begun our college teaching careers and progressed to full-time instructor and leadership roles, the authors of this chapter perhaps understand more clearly than most how important it is to have new adjunct instructors enter the classroom adequately prepared, fully supported, and appropriately recognized for their efforts.

References

Gappa, J. M., & Leslie, D. W. (1993). *The invisible faculty: Improving the status of part-timers in higher education.* San Francisco, CA: Jossey-Bass.

Leslie, D. W., & Gappa, J. M. (2002). Part-time faculty: Competent and committed. In C. L. Outcalt (Ed.), *New directions for community colleges: No. 118. Community college faculty: Characteristics, practices, and challenges* (pp. 59–67). San Francisco, CA: Jossey-Bass.

Lyons, R. E. (1996). *A study of the effects of a mentoring initiative on the performance of new, adjunct community college faculty.* Unpublished doctoral dissertation, University of Central Florida.

Lyons, R. E. (1999). Adjunct faculty: A priceless resource. *Community college week,11*(13), 4, 16.

Lyons, R. E. (2004). *Success strategies for adjunct faculty.* Boston, MA: Allyn & Bacon.

Lyons, R. E., Kysilka, M. L., & Pawlas, G. W. (1999). *The adjunct professor's guide to success: Surviving and thriving in the college classroom.* Boston, MA: Allyn & Bacon.

Lyons, R. E., McIntosh, M., & Kysilka, M. L. (2002). *Teaching college in an age of accountability.* Boston, MA: Allyn & Bacon.

Rodriguez, S. (2001). *Giants among us: First generation students who lead activist lives.* Nashville: Vanderbilt University Press.

Roueche, J. E., Roueche, S. D., & Milliron, M. D. (1995). *Strangers in their own land: Part-time faculty in American community colleges.* Washington, DC: Community College Press.

APPENDIX 12.1.

Instructor Effectiveness Training Syllabus
MNA 1330
Fall 200-

Class:
Saturday mornings, 8:30–12 noon
B building, room 111, Fort Pierce Campus
One-credit course, satisfies portion of recertification requirement

Textbook:
Success Strategies for Adjunct Faculty (part-timers; Lyons, 2004), or *Teaching College in an Age of Accountability* (full-timers; Lyons, McIntosh, & Kysilka, 2002), available at the IRCC Bookstore, or at www.amazon.com or www.bn.com. A three-ring notebook is recommended for organizing handout materials that will be provided.

Instructor:
Frank Harber earned his bachelor's degree at Barry University, an M.B.A. at the Florida Institute of Technology, and in 2007 his Ed.D. in Community College Leadership at the University of South Florida. He began teaching college courses as an adjunct instructor

at IRCC, and came on board full-time in 1998. He has served as chair of the Business Administration and Marketing Management Department since 2002.

Office:
Dr. Harber will be available following the end of each class meeting in B 102. He may be reached at school, 462-7659, or from Martin & Indian River counties at 1-866-866-7676, or by email, at iharber@ircc.edu.

Teaching Methods:
A wide variety of instructional methods will be used to provide you with meaningful learning experiences, and to provide a model for you to adapt for your classes. These include group problem-solving and self-analysis instruments, as well as more traditional methods.

Objectives:
Upon completion of this course, each participant will be able to:
1. Explain the function of the department chair.
2. Develop an effective course syllabus.
3. Describe the factors impacting the success of community college students.
4. Conduct an effective first class meeting.
5. Explain prudent classroom organizational skills.
6. Demonstrate a variety of instructional methodologies.
7. Plan, conduct, and follow up field trips and guest presentations.
8. Identify the factors impacting professionalism in the classroom.
9. Demonstrate Transactional Analysis techniques.
10. Compare and contrast test formats.
11. Analyze test results; take corrective actions.
12. Conduct formal and informal student evaluations.
13. Explain frequently misunderstood college policies and procedures.

Attendance Policy:
Although the instructor is providing opportunities for each participant's achievement of course objectives, please recognize the value that your experiences and insights offer others as well. Therefore, it is critical that you attend and participate actively in each session. An "S" will not be awarded to any student missing more than one class.

Grading Criteria:
Attendance, participation
Journal (standard provided), minimum of 6 entries

Schedule

Session 1
Planning the Course   *SSAF, TCAA 3 & 4*
The 8 Habits of Highly Effective Instructors
Utilizing your most critical resource: the department chair
Resources for planning: textbook, ancillaries, media, course outlines
Today's community college student
Developing an effective syllabus—your contract with students
Preparing for the first class meeting

Session 2
Managing Your Course Effectively   *SSAF, TCAA 5 & 6*
Introducing yourself effectively to the class
Using "icebreakers" and "student profiles" effectively
Establishing an appropriate atmosphere, professionalism
Effective communications techniques, "Transactional Analysis"
Managing class time effectively
Dealing with common teaching challenges

Session 3
Maximizing Teaching Effectiveness   *SSAF, TCAA 7 & 8*
Dovetailing instruction and evaluation
Asking questions, lecturing effectively
Using field trips, guest speakers and other activities effectively
Cooperative and experiential learning
Using audiovisual materials and equipment effectively
Infusing technology into your instruction

Session 4
Evaluating Success   *SSAF, TCAA 10, 11 & 13*
*Journals due
Comparing and contrasting test formats
Exam construction, debugging
Scoring exams, using Scantron system, analyzing test results
Students' and peers' assessments of teaching: informal and formal
Closing questions, discussion

INITIATING A SUPPORT SYSTEM FOR ADJUNCT FACULTY: THE FIRST YEAR

Laura Renninger, Shannon Holliday, Marie Carter

The Shepherd University campus is situated on 323 acres overlooking the Potomac River in historic Shepherdstown, West Virginia, 70 miles west of Washington, DC. A coeducational, state-supported university with a strong liberal arts emphasis, the institution was established in 1871 and currently serves approximately 4,000 students. It provides majors in more than 75 fields and has an average student-to-faculty ratio of 20:1. Over the past decade, enrollment has increased by 34% and the institution has completed capital construction projects totaling nearly $100 million. The student body composition is 57% female, 60% West Virginia residents, 71% traditional aged, and 91% white with about one-third of students living on campus and two-thirds commuting.

In March 2004 the West Virginia legislature changed the name of Shepherd College to Shepherd University and expanded its mission. The transition was accomplished in a very short time, and the most obvious change that occurred in conjunction with the name change was the implementation of master's degree programs. At the same time, the community college component was spun off into an independent, freestanding institution. With the name change came an immediate shift in the composition of our cross-applicants to students who had applied to other universities, unlike in the past when many of the cross-applications had been with community colleges. The average ACT score of incoming freshmen increased by two points over the two-year period following the change in status.

While the enrollment and physical plant of the university have grown dramatically, the primary mission of the institution has remained teaching and learning. The campus community does not envision growing into a large research institution. Highlighting this teaching and learning focus was the recent creation of a new administrative position—dean of teaching, learning, and instructional resources.

While Shepherd University has much—great students, great location, and great professors and administrators—like any other institution, it is not without challenges. From fall 2004 to fall 2005, only 69% of full-time, first-year students were retained for their sophomore year. In 2004 Shepherd's graduation rate after six years was only 43%. We also found ourselves becoming increasingly concerned that at-risk students were not being identified in a timely manner and that appropriate intervention strategies simply were not being implemented. Furthermore, we found that budget constraints prevented us from hiring an adequate number of full-time faculty members and, consequently, we were relying more and more on adjunct faculty members. By fall 2005, adjunct faculty members outnumbered full-time faculty members by almost 50%, and nearly 50% of 100-level courses and nearly 40% of our general education courses were being taught by part-time faculty. This was alarming given that they were teaching such a large number of critical courses even though they were typically much less connected to the institution and thus not always aware of campus resources available to assist our students. In short, it became clear that these adjunct faculty were on the front lines with our first-year students and yet were quite ill equipped to deal with many of the issues that confronted them. We were at a crisis point. We needed to change some things quickly. The good news was that these were things we could actually fix.

SHEPHERD UNIVERSITY ADJUNCT FACULTY TRAINING EVENT

In fall 2005 we proposed a training series for adjunct faculty members to provide a better understanding of campus resources available to assist our students. Through this pilot project, it was our intent to better prepare adjunct instructors to identify students who needed help and then connect them with the appropriate services. We also wanted to create a guidebook for our new faculty to make their transition to the institution much easier. To that end, we submitted a retention minigrant proposal to the West Virginia Higher Education Policy Commission. Excerpts from the mini-grant proposal follow:

Minigrant Objectives

The purpose of the proposed project is to train adjunct faculty members to recognize students who are experiencing problems that might interfere with their academic success and to connect those students with campus programs and services that could help to address the students' transition issues. An experienced consultant will be hired to provide this training and a resource book will be developed for the adjuncts to use throughout the academic year. There are three objectives included in this project. (1) The primary objective is to increase student retention. Students in the adjuncts' classes will be tracked for three years to see how many of them are retained compared with the retention rate of the general student body. We hope that training these important faculty members to help their students will pay off in an increased level of success for their students. (2) There will be a learning objective for the adjunct faculty members. This will be measured through a pre-test before and post-test after the training session is delivered. (3) There will be a learning objective for the students in the adjunct faculty members' classes. Students will complete an exit survey at the end of their participation in the adjuncts' classes evaluating what they have learned about the campus resources available to them.

Minigrant Plan

A training seminar will be conducted for adjunct faculty members prior to the start of the 2006–2007 academic year, featuring a speaker who is experienced in retention issues. The seminar will be organized to include an instructional component and a discussion period. Meals will be provided for participants and a stipend will be paid to participate in the seminar. Additionally, a resource book will be prepared and distributed to the adjuncts for their use as a reference tool throughout the year. We predict that over 2,000 Shepherd students per year will be affected by this program. This is a conservative estimate, based on the number of students who enroll in general studies courses taught by adjuncts. If 54 adjuncts teach two general studies sections each and if each course has 20 students in it, then over 2,000 students would benefit from this adjunct faculty training model. The number could realistically be quite a bit higher: If 54 adjuncts teach three general studies sections each and if each course has 30 students in it, then nearly 5,000 students would benefit from the program. While we recognize that training one segment of the campus population will not solve all of our retention problems, we believe that because adjuncts represent a critical link between the institution and students, arming them with appropriate information and preparation could make a measurable difference in our retention rate. Additionally, through this training, adjuncts will have an opportunity to form a community with other part-time faculty and, thus, they will feel more connected to the institution and be retained longer. If they are happier in their jobs, then it will carry over to their demeanor in the classroom.

Minigrant Applicability to Other Areas
One of the attractive aspects of this proposed adjunct faculty training project is its applicability to other areas of Shepherd University as well as to other institutions. If our adjunct training is deemed a success, then we will deliver similar training to other staff and faculty. Focused training could be delivered to specific academic departments, for example, with similar assessment measures used to evaluate its effectiveness.

Sustainability After the Grant
At Shepherd University, we are committed to improving our retention and graduation rates. Progress made through the adjunct faculty training model will be sustained through institutional resources. We will endeavor to deepen the connection that adjuncts have with the institution and to repeat this retention training each year for new

adjunct faculty members. We are fortunate to have many adjuncts who teach year after year, and we hope that they can mentor future adjuncts as a result of what they learn through this program.

Budget

The plan of this grant is to deliver training and resource materials to the adjunct faculty members who teach at Shepherd University. Long-range implications of this activity for West Virginia are the potential increased retention rates among students taught by faculty who have been well prepared to identify at-risk students and to assist those students in overcoming their obstacles to success. It is expected that between 2,000 and 5,000 Shepherd students will benefit from the proposed adjunct faculty training project. Funds being sought through this grant application ($7,125) would cover the cost of the consultant's stipend and travel expenses and the cost of paying adjuncts for their time. University funds will be used to supplement the income from this grant, should the grant be awarded. Shepherd will cover training materials, hospitality, presentation equipment, and advertising, and will provide employee time to coordinate the activities related to the program.

We were awarded the grant in fall 2005 and began the training event planning process in January 2006. A committee was created to discuss adjunct faculty issues and needs on campus. This committee included a cross-section of stakeholders: the vice president for enrollment management, the dean of teaching, learning, and instructional resources, department chairs who had large numbers of adjunct faculty members in their departments, and several adjunct faculty members themselves who represented different schools across campus. The committee decided that the training event should take place in early August well before classes began and should be held multiple times to accommodate adjunct faculty schedules (i.e., an evening session, a weekend session, etc.). The committee also decided to provide meals for the faculty immediately preceding each session—a perfect venue for a welcoming address by the president and vice president for academic affairs—and to pay all attendees for their time. The committee decided a $100 stipend was consistent with the budget and sufficient to demonstrate appreciation.

Our next step was to conduct campus-wide surveys of adjunct faculty members and department chairs asking about specific issues, needs, and requests that should be addressed at such an event. A copy of the survey results is included as Appendixes 13.1 and 13.2. To ensure the success of the event, the committee decided to invite a nationally known guest speaker, Richard Lyons, who is well versed in the field of adjunct faculty issues. His teaching workshop for our part-time faculty and department chairs ultimately proved to be highly enlightening and much appreciated by our faculty. We also decided to give our attendees complimentary copies of the presenter's book, *Success Strategies for Adjunct Faculty* (Lyons, 2003), and gold-plated, engraved badges that included their name and department to make them feel more connected to our university community. The agenda for our workshop is included in Appendix 13.3 and our subsequent evaluations are included in Appendix 13.4.

THE GUIDE FOR NEW FACULTY

Information gathered from our campus surveys was used to decide what needed to be included in our faculty guidebook. Creating the guidebook was an involved, monumental process, drawing resources from across all of the university's departments and offices. Most offices already had their own brochures or informative literature, but never before had everything been condensed into one helpful binder. We began the process several months prior to the workshop. This proved to be a wise move because we were still calling, copying, compiling, and collating in the days just before the training workshop. In the end, however, it all came together and the first 60 copies were carted off by workshop participants, grateful that such a resource was designed specifically with them in mind.

The "Guide for New Faculty at Shepherd University" is currently 150 pages of teaching suggestions, campus resources, and helpful hints for easing one's arrival to the school. Every department and academic support unit contributed in some way to the content. While practically all of the information was previously available on the Shepherd web site, few knew where to look. The handbook is an easy to use format: a three-ring binder with divider tabs highlighting 20 various topics such as Campus Map and Virtual Tour, Faculty Directory, Syllabus, Technology, Service-Learning and Internships, and Teaching Evaluations. Quick reference guides, a copy of the student handbook, and various forms (override, withdraw, copy request, outline of General Education Program) were included in the front and back pockets of the handbook.

Faculty response to the guidebook was overwhelmingly positive. Evaluation responses indicated that participants found it to be comprehensive and well organized. Those who had been teaching at Shepherd for several semesters expressed relief that they were finally receiving information that would have been helpful from day one. After the three-day workshop, we immediately compiled and distributed 25 more binders to other faculty who expressed interest. It is undoubtedly a popular resource and one that we will continue to update and expand upon in the semesters and years to come.

At the close of each of the three sessions during the adjunct workshop, we asked participants to complete a brief questionnaire and evaluation. The response to our event was overwhelmingly positive. Adjunct faculty finally felt that they were receiving information, recognition, and attention that had not previously been given to them. They found the seminar to be "very informative," "inspirational," and "much needed." Highlights for attendees were the ability to meet and collaborate with other adjunct faculty in an informal setting, the usefulness of the handbook, and the information provided by our guest speaker. Many attendees indicated that they intended to incorporate information gained from the workshop into their upcoming course syllabi and planning. One respondent found the information to be "practical, action oriented, and easily adapted across disciplines." We also asked for input for improving future workshops and received many good suggestions. The most common response to this inquiry was that the sessions be longer (these were three hours each with an optional, additional hour-long complementary meal prior to each session) and repeated. The evaluations revealed a heightened level of excitement and enthusiasm among those present and a true appreciation for any and all efforts made specifically with Shepherd University adjunct faculty in mind.

LESSONS LEARNED

Looking back on the entire planning process, we found it useful to reflect upon items that proved to be very useful. Our recommendations to others who may choose to adopt our method are the following:

- Definitely survey adjunct faculty and department chairs before assembling an institution guidebook or devising a training agenda. This provided us with the most complete picture of items we needed to address at our event.

- Involve as many administrators and full-time faculty as possible. It was a significant morale booster to have our president and vice president for academic affairs speak at the meals preceding the event. It was also highly beneficial to have chairs and other full-time faculty members present at each session to address specific departmental questions and concerns.

- Include a consultant or someone from an institution that has launched an initiative or who knows the special nature of adjunct faculty issues.

- Provide something that connects the adjunct instructors to the institution—whether it is a university bookmark, mug, or name badge. We chose to use the same formal name badges that our full-time faculty members receive. This greatly enhanced the sense of belonging and teamwork among the adjunct faculty members and was viewed as a gesture of appreciation.

- Feed people. The meals provided a wonderful opportunity for adjunct faculty members to get to know one another and to ask questions about the institution in an informal setting. It also reinforces how important we believe these instructors are to our institution. "Is this for us?" one professor asked me as she entered the dining hall, which was beautifully decorated and filled with delicious food. "Why, of course!" I replied, "We're so happy to have you here teaching at Shepherd."

- Provide a book dealing with adjunct issues. We have heard so many comments from our attendees about how helpful Lyons' (2004) book has been. This also demonstrates that we are serious about good teaching at our institution.

- Never underestimate how committed your adjunct faculty are. Some drove more than two hours each way to attend our training sessions. We also had more people attend than we planned for, so make sure you have more than enough materials!

So where do we go from here? First, we have created a web site for adjunct faculty, which includes helpful information, upcoming events, and copies of email bulletins with helpful teaching tips. We plan to survey the students in the classes of the adjunct faculty members who attended our session to see if they received help concerning available campus resources. We would also like to continue these training sessions each year, building upon the knowledge base and sense of community generated in the first year.

Reference

Lyons, R. E. (2004). *Success strategies for adjunct faculty.* Boston, MA: Allyn & Bacon.

APPENDIX 13.1.

Campus Survey for Adjunct Faculty Members

Dear Adjunct Faculty Members,

We plan to offer a professional development workshop for adjunct faculty members in August. The purpose of this workshop is to better acquaint you with various resources on our campus for you and your students. We would also like to create an opportunity for you to meet and interact with other adjuncts and full-time faculty. Please help us to better assist you by taking a few moments and answering some questions:

1. What specific topics, issues, or resources would you like to see addressed in such a workshop? How can we best support your needs?

2. We would like to accommodate your busy schedules. What would be the most con-
    venient time for you to attend such an event?
    ___ on a Saturday   ____ on an evening during the week   ____ on a weekday

3. We plan to provide food and a $100 stipend to attendees. Do you believe that these
    incentives will motivate you and your colleagues to attend our workshop?

Comments:

Thank you for your time and service to our institution. Please return this survey to:

Dr. Laura Renninger
Interim Dean of Teaching and Learning
Center for Teaching and Learning
Byrd Hall 212

APPENDIX 13.2

Adjunct Faculty Survey Response

1. What specific topics, issues, or resources would you like to see addressed in such a
    workshop? How can we best support your needs?
    *   Media resources (4); counseling resources (2); behavioral/disabilities (1);
        library services (5); bookstore ordering (1)
    *   Comprehensive tour and overview of resources at Shepherd (4)
    *   Tour of learning classrooms and specific features of different departments
    *   Outcomes research on the effectiveness of various educational/teaching prac-
        tices/classroom management
    *   How is SU organized? Chain of command? Maybe give us a flow chart of who
        does what and who is responsible to whom? (2)
    *   A list of all the offices and centers (all resources) that are on campus (6)
    *   A list of phone numbers to key people we may need to have contact with and
        their building and room number (3)
    *   Everything—how to get an ID card (4), RAIL (4), grading (3), add/drop, how
        to interact with department chairs and deans
    *   WebCT—general overview, online grading, class web site (4)
    *   Teaching, testing, and lecturing strategies (4); student motivation
    *   How to keep up with technology in the classroom (2)
    *   Pay raises (2); pay periods

- Ability to assign +/- to applied lesson grades
- Grading: When are grades due; OCR forms—where to get, how to use, what exam stats are available; midterms and finals policies (6)
- More frequent communication among members of departments—regularly scheduled department meetings
- Should receive SU handbook and schedule booklet to know what the school offers
- Info on student population and resources available for students
- An Adjunct Commons room with computers and a printer where we would not be charged! There is no place for us to work and print work. Office space is lacking.
- How do we communicate correctly to faculty? I've responded to two communications, only to be told "This is only for full-time faculty."
- Grants and scholarships available to students; grant-writing assistance
- Independent study venues for music students
- CTL does a good job of making training on technologies available.

2. We would like to accommodate your busy schedules. What would be the most convenient time for you to attend such an event?
   - on a Saturday (4)
   - on an evening during the week (14)
   - on a weekday (7)
   - It depends—maybe two times: once during day and once at night. I will only come if it's after the semester starts—earlier than that is vacation!
   - Weekday evenings after 6:00 pm
   - Any time with advanced notice
   - August 1–5 I teach in the morning hours

3. We plan to provide food and a $100 stipend to attendees. Do you believe these incentives will motivate you and your colleagues to attend our workshop?
   - Yes: 19.
   - I'd rather have more money and no food, unless it's organic and vegetarian. We could bring our own food.
   - Please have a vegetarian alternative and pork alternative.
   - I would come anyway, but these incentives do help (2).
   - Perhaps $200 would provide more motivation, especially if the workshop is over an hour long.
   - Yes, if it's during August 1–5 *afternoons, or Aug. 14–19.
   - No: 1.

4. Comments:
   - I'm enjoying my first semester as an adjunct, but this would help me to gain an understanding of any teaching resources that are available.
   - Please don't make it on a night that I teach class. You might consider offering two groups: those who are brand-new to Shepherd and those who have been here. In the past, the program was geared more toward first-year instructors.
   - The involvement of full-time faculty is crucial. Adjuncts, like freshmen, can feel isolated—the sense of community is refreshing.
   - Please let me know if you could use a set of National Board for Professional Teaching Standards for your library. I could bring you one or more of each discipline.
   - To feel more a part of Shepherd University, adjunct faculty members should welcome such an opportunity.
   - Thanks for asking!

Department Chairs Adjunct Survey Responses:

1. What specific topics, issues, or resources would you like to see addressed in such a workshop? How can we best support the needs of adjunct faculty in your department?
   - How to make use of Shepherd web site to access registrar, library, etc.
   - How to improve communication—individual mailboxes or electronic communication?
   - Using RAIL and OUTLOOK (2)
   - Getting a RAMBLER card
   - Discussion on handling class attendance issues
   - Discussion on how teaching undergrad courses is different than grad school or an adjunct's typical last education experience
   - Setting up Shepherd email accounts that will forward to personal account
   - When adjuncts teach classes that only meet once a week for 150 minutes are they meeting the required contact hours? Is this a realistic approach to teaching a class?
   - Accommodating and excusing SU athletes for college-supported events
   - Withdraws and incompletes
   - WebCT
   - The "flow" of the semester, i.e., midterms and finals
   - How to deal with plagiarism
   - Incorporating technology into class presentation
   - Conferences and interaction with students without having an office
   - Fundamentals such as organizing a syllabus, stress and time management, where to seek help if problems arise with students and/or colleagues
   - Who is who at SU?

2. Are there any problems with adjunct faculty that you commonly encounter?
   - They need office space and access to copiers and office equipment (2)
   - Many don't check their mailboxes
   - Don't know how to handle special situations that arise in class—i.e., add/drop
   - They should be given a complimentary parking pass
   - Cost of parking
   - Pay rates (3)
   - Sense of ownership instead of being "hired guns"
   - Overreliance on adjuncts
   - Submission of grades
   - Procedures of class cancellation
   - Access to classroom equipment
   - Adjuncts' lack of involvement in the academic life of the department

3. Do you currently have a mentor program for adjunct faculty in your deptartment? If so, how well has it worked? If not, would you be willing to adopt a mentor program?
   - Department chair informally monitors adjuncts.
   - We have few adjuncts, thus it is easy to work fairly closely with them.
   - Yes, it works inconsistently well (2): Some embrace it, some loathe it. I need to be more insistent and enforcing.
   - Reza would like to have a program such as this for his adjuncts.
   - Dr. Carter mentions that the English program has had a successful adjunct mentoring program for over 15 years, headed now by Betty Ellzey. He volunteers that she and he could provide some useful tips to other departments.
   - Not currently, but great idea (2)

4. Would you be willing to attend our workshop or to send a full-time faculty member representative from your department?
   - Contact Andy Henriksson when he gets back from sabbatical in August.
   - Possibly
   - We are planning an adjunct retreat of our own (? Don't know which dept.).
   - Yes: 5
   - Yes, so long as it doesn't conflict with our own (ENGL) dept. adjunct workshop at the beginning of the year. We require all adjuncts to attend at least one workshop a semester provided by CTL office or ENGL dept. We even pay them a stipend. (Charles Carter)
   - No, probably not

APPENDIX 13.3.

Shepherd University Adjunct Training Event Agenda

Thursday, August 3rd

5:00–5:50 PM Complimentary Dinner (Lower Level of the SU Dining Hall)
With welcome address by President and Vice President for Academic Affairs

6:00–6:30 PM Presentation and Question/Answer Session: "A Guide for New Faculty at Shepherd University" (Dr. Laura Renninger, 256 Library)

6:30–9:00 PM Teaching Workshop: "The 8 Habits of Highly Effective Professors" (Dr. Richard E. Lyons, 256 Library)

Friday, August 4th

12:00–12:50 PM Complimentary Lunch (Lower Level of the SU Dining Hall)
With welcome address by President and Vice President for Academic Affairs

1:00–1:30 PM Presentation and Question/Answer Session: "A Guide for New Faculty at Shepherd University" (Dr. Laura Renninger, 256 Library)

1:30–4:00 PM Teaching Workshop: "The 8 Habits of Highly Effective Professors" (Dr. Richard E. Lyons, 256 Library)

Optional WebCT Introductory Training Session from 4:00–5:00 PM for interested faculty. WebCT is our Learning Management System at Shepherd and we will provide information about it in your session. Please join us if you have the time (256 Library).

Saturday, August 5th

8:00–8:50 AM Complimentary Breakfast (Lower Level of the SU Dining Hall)
With welcome address by President and Vice President for Academic Affairs

9:00–9:30 AM Presentation and Question/Answer Session: "A Guide for New Faculty at Shepherd University" (Dr. Laura Renninger, 256 Library)

9:30–12:00 Teaching Workshop: "The 8 Habits of Highly Effective Professors" (Dr. Richard E. Lyons, 256 Library)

Optional WebCT Introductory Training Session from 12:00–1:00 PM for interested faculty. WebCT is our Learning Management System at Shepherd and we will provide information about it in your session. Please join us if you have the time (256 Library).

APPENDIX 13.4.

Shepherd University Adjunct Training Participant Evaluations

Shepherd University Adjunct Faculty Workshops
August 2006
Participant Evaluation

1. What are your thoughts on the handbook and guidebook overview?
    Overwhelmingly positive responses:
    *   Great idea and great resource
    *   Useful reference
    *   The tutorial was helpful
    *   Wish I had it when I started years ago
    *   Informative and helpful—should be followed up within departments
    *   Fabulous resource— I'm eager to read it
    *   Very helpful and well organized—will be easy to get info when I need it
    *   Well thought out
    *   Great resource—could have used more time for the guidebook session
    *   I like [this type of] well organized, quick reference
    *   More time to go over
    *   Excellent—I've been here four years and we needed this
    *   Discovered resources I wasn't aware of
    *   Resources and templates are helpful

2. Do you feel you have a better feel for what types of campus resources exist?
    *   Better understanding of student services
    *   It's nice to be able to inform students of what is available to them
    *   Better understanding of counseling services and web sites
    *   If I have questions, I know where to look to answer them
    *   Yes/Absolutely: 28
    *   A little: 2
    *   No: 1

3. How did you like the teaching workshop? What did you learn from it? Are there
    any changes you would suggest to improve it?
    *   Very interesting—I learned things I can do differently
    *   Perhaps have more small group activities to break the routine
    *   Lyons was good, but he could have been a little more on topic and a little less
        "entertaining." He digressed a good bit.
    *   Very stimulating

- I would definitely attend again.
- Met colleagues
- Inspirational
- Would like more from Lyons
- I have a better understanding and will use the information to improve the syllabus.
- Good but too slow—the Ethics worksheet was good
- Got ideas for classroom activities and assignments—wouldn't change anything
- As a mentor and new(er) SU faculty member I found it very helpful
- Workshop material interesting, Lyons was great, eliminate participants' personal examples and comments so that more info can be covered (2)
- Will use the 10 points in the book
- Lyons has good energy and helped me be optimistic about teaching
- Very informative—clarified difference between public school teaching and university—especially on ethical issues
- Stick to the point
- Reinforced some of my teaching philosophies
- Good tips for engaging/retaining students; helpful for developing syllabus
- Suggestions: Require attendance, hold it on a day when we can actually go get our Rambler card and parking permit and have department chairs attend for department-related questions
- More time (9)
- Interesting to see the evolution of education to a more collaborative effort
- Very much a mixed bag—I don't think we're necessarily doing students a favor by adapting everything to them. Info is still passed on by lectures in the real world
- Well focused—timely strategies to integrate into class planning immediately (4). Practical, action oriented, and easily adapted across disciplines. Thanks for the handbook. More please!

4. How were the facilities and service (room, equipment, food, etc.) throughout the workshop? What would you change and/or improve?
    - Very comfortable and conducive to learning
    - Flawlessly planned
    - Thank you for the good refreshments
    - A little chilly, but otherwise great
    - People without tables in the back
    - Have the meal closer to the lecture or discussion in the dining hall
    - Excellent technology
    - There was even half and half for the coffee!
    - Excellent: 20
    - Good: 7

5. Do you have any suggestions for future workshops? Any content or topic areas you think would be valuable to explore in a workshop? Please offer suggestions.
   - How to better manage large classes
   - Seminar on distance learning
   - More about WebCT
   - More small group interaction
   - Legal issues
   - Have a workshop for newest teachers and a separate one for continuing teachers
   - I would appreciate an opportunity to improve my computer skills
   - How to use student-engaging techniques in technical classes
   - Situational workshops
   - I would suggest a sharing session on special topics—full time and adjunct faculty have roundtable discussion or brown bag lunch discussion of issues like attendance and student athletes
   - Cover all of the 8 habits—ask Dr. Lyons to return.
   - Any forum such as this to get adjuncts together and offer support and open communication would be appreciated.
   - Felt we needed something like this for a long time—thank you
   - Sessions on test writing and syllabus writing
   - New strategies for teaching millennials
   - Keeping up with technology changes in instruction
   - Using SmartCarts
   - Little more on RAIL, Smart Technology, Parking, and WebCT
   - Our full-time department heads need to attend

6. Please provide an overall commentary/evaluation on the workshop and/or its facilitators. Use the back if necessary.
   - All was very interesting and informative.
   - Thank you so much for doing this!
   - Excellent reference material
   - Dr. Lyons was very interesting—good resource for future trainings.
   - This was great for me, I've been an adjunct four years and didn't realize how much I didn't know.
   - Very useful—good job all around
   - I am much better prepared to work at Shepherd and facilitate my students. Thank you.
   - You're doing great work, Laura! Thanks so much. (4)
   - Guidebook session was particularly useful
   - Stay on track—wandered off point too often
   - Nice to have something for part time faculty
   - More time—longer session—very valuable
   - Excellent first effort—much needed

- Very thoughtful and well organized—helps with adjunct morale
- I didn't always like Lyons's interaction with the group—too pedagogical or something.
- Well planned and executed—Shannon and Laura are awesome! Dr. Lyons is a great resource.
- Dr. Lyons is an experienced and engaging facilitator—gave me ideas to incorporate into my classes and made me aware of (legal) issues I had not considered
- While much was valuable tonight, I have one overriding concern: We are a university, not a corporation. Framing pedagogy in a corporate mold is dangerous. Corporatism running life is just another word for fascism.
- Good info—also nice to talk unofficially with other adjuncts

14

THE TWO-YEAR EFFORT TO BUILD A PROGRAM THAT PROVIDES PART-TIME FACULTY PEDAGOGICAL SUPPORT, COMMUNITY, AND A SENSE OF MISSION

H. Edward Lambert, Milton D. Cox

While engaging in a cooperative learning exercise at a workshop sponsored by the Miami University's (Ohio) Center for the Enhancement of Learning and Teaching (the Center) three years ago, the Center director discovered that one of the group members—a visiting faculty member at our institution in the department of sociology—wrote her dissertation on part-time and adjunct faculty. That small group immediately began discussing part-time faculty and their academic lives and culture at our institution, and the director realized that the new colleague offered an excellent opportunity for the Center to begin to address pedagogical issues connected to part-time faculty. For many years the growth and teaching of this cohort of faculty had gone almost unnoticed. The Center director now moved quickly to invite our new colleague to help initiate a program for our part-time faculty, and when she enthusiastically accepted the offer to become one of our Center's faculty teaching associates for the 2004–2005 academic year, our efforts were underway to address part-time faculty teaching issues and opportunities.

This chapter reports on our initial efforts to establish a program to support the part-time faculty at Miami University: the experimental first year, learning as we went; the information-gathering second year, expanding the program from a teaching focus to a broader outreach; and the upcoming potential-filled third year, attempting some unusual new directions to try to engage a critical mass of our part-time faculty. After describing the context, the initial program, and its results, we then describe our new comprehensive program that will address the shortcomings of the first attempt. Finally, we provide recommendations for universities contemplating similar issues and opportunities for part-time faculty.

Community colleges are experienced at providing support for their part-time faculty, but most research universities have focused their energies on other faculty cohorts: new and junior faculty, graduate teaching assistants, and (although infrequently) midcareer and senior faculty. And the research mission often takes top priority. We begin with the context for our initiative. Miami University is a research-intensive, state-supported institution with approximately 750 tenured and tenure-track faculty, 750 visiting and part-time faculty, 14,000 undergraduates, and 2,000 graduate students on a residential campus in Oxford, Ohio, with two nearby regional campuses, each offering mostly two-year programs to around 2,000 commuting students.

Miami University is in the same position as most other colleges and universities with respect to part-time faculty. Growth in the use of this faculty segment has occurred on a steadily increasing basis. Relatively recently, it reached the point at which the realization dawned that a significant change had occurred: Part-timers exist in such numbers and on such a continuing basis that as a group they can no longer be considered as casual labor. They have become a segment of the faculty and a constituency in their own right.

In framing a discussion of how Miami University is adjusting to this phenomenon, it is instructive to review a bit of its history. Having traditionally been considered casual labor, there is little definitive information on the history of part-time faculty at Miami University. Recruitment and retention have been handled on a department-by-department basis with little institution-wide coordination and few standards. No records exist on matters such as turnover, the average number of credit hours taught by individual part-time faculty members, the length of time individual part-time faculty members have taught at Miami, or, indeed, the growth in the use of part-timers vis-à-vis other nontenured faculty over the years. However, all indications are that the issues concerning part-time faculty are the same at Miami University as they are throughout academia. For example, with very few exceptions, the experience of part-timers at Miami has been similar to that reported in the literature on this subject. Jacobs (1998) notes:

> At many institutions more than two-thirds of the appointments made for any semester are made in the thirty days preceding the start of the semester; in one regional survey several years ago, 10 percent of part-time appointments were made after the start of classes. (p. 13)

Consistent with its casual labor treatment of this group, Miami did not record statistics of this nature. However, a significant number of contracts (that confirm appointments) are completed within 30 days preceding the semester, and appointments are known to have been made after the start of the semester.

The First Year: The Initial Program

For 2004–2005 Susan Weaver, a new colleague and Center faculty teaching associate, and Milton Cox, the Center director, selected an opening strategy that would draw on a unique strength of our Center: our experience with designing and implementing faculty learning communities. We digress here to describe them.

A faculty learning community (FLC) is a special type of community of practice (Wenger, 1998). It is a multidisciplinary group of 6–15 voluntary members (8–12 recommended), consisting of faculty or a mix of faculty, graduate students, and administrative professionals. They work collaboratively on nine-month scholarly projects to enhance teaching and learning. Specific activities include retreats and triweekly seminars to build capacity and develop competence in the scholarship of teaching and learning. Each FLC participant may select a focus course or project in which to try out innovations. Participants also assess outcomes connected to their projects, including student learning, and may prepare a miniportfolio to chronicle results. They may select and work with student associates to engage student perspectives. Finally, they present project results to their institutions and national conferences. An FLC program is the system of FLCs that an institution has in place and the administrative structure that manages it. This is usually a teaching or faculty development center.

FLCs may be cohort based or topic based. Cohort-based communities address the developmental needs of a particular cohort of faculty. Examples include graduate students preparing to become faculty, early-career faculty, senior and midcareer faculty, and chairs of departments (note that a part-time faculty cohort is not mentioned). A cohort FLC curriculum is shaped by the participants and includes a broad range of teaching and learning matters. In contrast, a topic-based FLC has a yearlong curriculum designed to address a special teaching and learning innovation for the participants, such as the introduction to and use of problem-based learning. When the topic or cohort is set, the FLC program management works to find interested, multidisciplinary, and committed participants, a qualified facilitator, and funding.

An FLC is more than a committee, seminar, or action-learning set precisely because it is a multidisciplinary community—with everything this term implies in terms of bonding, safety, and support. However, the associated objective of taking a scholarly approach to teaching and developing a scholarship of teaching and learning does mean that FLCs are more structured and scholarly than discussion groups or informal teaching circles. FLCs work because of trust, sharing, and the cross-fertilization of ideas (Cox, 2004).

Miami University's FLC Program has been in place for 27 years. Each year the Center manages 10 FLCs. Forty percent of Miami's current faculty have participated in FLCs as well as 40% of department chairs. The FLC Program received a Hesburgh Award in 1994 and a Certificate of Excellence in 2003. The model's dissemination has been funded by grants and has been successfully adapted and assessed at several institutions (Beach & Cox, 2005; Richlin & Essington, 2004).

Not surprisingly, until 2003 part-time faculty had never been eligible to join FLCs. The administration chose to invest support only for tenure-track and tenured faculty, graduate students, and, recently, professional staff. However, in 2004–2005 we decided to use a modified FLC model to initiate the Center's program to support part-time faculty.

Because FLCs involve intensive, yearlong commitments, some feel that they required too much of a time investment for first-year faculty and graduate students. To address this concern, a one-semester variation of an FLC, which we called an "FLC lite," was established in 2003 for the new faculty and the graduate student cohorts to provide an initial teaching enhancement opportunity for those desiring it. Each FLC lite required participating in eight (for new faculty) or six (for graduate students) teaching and learning seminars and writing a report on how participants incorporated what they learned into courses they taught. Production of the scholarship of teaching and learning was not required so that participants could focus on their disciplinary scholarship and adjusting to their departments. The FLC lite did, however, provide multidisciplinary approaches, community, and an opportunity to meet peers and form networks across departments. Those completing the FLC lite received professional expense money in the amount of $400 (new faculty) or $200 (graduate students).

With the FLC lite model already in place, the Center then established a similar kind of cohort program for part-timers, the Part-Time and Adjunct

Faculty Teaching Program (PTAFTP). This FLC lite required participation in five Center seminars or workshops, three of which were to be provided specifically for part-time faculty. Participants completing the program were offered $200 to use for professional items that might enhance their teaching, such as purchase of books, videos, software, or travel to conferences. The goals of the program were established to be consistent with the Center's teaching mission and the pedagogical needs expressed by part-time faculty. The primary goals were to:

- Provide teaching opportunities for training, interaction, and support for part-time faculty

- Share information about opportunities available for part-time faculty

- Include part-time faculty in the Miami culture

- Provide links among the part-time faculty on Miami's three campuses

- Provide opportunities to brainstorm to address classroom issues such as individual student needs, grade distribution, and motivation

- Provide personal invitations to join in campus-wide professional development opportunities such as the Lilly Conference on College Teaching

- Provide a venue to share ideas and opportunities for career development

- Provide consultation as requested by part-time faculty

A web page dedicated to part-time faculty (www.units.muohio.edu/celt /cohort/patep.php) was developed by facilitator Weaver and the Center. The information includes background about Miami, grant opportunities, campus policies, links to non-Miami resources for part-time faculty, and frequently asked questions.

A sample PTAFTP meeting session is described here:

Saturday, January 15, 10:00–12:45 p.m. in Shriver Center (Oxford): Lunch provided.
Topics and Activities:

- Resources to support teaching and research at Miami

- Different concerns but common goals: Addressing student needs in making the transition from the Hamilton and Middletown regional campuses to the Oxford campus

- Approaches that have worked for you in keeping students engaged and challenged

- A brief overview of Blackboard

- Increasing writing and critical thinking in the classroom—Idea share and new ideas, including jigsaw and problem-based learning approaches

- BONUS: After the session, we will offer an optional tour of the Oxford campus

During the year, sessions were offered at each Miami campus and in Cincinnati, where some part-timers lived. Email was used to encourage participation. Messages were sent to department administrative assistants, part-time faculty, and the Center's department teaching liaisons. Staff members at the regional campuses put fliers in each mailbox, and this means of communication seemed to generate the best attendance.

Attendance at sessions, however, was disappointing, and only five part-time faculty completed the program. In her final report, facilitator Weaver provided informal feedback from part-timers who did not participate. Their reasons included lack of time; costs of traveling to meetings; lack of departmental encouragement for participation; a sense that the program seemed to be aimed more at new part-time faculty while ignoring the skills, experience, and diversity of many (or most) part-time faculty; and that most of the sessions were on the Oxford campus, while most of the part-timers were on the regional campuses. Suggestions for improvement included providing a schedule earlier in the academic year, asking department chairs to encourage participation and recognize the efforts and interest of participants, offering the same sessions on all campuses, paying transportation costs, and having campus-wide session presenters meet with part-timers afterward to discuss part-time faculty issues and challenges.

Because the new program was sponsored by the Center, the program goals were connected to teaching and learning. The other logistical issues cited by part-time faculty were not the focus of the sessions, but the concerns still emerged. Nonparticipants also contacted program facilitator Weaver in hopes that the program would lead to development of a vehicle for input from part-time faculty to improve the climate for part-timers at Miami. The compilation of this informal feedback contained in Weaver's final report appears in Appendix 14.1 of this chapter.

THE SECOND YEAR: GATHERING INFORMATION

During the summer before the second year of the program, facilitator Weaver accepted a position as director of a teaching center at another institution. Upon her recommendation, H. Edward Lambert (a part-time member of the Department of Educational Leadership) replaced her for 2005–2006 as a Center faculty teaching associate and facilitator of the Part-Time and Adjunct Faculty Teaching Program, which was renamed the Part-Time and Adjunct Teaching Enhancement Program (PATEP). Having retired from a career as a business executive and attorney, Lambert taught career development courses on the regional Middletown campus of Miami University. His interests included teaching techniques based upon recent developments in brain research as well as scholarly teaching techniques in general and scholarly teaching of part-time faculty. He was also a member of the Middletown campus Center for Teaching and Learning.

Recognition of the scope of the part-time faculty issue throughout the Miami community had been slow to develop. In the typical fashion of academia, committees were formed in various schools and divisions to study various part-time faculty concerns. However, there was no university-wide coordination or consensus on an overall program to address the matter. This was brought to light in August 2005 in the university president's annual State of the University Address that noted the trend of retirements among senior faculty and the increased use of nontenured faculty throughout academia. The president startled many in the community when he revealed that only 49% of undergraduate student credit hours were being taught by tenured and tenure-track faculty. He referenced a concern that faculty ranks have become "two-tiered institutions of winners and losers," and stated, "it is important that we not allow a caste system to evolve in our teaching ranks" (Garland, 2005).

In the context of this history and with a presidential focus now on the matter, the issue became determining how the needs of part-time faculty should be addressed. The Center voluntarily assumed a major role in the endeavor. One of our first priorities was to gather information. Working with the Office of Academic Personnel and the Office of Institutional Research, the Center began a database related solely to part-time faculty. This was the first time that a comprehensive record of this nature had been maintained.

Lambert continued to facilitate the program that Weaver had implemented in the first year, but pushed for new avenues to address the part-time faculty concerns expressed in her final report (Appendix 14.1). He designed, and the Center published, three part-time faculty newsletters (see www.units.muohio.edu/celt/library/patep_newsletter/index.php) during 2005–2006. Lambert and Center director Cox met with associate deans, regional campus associate executive directors, and others to seek support for a part-time faculty program that would include, but go beyond, a teaching support program and would have a full-time administrator who would be dedicated to supporting part-time faculty. Although listeners were sympathetic, funds were (always) in short supply, and other issues were a higher priority. Thus, nothing major happened.

Progress was made in some areas of programming and information gathering, however. Because Lambert also cofacilitated the Faculty Learning Community to Study and Implement Teaching and Learning Techniques Based on Recent Developments in Brain Research, at his urging part-time faculty were urged to apply, and four of the 16 successful FLC applicants were part-time faculty. Other FLCs then changed their eligibility requirements, and three part-timers joined two of them as well. Four new part-timers joined the new-faculty FLC lite rather than the FLC lite for part-timers. As a result of the broadened participation of part-time faculty in these other Center programs, the part-time FLC lite had only two faculty who completed that program. This was disappointing even though the total number of part-timers involved in Center Programs was 11, more than double the five from the previous year.

One of the part-time faculty members in the Brain FLC, Alana Van Gundy-Yoder, became very interested in the Center's programming for part-timers. As a trained focus group facilitator, she volunteered and led a focus group session of part-time faculty to provide qualitative evidence that could be used to strengthen the program. Her focus group report appears in Appendix 14.2. It is interesting to note how it confirms the concerns raised in Weaver's informal report from the previous year.

At the request of the provost, the Center's advisory committee (a sub-committee of the university senate) devised a questionnaire about teaching practices and evaluation of teaching to be sent by the provost's office to department chairs and deans. It included a section that gathered information about department chair perspectives of and policies for part-time faculty. This survey is currently being completed, and the results will be analyzed and available later from the authors.

Lambert also engaged in an informal survey and conversations with some part- and full-time faculty during 2005–2006. Discussion points included the quality of their teaching, teaching obligations, other academic community obligations, and their view of their relationship to the community and with each other. One of our resulting impressions was that a gulf existed between part-time and full-time faculty, and that some responsibility for the gulf resided in both camps. We conjectured the following:

- The use of part-time faculty has become intermixed with the debate over the feasibility of the continuation of the tenure system. This has led some tenured faculty to look upon part-time faculty as a threat to the tenure system.

- Many part-time faculty members do not have terminal degrees, and this raises questions about their teaching abilities.

- Part-time faculty are viewed as casual labor, and they tend to respond to that perception by actually taking on the attributes of casual labor.

- Part-time faculty do not become invested in the goals and mission of the university.

These perceptions may result in the following outcomes:

- The potential of part-time faculty to enhance the educational mission of the university is not being optimized.

- Optimization of part-time faculty will require recognition of and better integration of the part-time segment into the university community.

- For part-time faculty to become a more cohesive, integrated segment of the university community, cultural change is necessary throughout the university community—including the part-time segment itself.

THE THIRD YEAR: THE NEW PLAN

Based on the results of the information gathering in 2005–2006, for 2006–2007 the Center will engage an extended program, the Part-Time and Adjunct Teaching Scholars Program (PTATSP). Lambert and Van Grundy-Yoder will cofacilitate the pilot phase.

After careful study, we determined that effecting the needed cultural change should begin with a two-part program. The first part of the program involves enhancing the educational expertise of part-time instructors. The second part involves establishing a climate in which part-time instructors can function as an integrated segment of the university community. Both parts of the program are interdependent; neither can succeed without the other.

In the first part of the program, we are concerned not only with part-time faculty expertise as instructors, but also with their expertise as educators. There is a subtle but distinct difference. One can be an expert *in* one's discipline, and one can be an expert at *teaching* the discipline. However, as an educator, the instructor furthers a higher goal of ensuring that students can translate disciplinary learning into an integrated knowledge base that includes their entire learning experience. Thus, of concern is the holistic professional development of part-time faculty. Center activities span the disciplines and, in that sense, are holistic. Yet the Center found that only 6.2% of part-time faculty had attended Center-sponsored faculty development activities, compared to 26% of full-time faculty.

This disparity in participation is significant. Part-time faculty responses to our inquiries into the reasons for this difference were varied, ranging from the time at which activities are held not being conducive to part-timers' schedules to concern that in the culture in which they teach, part-timers are unaware of the need for pedagogical and professional development. When questioned further, part-timers noted that even at the Center, professional development activities were designed primarily to accommodate full-time faculty without regard for differing priorities of part-timers. This underscores the important lesson that part-time faculty are not "partial editions" of full-time faculty, but unique contributors to the educational enterprise (Maguire, 1984). Realizing this, the Center undertook the design of a program exclusively for part-time faculty.

The new program continues to follow the FLC lite model in which participants interested in a particular subject meet to study, investigate, and discuss subjects. However, the program involves more rigorous study pursuant to a schedule of professional development activities. The program is, in effect, a study of pedagogy in higher education. Eligibility for participation requires having completed at least six consecutive semesters of teaching at Miami. This serves to ensure that resources are directed to those who have a continuing connection with the university. Upon completion of the program, participants will be awarded the title of Part-Time Teaching Fellows. The award will be presented at a banquet attended by the provost and the recipient's department chair. Participants will also receive a professional expense stipend of $500 during the course of the program.

The new program will require at least eight meetings for each of three part-time FLC lites (one on each Miami campus, although the pilot year will have only one FLC lite) over an academic year with each meeting lasting at least two and one-half hours. The meetings will begin with a short greeting and presentation by a university official such as the provost or a dean. The objective is to include participants in the university culture as well as to provide practical information about university structure, operations, and goals. To enhance their sense of identification with the university, participants will, from time to time, receive a token gift such as a coffee mug, pen, or T-shirt bearing the university logo.

All meetings will involve in-depth and comprehensive pedagogical study of a specific teaching/learning subject. Topics might include teaching and learning styles, creating inclusive classrooms, assessment of student learning, and other topics determined by the group's interest and needs. Guest presentations on selected pedagogical topics at meetings will be given by full-time faculty members distinguished in those respective areas (who also may receive a small professional expense account for their efforts). In addition to their pedagogical benefits, the presentations will help build rapport between part-time and full-time faculty.

The cohort will also read and discuss at least two books per semester. Examples of books are Bain's (2004) *What the Best College Teachers Do* and Richlin's (2006) *Blueprint for Learning.* Participants will be expected to attend other workshops and seminars, for example, sessions at the Lilly Conference on College Teaching. In addition to meetings and instructional sessions, program activities may include attending classes of other cohort participants, videotaping classes taught by participants, and team teaching.

In crafting the new program, the Center considered and wrestled with ways to address the complex connections between campus climate, perceptions and relations between part- and full-time faculty, expectations for increased commitments from part-timers, and pay. We now explore our strategies to address these connections through the new program.

Increasing the pedagogical expertise of part-time faculty will not be effective unless and until part-timers can put their expertise into practice. This involves creating the proper university climate and changing the perceptions of part-timers' role by all university segments, including administrators, full-time faculty, and part-timers themselves. Part-timers are not hired to conduct research. Their role in governance activities is limited. The primary mission of part-time faculty is teaching, and they can support and further the core goal of providing a quality education to the student population. If they are equipped to perform their role well, they will create increased time for full-time faculty to engage in long-term planning, implement new programs, and conduct research. They will enhance all areas of the university's mission. As one department chair at Miami observed, part-time personnel teach introductory courses. If they do a bad job, students are turned off from majoring in the discipline. Thus, it is essential that part-timers be empowered to realize their full potential.

An impediment to giving part-timers additional responsibilities is a belief that they are underpaid. Some administrators and department chairs are hesitant to ask part-timers to do more than attend to classroom instruction. Some part-timers also complain that they are too busy earning a living and/or caring for their families to do more than classroom duties such as attending professional development sessions.

Part-time pay is significantly lower proportionally than that for full-time faculty and needs to be increased. Across-the-board pay increases are problematic, however, because part-time faculty exist in such large numbers. Nevertheless, low pay should not become an excuse either by the administration or by part-timers for substandard performance. In a way, the situation becomes a chicken-and-egg matter. Part-time faculty will become more deserving of a pay increase by having their status increased within the community. Furthermore, pay is not the impediment to obtaining qualified instructors that some perceive. The National Center for Education Statistics (NCES) reported that 70% of part-time faculty indicated that being a part of academia was the main reason for holding part-time employment, and 54% of faculty in four-year institutions *preferred* working part-time (Conley & Leslie, 2002). From a purely free-market standpoint, there is no shortage of potential instructors, and lower pay should not be used to justify lowered professional expectations for part-timers.

At the same time, this disparity in pay should be addressed. To enhance the attractiveness of the Center's new program, part-timers will receive a wage increase of $50 per credit hour for all courses they teach after successful completion of the Part-Time and Adjunct Teaching Scholars Program. From the university's standpoint, this plan not only allows for an incremental pay increase without the severe budgetary impact, but it also links the increase to professional development.

Addressing pay and collegiality issues, Haeger (1998) notes the importance of making part-timers part of the mainstream institutional environment:

> Large numbers of part-time faculty who are paid less and have a nearly invisible role in the departments disrupt the departmental culture of teaching and research. Most departments do not understand the problems created by the use of part-time faculty and lack policies to ensure an integration into the culture. Ultimately this affects the learning community, as well as efforts at assessment and at interdisciplinary teaching and research. (p. 86)

Haeger concludes that "the university must control the negatives of part-time faculty employment and ensure support for the learning environment by placing part-time faculty in the mainstream of public life" (p. 87). One of the ways to mainstream part-timers is to promote collegiality. Toward this end, the Center sponsors a monthly social get-together with complimentary refreshments for all faculty at a local inn. There is no formal agenda, and faculty have the opportunity to meet on an informal basis. In the past, this function was lightly attended by part-time faculty. The Center will embark on a program to attract the part-time cohort through special invitations to specific departments. For example, on a given month the English department will be featured. The Center and the department chair will send invitations to each department member with special emphasis on part-time faculty. In addition to the department chair, the dean and assistant deans of the College of Arts and Science will be invited. This approach offers a unique opportunity for department members to meet on an informal basis.

RECOMMENDATIONS FOR DESIGNING AND INITIATING PART-TIME FACULTY PROGRAMS AT RESEARCH UNIVERSITIES

The following steps for ensuring a successful part-time faculty program are recommended:

1. Initiate a bottom-up approach with top-down endorsement. A faculty development office/teaching center is a good base for designing and implementing a program to support part-time faculty.
2. Add funding and support for this part-time faculty effort to the center's budget without decreasing support for the traditional cohorts: new, junior, midcareer and senior faculty, and graduate students.
3. Look for grant and financial support in your local community and state funding institutions.
4. Draw on the particular and distinctive strengths of your center and the expertise of its staff.
5. If no center staff members are experienced or experts in part-time faculty matters, look for faculty members who have expertise and interest in the subject to lead or cofacilitate the initiative. An experienced and interested faculty member may be found, for example, in the sociology department or in the ranks of part-time faculty who are passionate about teaching and part-time faculty issues and opportunities.
6. After they are located, find a way to encourage and reward these faculty, providing them with appropriate membership in your center.

7. Prior to designing the program, collect related information that is available from your office of institutional research. Also, investigate the needs of your part-time faculty using focus groups and part-time faculty and department chair surveys.
8. Communicate with part-time faculty via email (establishing a database may be challenging), a Listserv, newsletters, and a web site.
9. At meetings of part-timers, be prepared for part-time faculty issues to be raised that may not be related to the meeting topic.
11. Provide recognition for participating part-timers who complete your program: a certificate from your provost and president and a modest professional expense account. Find out what part-timers value and appreciate and try to provide that.
12. Address, in a way appropriate to your institution, the complex connections between campus climate, perceptions, and relations between part- and full-time faculty, expectations for increased commitments from part-timers, and pay.

The need for addressing part-time faculty issues and opportunities has reached a point that research universities must acknowledge and offer support and climate change. This chapter offers some possible solutions to consider in designing and implementing programs for this important cohort.

References

Bain, K. (2004). *What the best college teachers do.* Cambridge, MA: Harvard University Press.

Beach, A. L., & Cox, M. D. (2005, October). *Faculty learning communities' impacts: Results of a national survey.* Paper presented at annual meeting of the Professional and Organizational Development Network in Higher Education, Milwaukee, WI.

Conley, V. M., & Leslie, D. W. (2002). *Part-time instructional faculty and staff: Who they are, what they do, and what they think* (Rep. No. NSOPF-93, Project Officer L. J. Zimbler). Washington, DC: National Center for Education Statistics.

Cox, M. D. (2004). Introduction to faculty learning communities. In M. D. Cox & L. Richlin (Eds.), *New directions for teaching and learning: No. 97. Building faculty learning communities* (pp. 5–23). San Francisco, CA: Jossey-Bass.

Garland, J. (August, 2005). *State of the university address.* Oxford, OH: Miami University.

Haeger, J. D. (1998). Part-time faculty, quality programs and economic realities. In David W. Leslie (Ed.), *New directions for higher education: No. 104. The growing use of part-time faculty: Understanding causes and effects* (pp. 81–88). San Francisco, CA: Jossey-Bass.

Jacobs, F. (1998). Using part-time faculty more effectively. In D. W. Leslie (Ed.), *New directions for higher education: No. 104. The growing use of part-time faculty: Understanding causes and effects* (pp. 9–18). San Francisco, CA: Jossey-Bass.

Maguire, P. (1984). Enhancing the effectiveness of adjunct faculty. *Community College Review, 11*(3), 27–34.

Richlin, L. (2006). *Blueprint for learning: Constructing college courses to facilitate, assess, and document learning.* Richmond, VA: Stylus.

Richlin, L., & Essington, A. (2004). Overview of faculty learning communities. In M. D. Cox & L. Richlin (Eds.), *New directions for teaching and learning: No. 97. Building faculty learning communities* (pp. 25–39). San Francisco, CA: Jossey-Bass.

Wenger, E. (1998). *Communities of practice.* Cambridge, U.K.: Cambridge University Press.

APPENDIX 14.1.

Informal Feedback From Year One

Center for the Enhancement of Learning and Teaching (CELT)
Part-Time Faculty Initiative
July 5, 2005
Susan Weaver, Facilitator
Part-Time and Adjunct Faculty Teaching Program (PTAFTP)

Introduction

Gathering information about faculty frustrations was *not* a goal of the PTAFTP. The focus was intended to be on the positives. However, non-participants' negative feedback came from a variety of sources. The majority of this frustration was expressed by those who felt that they had major issues but did not know where to vent. They hoped that the PTAFTP would be a venue for them. Information gleaned from these faculty is shared in this section in recognition that there does not seem to be an institutional mechanism for resolving such issues.

Although the content of this section seems largely negative, it is to be noted that most of the views of part-time faculty at the Hamilton and Middletown campuses were positive. Both of these campuses have made great efforts to accommodate part-time faculty through meetings where they meet administrators and offer Part-Time Faculty Handbooks and attempt to provide access to office space, telephone, and support services. The Oxford campus faculty seemed less likely to feel supported.

There is a prevailing sense of invisibility or even disrespect for part-time faculty at Miami. There is a feeling that barriers exist both in attitude and policy. This narrative attempts to outline some of the particular features of the part-time faculty experience that could be remedied. The invisibility is especially apparent on the Oxford campus, which does not have a handbook or central contact person for part-time faculty.

Nomenclature and Compensation

The titles used for part-time and adjunct faculty do not reflect these individuals' experience or contributions to the university outside of the classroom. Although there is a national movement toward differentiated titles and appropriate compensation for lecturers, senior lecturers, and part-time assistant professors, Miami uses only the undifferentiated term "part-time." Several respondents indicated that the terms "part-time" or "casual" faculty imply a lack of dedication or professionalism. These terms do not reflect the effort that many put into combining multiple positions and career sacrifices because of their dedication to teaching and to their discipline.

Many universities base compensation for part-time faculty on their years of experience and their responsibilities. Miami differentiates only by highest degree held by the person. One person told me that Miami has raised base pay for part-time faculty only one time in twelve years. Further, class size doubled in this person's department during this time, so that grading and activities needed to be planned for twice as many students and required twice as much time for grading assignments and tests.

Professional Development

Part-time faculty members are not rewarded for their professional development, publishing, grant-writing, and community service. In fact, they are denied opportunities to participate in most faculty programs. These include basic recognition, funding for conference participation, and training opportunities.

Collegiality

Part-time faculty have both professional credentials and dedication to their disciplines. However, they are isolated from others within their departments. They are not assigned mentors, not invited to department meetings or social events, and often meet only a few, if any, other faculty in their departments. The only departmental contact is often by mail or messages from administrative assistants. They do not have opportunities to engage with others within their disciplines to learn or share innovations and ideas or ask questions. Many do not know their department chairs or other faculty.

There is a sense that the part-time faculty are perceived as unprofessional and less qualified. Students making grade appeals receive greater consideration than the instructor.

Policies and Procedures
Part-time faculty would like to be notified about seminars or honor societies for their students. They would like to be included on department listservs and given input or at least information about university or departmental policy or procedure changes.

Evaluations
For many part-time faculty, especially those on the Hamilton or Middletown campuses, the only contact they have with their department in Oxford is when it is time for evaluations. Since they are denied opportunities for collegiality or recognition, student evaluations become their only feedback. If the evaluations are good, then they are invited back. If evaluations are weak, then they risk losing their jobs. Absurd or callous feedback from a student takes on disproportionate weight because it adds insult to the career injury that many part-time faculty experience as a result of teaching part-time. Evaluation comments such as "I even hate your boots" create stress among an already unappreciated and vocationally insecure faculty.

Professional Consideration
Part-time faculty represent a diverse population. Some are retired from other areas and prefer to work part-time. Some enjoy the opportunity to mentor, the contact with younger populations, and university affiliation. For others, part-time teaching is seen as a stepping stone to opportunity. Others find part-time teaching to be the only employment that they can find. There is a surplus of Ph.D.s in many disciplines and a limited number of positions due to restructuring, delayed retirements, and university adoption of corporate models that value administrators more than professors.

Regardless of the reason for teaching part-time, virtually all are surprised at the marginalization and stigma that comes with the position. Denigration of part-time faculty occurs in several ways:

- Many part-time faculty are frustrated that full-time administrators, faculty, graduate assistants, staff, and even their families can take classes without paying tuition, but part-time faculty must pay for every class that they take, regardless of how many classes they take or how many years they have taught at Miami.

- Part-time faculty experience and commitment to the university as part-time faculty are held against them when applying for positions within their departments. Many would like help with career development so that they are not penalized for their experience with Miami.
- Part-time faculty would like and need travel support to attend conferences. They need access to paid or unpaid sabbaticals without jeopardizing their part-time positions.
- Increasing class size has become a problem for many part-time faculty. There should be an opportunity for feedback or at least acknowledgment of the extra work.
- Part-time faculty would like to be compensated for travel mileage, especially to attend training or meetings on other campuses.
- Part-time faculty would like to be permitted to get a laminated plastic parking pass as is given to students, faculty, and staff, instead of a cardboard pass.
- Part-time faculty would like to be permitted to have business cards. One person offered to pay for his own cards but was told that he was not eligible to have them. Thus, when meeting with others or presenting at conferences, they do not have cards to give out.

Teaching Needs

There are several concerns that emanate from a sense of being in perpetual transition. Many part-time faculty would like office space and access to a telephone and computer. They would like to be able to get faculty/staff directories without being charged for them.

The policy of discontinuing e-mail with the end of employment means that part-time faculty who teach only one semester a year always have a lag time without e-mail or access to departmental communications that might come before the next semester begins. It also means that students are unable to contact them if there is a desire to discuss a class or a need for a letter of recommendation.

Many faculty would like a contact person or personal instruction in library resources, Blackboard, and IT services. There are many supports and training classes that they do not receive information about or an invitation to participate.

Several part-time faculty indicate that they would like to have a say in what courses they teach and the opportunity to propose courses or to teach different courses.

Several part-time faculty report that they have purchased texts and other textbooks out-of-pocket, because they do not know what their departmental resources are and they are not in contact with book reps or with other faculty teaching similar courses.

It would be helpful to have a syllabus template and a handbook of university and departmental policies.

Personal Needs

In addition to a need for counseling to assist in attaining their professional goals, part-time faculty face difficulties and stress that are not experienced by full-time faculty. Many do not have insurance and would like at least pro-rata benefits. If this cannot be done, then they would like a resource list so that they can find reasonably priced insurance or Medigap policies.

Job insecurity of part-time faculty is a problem for long-term planning. It is impossible to plan ahead when one is hired semester to semester. Some institutions have part-time policies that provide preference based on seniority or extended contracts (five-year contracts) as well as the opportunity for sabbatical or personal leave without losing standing with the department.

There is some confusion about the ability to recover funds contributed to retirement while at Miami. It would be useful to have a summary of such policies for quick reference.

Part-time faculty would also like a contact person to reach when there are questions or issues arise. Sometimes asking questions within their departments only serves to get them in trouble.

Discussion

This report is based on input from many part-time faculty and does not represent situations faced by all part-time faculty. Most of the more frustrated part-time faculty did not attend PTAFTP meetings, but contacted me personally or conveyed messages through the meeting attendees. It is encouraging that they take the time to convey their concerns. The persons who contacted me seemed genuinely interested in teaching and in their disciplines. They spoke of projects and additional training that they've completed on their own to enhance their credentials. Also, taking the initiative to make contact indicates that they feel there is hope that their concerns will be addressed in a positive way. In fact, the concerns listed here can be seen as reflections of people who have spent time envisioning Miami at its best.

Many of these sources of frustration can easily be remedied through greater retention efforts, including recognitions. Others require long-term changes, such as the creation of an ombudsman for part-time faculty. The bottom line, though, is that there are many persons on campus who are teaching within a climate that is not nurturing, affirming, or progressive. Instead of the collegiality anticipated by part-time faculty, they find that they are isolated as they negotiate a chilly environment. When they have issues with the department or with students or need assistance, it is a challenge for them to know what resources are available or whom to ask for information.

Research supports the idea that part-time faculty see themselves as professionals and take their responsibilities seriously. They tend to put a lot of thought and energy into the classroom, as it is their sole responsibility. CELT and Miami University can be credited with the innovation of implementing this program for part-time faculty. I hope that this report meets the expectations of the committee and serves as a springboard to make the Miami experience for part-time faculty as positive as it is for the rest of the Miami community.

APPENDIX 14.2

CELT Part Time Faculty Initiative at Miami University Focus Group Results
Alana Van Gundy-Yoder, Facilitator
August 10, 2006

Focus group discussions were conducted with part-time faculty employed at Miami University's Oxford, Hamilton, and Middletown campuses. Two focus groups were conducted, and a total of 13 part-time faculty volunteered for participation. All names and identifying information have been removed from the data utilized in this report in order to obtain participant confidentiality. Participants were asked to reflect on their experiences as part-time faculty at Miami University and to answer the following questions:

- How did you become part-time faculty at Miami University?
- What do you like best about being part-time faculty?
- What do you like least about being part-time faculty?
- What, if any, specific needs do you feel that part-time faculty here at Miami have?
- Based on your experiences, what changes would you suggest for addressing those needs? [Was rephrased as the following probing question: What kinds of initiatives would you like to see address these issues?]
- If you had the opportunity to become full-time faculty, would you? Why or why not?

Results
The results section presents a concise summary of the discussions held in each focus group.

How did you become part-time faculty at Miami University?
The respondents unanimously agreed that the hiring process was very informal. The majority of participants reported being approached on short notice by a friend or colleague at Miami who needed to "fill the spot." Many reported transferring from other schools, moving to Oxford because their spouse is a full-time employee, or utilizing this position as a transition from graduate school. Three participants were full-time staff in other offices within Miami University and responded that their colleagues had requested their help "out of desperation."

What do you like best about being part-time faculty?

Respondents reported liking the flexibility of being part-time and the lack of political expectations for their position. Along with providing more family time, participants felt a large benefit was the ability not to attend department meetings, not having to play department politics, few or no research expectations and, in general, less pressure to be part of the academic culture.

Importantly, a common theme throughout each focus group was the love for teaching. Participants agreed that they love to teach, they provide a student-focused course, and they are stimulated by high-quality interaction with their students. The part-time faculty felt that they provided the benefit of particular expertise to the students, because they work within their career field and then transfer that hands-on knowledge to their students.

What do you like least about being part-time faculty?

Consistent with research on part-time faculty, participants in each focus group disliked not having an office. Without an office they are unable to provide office hours to students, keep anything on campus, or have privacy when speaking with their students.

The part-time faculty reported a lack of research and travel funding for those in their position. Many hoped to engage in academic research, but reported access to little or no funding for their ideas because funding is reserved for full-time faculty.

Although they enjoy not feeling the pressure of the academic culture, participants unanimously agreed that they do not feel like part of the faculty culture. They feel disconnected with the campus, that no one pays attention to them, unsure of acceptance if they attended department meetings, and a general discontent with the lack of administrative support for part-time faculty. An example they provided was that in the State of the University Address, grade inflation within Miami University was attributed to part-time faculty when, in fact, many stated they are giving out lower grades than they feel is necessary. Another example discussed, was that although they are asked to provide more work than a graduate student, they make less money than a graduate student and have less travel support available than graduate students do and, thus, feel even less important than graduate students.

Lastly, participants felt there is a lack of communication between part-time faculty and all other aspects of the university. Some were never told when department meetings were held or provided an option to attend. They were concerned about student evaluations, yet they had no academic support personnel to discuss their course content or structure with them. They felt a lack of respect from colleagues, administration, and students because they are low on the "hierarchy" of classification systems. Participants described their relationship with the university as a "love-hate" relationship. They love to teach, and hate how they are treated by others.

What, if any, specific needs do you feel that part-time faculty here at Miami have?

Part-time faculty requested that they receive a formal orientation to their environment. Due to the informal way they were hired, many did not know their supervisors or colleagues, and many had no idea what to do about particular problems (student evaluations, faculty support, or someone to help them with particular resources).

Participants also felt that part-time faculty need the option of being assigned a mentor. Because they feel so disconnected with the campus in general, have few resources and no office space, they felt the need to have someone aid them in navigating the academic environment. For example, part-time faculty often are assigned classes with a large number of students (because they are asked to teach introductory level courses), and they would like to have another part-time faculty member help them with time management, syllabus construction, and general questions they may have.

The most important need that participants identified was the need for benefits. Those working in part-time positions receive no benefits and little pay. Therefore, faculty felt that they should have the option for specific types of benefits commensurate with their experience. For example, a few of the participants have been teaching on the campus for more than ten years, yet they receive no tuition reimbursement for themselves or their family. Participants were willing to pay a percentage of academic benefits, but felt that they should be able to have access to research and grant funds, conference and travel money, and possibly a pay increase with experience. Similarly, those in fields which mandate continuing education expressed a need for stipends to use for travel or certification. Those who already had full-time staff positions within the university stated that they were unable to believe that part-time faculty were willing to work with no health care and no employment stability.

Based on your experiences, what changes would you suggest for addressing those needs?

The participating faculty provided a number of suggested changes, or university-wide initiatives, they would like to see. These included:

- A part-time faculty orientation through the university and through their department
- Preference for full-time slots when positions become posted
- Access to benefits, such as tuition reimbursement, travel funds, etc.
- Administration awareness of the special needs of part-time faculty
- Higher pay with experience
- Greater access to scholarly pursuit, including grant and research funds or stipends for continuing education
- The creation of a "part-time administrator" with the idea that the individual would be the spokesperson and "go-to" person for part-time faculty that have questions

- An evaluation of other universities which have a high rate of part-time faculty, such as Sinclair Community College, for what they offer as part-time initiatives
- Clarification of the classification system
- Expanding the part-time contract to a year versus semester-by-semester to provide some job stability

If you had the opportunity to become full-time faculty, would you? Why or why not?

Participants who already held staff positions within the university reported not having a desire to become full-time because they enjoyed their current position. Four part-timers expressed interest in becoming full-time and hoped to have the opportunity to do so. The remaining part-time faculty participants reported not seeing full-time as an option because they would take a severe pay decrease if they were to leave their current position. Similarly, they enjoyed teaching so much as a part-time job they did not want to attempt to work in that position full-time.

Conclusion

Many interesting findings emerged from these discussions. It is imperative that the administration examine, advance, and clarify the position of part-time faculty within the hierarchy of Miami University. Participants in these focus groups expressed a passion for teaching their courses as well as an interest in scholarly pursuits. They felt that by improving communication between part-time faculty and full-time faculty/administration, assigning a position devoted to part-time faculty, clarifying classification issues, and providing access to academically oriented benefits, the university would show an unprecedented level of support for part-time faculty. This support would address what they feel is the devaluation of part-time faculty on the Miami University campuses.

15

PROFESSIONAL DEVELOPMENT GEARED TO PART-TIMERS' NEEDS: AN ADJUNCT PROFESSOR'S PERSPECTIVE

Jason Schwartz

Unlike others in this book, this chapter provides the first-hand impressions of a part-time instructor. Currently employed at two different colleges—one with a well developed, comprehensive program for preparing and supporting part-time instructors, and another that has taken only some very modest steps—I will seek to compare the two teaching cultures and identify the benefits accruing to the one that has developed its program most fully. Wanting to be as clear and objective as possible while shielding both from undue criticism, I refer to the one with the well developed program as College A and the other as College B.

The anxiety that I experienced as a college freshman on the first day of my classes paled in comparison to the self-doubt overwhelming me on my first day of teaching as an adjunct instructor some five years ago. I suspect my feelings were common and even greater among the many adjunct professors, who, unlike me, had received no orientation to their instruction nor training in teaching and classroom management methods prior to entering the classroom. After all, few of us are professional teachers—a fact that many department chairs and deans seem to forget sometimes. Instead, we are hired because of our expertise in our chosen field, the flexibility we add to their staffing decisions, and our relative low cost. Most of us adjunct instructors therefore, at least at first, are challenged to feel connected to our institutions—to feel like real professors. The more that can be done to help us anticipate and address this alienation and anxiety, the better our classroom performance will be, and the greater likelihood that our instructional leaders and we will want to improve the situation.

In 2001 after 24 years as a practicing physician, an injury necessitated my retiring from clinical practice. I sold my practice, helped the office with the transition to the new doctor, and then what? At 48, retirement did not fit. Entrepreneurship and that creative "can do" energy still drove me. To go from running my own successful practice to retirement was too drastic a contrast; it did not fit. I did enjoy the more flexible daily schedule that it gave me and the additional time provided for my family, but I knew this was not the time for real retirement.

I believe that boredom is the result of resisting that creative flow within all of us. So when a long-time friend, a professor at College A, suggested I seek a part-time teaching position there, I listened intently. "You love to teach your patients. Why not teach preprofessional students at the college?" Within a week I was interviewed by the department chair about teaching a daytime section of anatomy and physiology that was to begin in a month. After discovering that I was a physician, he said that he welcomed practitioners to teaching and that another physician was teaching a section of the same course that we were discussing for me.

At that moment, the phone rang, and the department chair asked if I could step outside his office for a moment. As I did, the door of the classroom next to the office opened, and a professor emerged. I asked if he was the physician mentioned by the chair. He said "yes" and introduced himself. After a brief chat, I knew that I would accept the job offer.

Returning to the interview with the department chair, I was informed that, contingent upon my satisfying the standards of the regional accrediting association, I would be hired as an adjunct professor. I was excited! Yet, driving home, I sensed a nagging resistance to this golden opportunity. There was a feeling that I was making a big mistake.

Arriving home, I sat down and contemplated the situation, searching for insights about why I was not totally comfortable with the job decision. Within moments a phrase formed in my mind, "He who can, does. He who cannot, teaches." Thinking back, I remembered that phrase from my early school days. Perhaps it was during sixth grade when someone said it, and I accepted it as true. I then went on the Internet and researched the phrase and found it was attributed to the late George Bernard Shaw, an Irish playwright and critic.

Reflecting upon the phrase more objectively, I realized it obviously was not true. I do not want my child taught by people who cannot achieve in life, just as I do not want the bridges over which we drive to be built by engineers trained by engineering failures, nor my lawyers, accountants, doctors, and nurses taught by professors who were failures in their fields. I had accepted and internalized this false belief as a child and it almost sabotaged a wonderful opportunity. I went back into contemplation and replaced the destructive, limiting phrase with a more constructive one, "He who can does, and he who can and cares, shares."

My fellow physician/adjunct instructor colleague became a mentor who invited me to sit in on his classes. His were scheduled a few hours earlier in the day than mine, and I observed perhaps eight of his class meetings. His insights proved invaluable as I began this new career and even later as I sought to continually improve the effectiveness of my teaching.

Interestingly, he was teaching for very different reasons than I. I was a *career ender* with a hint of a "perhaps I would go full-time if this works out well" attitude. The other physician attended medical school in the U.S. and then moved to Europe where he joined an established clinical practice. Finding that environment a poor fit, he returned to the U.S. and began the process of completing various state and national required examinations. During that period he accepted a position teaching high school science and taught as an adjunct college instructor in the evening to earn additional income until his license was issued. Therefore, he fit most closely into the category of *specialist/expert/professional.*

Later, upon being introduced to Gappa and Leslie's (1993) typology of part-time instructors, I wondered if the category into which adjunct instructors fit is an indicator of their dedication to teaching. As time passed, my commitment increased, while the opposite seemed to be the case with my colleague. Many part-timers, I later discovered, do not fit neatly into one of the categories of *aspiring academics, career enders, freelancers,* and *specialist/expert/professional,* while others seem to move between categories over time.

Besides that provided by my adjunct colleague, mentoring was also provided by a full-time instructor who also taught the same course as I. Her very different teaching style contrasted dramatically with his. I found the ability to observe two gifted instructors an invaluable tool in helping me develop my own teaching style. In addition those two relationships played a big role in helping me assimilate into the teaching culture of College A, and I began to feel like a fully contributing member of the faculty.

As I started my teaching career at College A, I was required to complete a short course for new adjunct instructors. Titled Instructor Effectiveness Training, it met four times on Saturday mornings and focused on developing basic teaching and classroom management skills. Although there was also an online version, I decided to enroll in the face-to-face version, because I believed it would be a richer learning experience.

As my adjunct faculty colleagues introduced themselves at the first Saturday session, a bond with my new colleagues, the college culture, and the course instructor began to develop very naturally. As the course progressed, I began to feel informed, supported, and connected to the college in a way that would not otherwise have been possible. I realized that each of my classmates brought a unique, deep, rich, and colorful wealth of experience to the college that enriched our in-class dialogue as well as our collective interchanges with students that would follow. At the opening of each session, we discussed the challenges that had arisen in our individual classrooms since the previous Saturday session. The course emphasized sound planning, the need to deeply understand our students, utilizing active learning strategies, and effective techniques of assessing student learning.

Driving home from each class meeting, I felt more and more comfortable with my new identity as an adjunct professor. The insights that my Instructor Effectiveness Training professor shared—the challenges of teaching, students' varied learning styles, expectations of the college and its external stakeholders—no doubt saved me a lot of time and frustration. One insight that made a special impact was that new instructors rely on two factors to establish the foundation of their teaching style—the way in which they have been taught themselves, especially by those in their own discipline, and their own learning styles. Aware that I learned best through auditory instruction and reading, which were the primary methods used by professors in my medical training, I realized the importance of resisting that approach and using tactile methods with my students. This proved to be one of many benefits of investing four Saturday mornings away from my family.

Beginning my teaching while enrolled in the Instructor Effectiveness Training course also helped me achieve confidence in front of my students much faster than would otherwise have been the case. The course helped me realize that a primary asset that adjunct instructors typically contribute to today's students is their real world experience. I have speculated that if I taught these same classes with a Ph.D. instead of a clinical doctorate, I would not be able to establish the same rapport with the students. While Ph.D.-trained professors contribute a different set of assets, students most likely achieve a more rounded education through their instructors' varied backgrounds.

Some five months following the launch of my part-time teaching career at College A, I saw an employment opportunity on the online human resources web page of another nearby college (College B). They had an emergency need for an adjunct instructor to teach an anatomy and physiology lab similar to the one that I was already teaching. Apparently the part-timer assigned to the course had given notice that she was moving and would not be available the following semester. Having caught the teaching bug, I was motivated to pursue this second opportunity out of simple curiosity and to broaden my experience base.

During my interview, the department chair displayed much more of a sink-or-swim approach than the supportive one that I had experienced at College A. He mentioned, in a matter-of-fact manner, that the students have a standard department syllabus, much as if it were a recipe, and lab textbooks and assignments that are laid out plainly for them. The chair viewed my role, it seemed, as being a rather passive resource in the room available to answer questions only if students approached me. Still curious nonetheless, I accepted the chair's invitation to begin teaching the course at the start of the following term, a few weeks hence. The fact that College B paid their adjunct instructors at a significantly higher rate made the decision easier.

Before entering the classroom at College B, I, along with other new part-timers, was required to attend a two-hour department meeting. The agenda included a welcome orientation by the campus provost that was delivered via television broadcast. The dean stopped in briefly to offer greetings. The department chairperson gave a general game plan for the term, provided each of us with an adjunct faculty handbook, announced the requirement that we each complete an online sexual harassment module, and answered our questions. We adjunct instructors introduced ourselves, and the meeting ended. With no further training or an introduction to someone who might have served as a mentor, we were each thrown into our assigned course sections. Any bonding between faculty members or with the college would be at the initiative of the new adjunct instructor.

By then, with some five months of teaching experience at College A, I decided to take a proactive approach. I created PowerPoint presentations, diagrams, and other audiovisual aids that would begin each lab session. I also proactively approached students one-on-one as they completed their assignments using some techniques that proved to be successful for me at College A. Late in that first term at College B, the chair stopped by the lab to tell me with a grin that I was being offered an opportunity to teach the following term, because I did not just sit in the class reading a newspaper. Apparently, the strategy for continuing the employment of adjunct instructors in the department was to give them enough rope to hang themselves then reward those who did not step into the trap.

As a new instructor, it was interesting to compare the strategies of the two department chairs and the different institutional approaches taken by the two colleges. I sometimes wonder about the attrition rate of adjunct instructors and can only speculate that the rate at College B is much higher than at College A.

Working in close proximity to the administrators, chairperson, and tenured professors, as I do at College A, no doubt contributes to a sense of greater support for a new adjunct instructor and perhaps helps them feel like a more important part of the instructional team.

Despite the lack of training and programs to encourage a satisfying new career, College B seems to have little trouble recruiting adjunct faculty members. Located in a much larger metropolitan area that offers a larger pool of potential professors and paying at a higher scale than other nearby colleges seems to solve the problem that so many other colleges experience. Pragmatically, I will admit, if my salary was needed to put food on the table, College B is where I would remain, but not without regrets. The responsibility of providing for one's family—as many aspiring academics must no doubt do—often necessitates compromising our wishes and dreams.

Teaching anatomy and physiology to students seeking health care careers presents a unique opportunity to an instructor who has had a clinical career himself. So I must admit that I approach my preprofessional students as my future colleagues. Relating to these students as potential future clinical colleagues demonstrates a level of respect and my honest acknowledgement of the demands of the courses I teach. This sets up a relationship perhaps rarely found in undergraduate education. Often in graduate schools and trade schools these relationships exist among students and insightful instructors. I remember the professors I had in medical school who treated us as future colleagues. They established a relationship with the students that was very conducive to learning.

The professional relationships I develop with the students seem to work. During my first semester teaching, I gave a student a failing grade in a class. The student showed up the next semester to retake the class with me. I asked why she did not try another instructor this semester, and she said, "You did your job great; I was the one who didn't do my job." For me, that demonstrated this approach was a success.

There is no easy way around the depth and breadth of the material that must be comprehended in the anatomy and physiology curriculum to be qualified for a health care professional program. Thus I take a two-pronged approach. My two goals are to clearly present the material and also clearly acknowledge how challenging the material is. I continually offer creative options and motivating ideas to aid the students. I find, for example, discussing the relevance of the specific material to clinical situations may for some be that shining light at the end of the long studying tunnel.

There are many challenges that colleges face in utilizing adjunct instructors' talents effectively that may not be present with full-time faculty. The majority of us still pursue another career full-time, and being freed from those obligations can often be problematic, even if, like me, we are self-employed. Adjunct instructors who are retired or near retirement often seek a limited teaching load to free up quality time with family members and friends or to pursue community obligations or other interests. Those of us who believe we might want to teach full-time some day may teach at more than one institution and thus must not only balance conflicting schedules that factor in travel time, but we must also compare the relative rewards of teaching at disparate institutions. In addition, we may be qualified to teach only a narrow selection of courses and thus must make critical decisions about accepting assignments within what is often a tight time frame.

Still another challenge for adjunct instructors and the institutions employing us occurs when we take a term off from teaching, either by our own choice or because of institution-based factors such as insufficient enrollment or the need to enhance a full-timer's load. If our teaching performance has met or even surpassed expectations, we typically expect some consideration for our previous service to the institution and may feel left in limbo while needing to take advantage of competing opportunities.

These and other issues have given rise to the growing trend to designate key personnel dedicated to coordinating the teaching of adjunct instructors. The two colleges at which I teach have taken very different approaches to this issue. At College B, the department chair plays this role exclusively—enforcing an unwritten policy that full-time faculty members select the schedules they want with no consideration for the adjunct faculty's availability. The department chair then fills in the gaps with adjunct faculty with little regard for the adjunct instructor's scheduling conveniences, such as assigning one class one day and another the next day versus assigning two classes in the same day to save travel time or not to tie up two days of the instructor's time. While this widely known policy displays no concern for the individual adjunct instructor, it also achieves a less than ideal overall learning environment for students. If the whole assignment process were looked at more strategically, full-time faculty members would need to make only token sacrifices that achieve a more strategic learning environment.

Each college at which I taught initiated programs for recognizing the contributions of their adjunct faculty. College B gives out awards to outstanding adjunct faculty by having the dean and department chairperson arrive unannounced in the classroom while the instructor is teaching. The criteria for selection and the process details are not well communicated. The award is presented in a two-minute ceremony with the students serving as the audience. During my first year teaching there I observed this first hand; an efficient thank you.

College A, on the other hand, invites all its adjunct instructors to an award reception where refreshments are served, and the college president expresses his gratitude for the contributions that adjunct faculty make to the college mission. Several years ago that recognition was expanded to honor a half dozen of the adjunct instructors attending as "Outstanding Adjunct Faculty Members." Nominated by faculty, administration, and students, the nominees' credentials are reviewed by a committee of full- and part-time faculty and instructional administrators. At the ceremony, the college president delivers a personalized recognition of the recipients that includes biographical information and a listing of their contributions to their instructional departments. In my second year of teaching at this college, I was one of those honored to receive the award. Forewarned of the impending honor, I was encouraged to invite my family and friends, which really served to make it a big event. Having my wife and children witness the appreciation the college felt for the efforts I put forth made it an event we will never forget.

Having been recognized at both colleges, I must admit that the ceremony of College A was significantly more memorable. Yet the downside of presenting the awards at a reception to which all adjuncts are invited is that those who are not nominated or who were nominated but were not selected by the adjunct faculty advisory committee to receive the award may be disappointed and disenfranchised. But that is the flip side any time we recognize outstanding performance; those who are not recognized may get hurt. The alternatives are to recognize faculty in a stealth manner, such as College B, or accept average as the goal.

College B sponsors an adjunct appreciation week during which all the part-time instructors can get free cosmetology services at the college's cosmetology school, extra discounts at the bookstore, and free massages given at the physical therapy assistant department.

I have found at College B, perhaps due to the lack of required training such as the Instructor Effectiveness Training course, that the adjunct faculty attrition rate seems to be much higher, and there are more adjunct faculty disasters. One that I personally witnessed involved a very nice adjunct instructor who had earned a doctorate in genetics and offered his services to teach an anatomy and physiology lab that focused on cat dissection. He was so poorly prepared for the actuality of dissecting the cats that he had the lab prep person teach his lab while he stood by as a spectator.

The reason I mention this misadventure as perhaps related to the lack of a required adjunct instructor training program is that one of many benefits of such a course is to transform the adjunct instructor's identity from being a professional specialist to being a teacher. Adjunct instructors, almost by their nature, identify themselves as the "can do anything Ph.D.," or whatever else their expertise is or was in the nonacademic world. This attitude must be melded into a new identity as a professional/teacher or teacher/professional.

College A and College B use different means to evaluate their adjunct instructors. At College B, the department chairperson observes the adjunct instructor while he or she conducts a class then writes up a performance evaluation. Within a week, the evaluation is reviewed with the instructor. The instructor is asked to sign the evaluation, and it is sent up the administrative chain. I felt that the chairperson got a snapshot view of my class. My evaluations have always been reasonable. I have received the highest review grading that can be given, and the chair people have written superlative comments. I bring this up because I cannot comment on how I would have reacted if the department chairs had given me either a poor review or commented with remarks that I felt were unfair.

College A asks students to complete evaluation forms during one of the class sessions midway through the semester while the instructor is out of the room. A student collects them and delivers them to the dean. They are anonymous, yet the instructor cannot view the evaluation until the next semester. The administration realizes that there will be a few grudge evaluations, yet I feel it does give the administration reasonable feedback.

Of the two methods I experienced, the student review helped me to improve the quality of my instruction the most. College B's approach did not document areas that needed fine tuning. College B's approach seems to be more effective in discovering midsemester if some adjunct faculty are failing to adequately meet their teaching responsibilities so the department can respond. Considering that almost no training and teaching guidance is given to the new adjunct instructor at College B, this may be a pragmatic approach.

College A's approach of using student evaluations was not as effective as it could have been in allowing me to improve the quality of my instruction, because adjunct faculty are not allowed to read the evaluation until after the final grades for that semester are posted. This does not make midsemester improvements possible. Thus if some aspect of the course is not working, that group of students cannot benefit from any changes the instructor may make after it is brought to his or her attention.

I teach at two colleges with very different philosophies and attitudes toward the adjunct sector of the faculty. College A demonstrates that they value the adjunct faculty as an important part of the whole faculty. They show this by the training they require and offer as well as the more subtle aspects such as the adjunct faculty appreciation awards.

College B appears to view the adjunct faculty as the "hired help" that does not deserve additional benefits. Also, because the adjunct instructors are well compensated there, but the full-time faculty has a pay scale one-third less than that of College A, there is a palpable tension between many of the full-time faculty members and the adjunct faculty. This may be part of the reason so little regard is given to the adjunct instructors' scheduling needs when planning the full-time faculty's schedule.

College A compensates its full-time faculty very well, and both they and the administrators are openly embarrassed about the low pay provided to adjunct instructors. While I do not believe that the heart-felt support the administration and full-time faculty give to the adjunct faculty is due to a guilty conscience for the low salaries we receive, they would do well to be sensitive to the perceived inequity and provide a similar percentage increase to adjunct faculty as the full-timers receive annually. Doing so would foster a sense of equity and thus deepen the sense of collegiality among part-timers.

After several terms of splitting my weekly teaching schedules between both colleges, I contemplated which college I would be more willing to walk away from. I would much rather teach at College A despite the lower pay scale directly due to the training and attitude of appreciation demonstrated by the administration and the full-time faculty. That one course, Instructor Effectiveness Training, set the foundation for a deeper loyalty to College A than I ever developed with College B. College A demonstrated their commitment to my success and a high standard of teaching for their institution by requiring that course as well as additional coursework during the five-year certification window.

Today as I walk the campus and the halls of College A, I feel at home, comfortable, welcomed, and appreciated. I expect and receive warm cooperation from my coworkers. This feeling of belonging aids my ability to function as an effective and efficient teacher—something that cannot be said of the more widespread situation that exists at College B. I look forward to growing further as a professor and contributing to the knowledge base of my students—our future health care professionals.

Reference

Gappa, J. M., & Leslie, D. W. (1993). *The invisible faculty: Improving the status of part-timers in higher education.* San Francisco, CA: Jossey-Bass.

INDEX